WADING IN

WADING IN

Desegregation on the Mississippi Gulf Coast

Amy Lemco

University Press of Mississippi / Jackson

The University Press of Mississippi is the scholarly publishing agency of
the Mississippi Institutions of Higher Learning: Alcorn State University,
Delta State University, Jackson State University, Mississippi State University,
Mississippi University for Women, Mississippi Valley State University,
University of Mississippi, and University of Southern Mississippi.

www.upress.state.ms.us

The University Press of Mississippi is a member
of the Association of University Presses.

Any discriminatory or derogatory language or hate speech regarding race, ethnicity,
religion, sex, gender, class, national origin, age, or disability that has been retained
or appears in elided form is in no way an endorsement of the use of such language
outside a scholarly context.

Copyright © 2023 by University Press of Mississippi
All rights reserved

∞

Library of Congress Cataloging-in-Publication Data

Names: Lemco, Amy, author.
Title: Wading in : desegregation on the Mississippi Gulf Coast / Amy Lemco.
Description: Jackson : University Press of Mississippi, [2023] | Includes
bibliographical references and index.
Identifiers: LCCN 2023022685 (print) | LCCN 2023022686 (ebook) | ISBN
9781496847164 (hardback) | ISBN 9781496850348 (trade paperback) | ISBN
9781496847171 (epub) | ISBN 9781496847188 (epub) | ISBN 9781496847195
(pdf) | ISBN 9781496847201 (pdf)
Subjects: LCSH: Mason, Gilbert R. | African Americans—Civil
rights—Mississippi—Biloxi—History—20th century. | African American
physicians—Mississippi—Biloxi—Biography. | African American civil
rights workers—Mississippi—Biloxi—Biography. | Civil rights
movements—Mississippi—Biloxi—History—20th century. | Biloxi
(Miss.)—Biography. | Biloxi (Miss.)—Race relations.
Classification: LCC F349.B5 L46 2023 (print) | LCC F349.B5 (ebook) | DDC
323.1196/0730762130904—dc23/eng/20230526
LC record available at https://lccn.loc.gov/2023022685
LC ebook record available at https://lccn.loc.gov/2023022686

British Library Cataloging-in-Publication Data available

*To the memory of Dr. Gilbert Mason Jr.
and all the generations who live a freer life
because of those who have gone before.*

CONTENTS

PREFACE. IX

CHAPTER ONE. Black in Biloxi: Back-of-Town 3

CHAPTER TWO. Still Waters Run Deep:
The Beginning of a Hero's Journey 10

CHAPTER THREE. Riptides:
How Black Taxpayers Were Forced to Fund Their Oppression 17

CHAPTER FOUR. Wading In:
Petition, Rejection, and "Operation Surf" 25

CHAPTER FIVE. Blood on the Sand, Cause of Injury: "Integrational". . . 39

CHAPTER SIX. From Ripples to Waves:
Shifting Blame, Calls for Peace, and the National Campaign 49

CHAPTER SEVEN. White Sand, White Solidarity:
The Continued Policing of Harrison County Beaches
and *United States v. Harrison County* 59

CHAPTER EIGHT. Many Oars:
The Other Avenues of Civil Rights Progress in Harrison County. . . 67

CHAPTER NINE. Tides Turning:
Resuming the Federal Trial and the Final Wade-In. 78

CHAPTER TEN. High Tide, Low Tide:
Progress, Pushback, and Desegregation 87

CHAPTER ELEVEN. Sand between My Toes:
   Continuing Work for Racial Equity 102

EPILOGUE. Flotsam, Jetsam:
   The Demise of the State Sovereignty Commission,
   Unforeseen Consequences, and Horizons Ahead 108

ACKNOWLEDGMENTS 111

NOTES 113

SELECTED BIBLIOGRAPHY 158

INDEX 173

PREFACE

As the civil rights movement is taught in history class, it may create the impression that a line was drawn in time, the event is over, and the oppression, aggression, fears, and desire for respect, safety, and opportunity are settled. It has become the stuff of multiple-choice and short-answer quizzes. To the contrary, such a close history can never be less than a living thing, still evolving, affecting and being affected by us. It is like an ocean, which none of us observes from the shore, counting the waves as they roll in. We are in the water together. Some of us believe we are safe in boats on top of the waves, while some tread in exhaustion, up to their necks, fearing—or hoping—for the next storm. Sometimes, the currents drag us backward before we surge forward again.

 I was raised in Biloxi, Mississippi. I love the water and my childhood memories of horseshoe and hermit crabs, seagulls and terns, wading in the silty water, fishing off the long piers, rowing to the strip of islands, watching shrimpers chug home with trawlers dripping dry in the breeze, and seeing the lantern lights of the fishermen casting nets for flounder at night. It was not until decades later that I would realize the information skipped or patched over in our local history of pirates, explorers, and (hastily relocated) native peoples. I knew more about the slave market in New Orleans than the ancestors of those who lived, literally, on the "other side of the tracks," much less how such a dividing line had been enforced in Biloxi. Through my genealogical research, I began to realize how often local histories employ euphemisms like "farmer," concealing numerous unnamed enslaved individuals who had helped build the community. I became aware that even the poorest and most uneducated European immigrants, who amazed later generations with their pioneer spirit, nonetheless benefited from centuries of genocide and a government that supported their claim to the violently depopulated land and its attending upward mobility, which had not existed in the countries they left behind. It was a mark of my own privilege that I could be raised so naively, trusting that the authorities who produce our histories (so instrumental in forming our modern consciousness) had done so with due diligence, without question of their bias or motivations.

Some people object that reexamining and critiquing our national myths and figures constitutes "rewriting" history. It certainly can be disturbing to find our heroes or mottos flawed; it may prompt us to reexamine our own identity. From a historian's point of view, I find scraping off the whitewash to be deeply satisfying. It is the purview of historians to notice and seek to fill gaps, to broaden perspective and tell as complete a history as possible, so that we may be as complete a people as possible (individually and as a collective). As a writer, I know the first draft is never the most complete, complex, or true. From the sociological perspective, I believe unearthing the histories of marginalized people is an integral, intellectual, and emotional part of reparations.

One core issue that arose in writing this text was the use of racial designations and signifiers. In quotes from older sources, I retained the historical term "Negro." Otherwise, I chose to use "Black" over "African American" or "People of Color." Never before has a circumstance so revealed to me the problem inherent in words as imperfect conduits of meaning. "Black" lumps together and "color-washes" a multitude of individual experiences and heritages. "African American" runs the risk of obscuring contemporary immigrants from Africa, not to mention the variety of countries and cultures within that vast continent, and may mythologize an innate connection to Africa, though generations of suppression and assimilation had resulted in the loss of much of the culture for those enslaved and their descendants. On the other hand, "People of Color" is too inclusive, embracing individuals of other marginalized ethnicities who may or may not have received the same treatment on the Biloxi beaches. For this book, I chose the signifier "Black," despite its flaws of communication, because it seems to straddle, as nearly as possible, historical and modern linguistic preferences, while embodying connotations of institutionalized oppression as well as personal and collective dignity.

A related issue arose. My capitalization of "Black" (which is consistent with the publisher's style) led to the consideration of whether or not to treat "white" similarly. In the end, I realized that those of European descent had multitudes of capitalized designations to indicate their ethnic or national heritage. Before (and even after) the concept of "whiteness" was formed, many Euro-Americans of different ethnic backgrounds wielded bias, animosity, and violence against one another. As colonizers, living alongside a competitive population of nonwhite ethnicities, "white" identity (and its attendant colorism) was mobilized selectively to prevent the marginalized classes from uniting across "color lines," in order to maintain the intersecting hierarchies of wealth and racialized, gendered power in post-contact America. In other words, a poor white walking down to the beach might say, "I have a right. I am an American, born and raised southerner, a Biloxian every day of my life." If turned away, this person might rationalize, "Well, I am not a beachfront homeowner." It would be an economic class issue. Whiteness would not come into it until a Person of Color came alongside the white person. Only then is it likely the first individual would become conscious of his or her "race," as belonging to the list qualifying them—not the Other—for the right to be there, whereas the Person of Color would have been aware, pretty constantly, that his or her designated racial identity had been assigned *in order* to supersede all their claims to "American, southerner, Biloxian." For worse or worse, "white" has been treated as a default, written in invisible ink, becoming conscious and capitalized only when it is used as a weapon, signaling a claim to superiority. Conversely, "Black" identity was first imposed for the purpose of exclusion, later reclaimed as a title of pride through acts of collective will and leadership. (Perhaps, in the context of the period and events covered in this book, it is appropriate that the label bridges the two connotations.) Finally, the distinction of capitalization reflected in this text mirrors the historical, frequently similar treatment of "white," "Negro," and "Colored" in the press during the era.

A note on sources. Memory is fallible and subject to bias, even when immediately recorded. Most of the Mississippi State Sovereignty Commission records and even newspaper articles read like a game of "telephone," replicating each other ad nauseum and imperfectly, quoting or summarizing conversations days after they had taken place—not to mention the slant that might be placed on them by unconscious bias or intentional agendas. The court documents, interviews, and subsequent writings were recorded years or even decades after the fact. There are contradictions even between primary sources, usually over small matters, such as the exact wording of a reported incident. Names, in particular, are notorious for a variety of spellings from source to source. Obviously, I must assume myself capable of creating new errors or overlooking others. I hope that awareness has kept me alert and, therefore, any mistake on my part may also be small and not contradictory to the events and personalities I hope to honor by this work. I remind readers, as I remind myself, that everything in the text and sources should be scrutinized with your own capabilities. Neither history nor authority must ever turn away from scrutiny.

A secondary failing of the sources (and, no doubt, my own unconscious biases) must be acknowledged. Like any historical record, this book can only aspire to but never achieve a complete representation of events. I regret every relevant biography that is incomplete or absent within these pages, particularly of those figures for whom other scholarship does not redress this injustice. The gap I am most conscious of pertains to the women of the Biloxi wade-ins and other desegregation events. The absence of visibility is not the absence of action. I hope future research will illuminate their efforts and remove these chasms and that what information is accumulated here may be helpful to that end.

Just as this account cannot represent the fullness of one event, it cannot even approach the fullness of a person. This is perhaps especially important to remember as some participants of the fight for and against desegregation, and their direct descendants, are still living. This text is not a representation of any person, place, era, or culture in its entirety. It is a rough sketch, penciled in, in the hopes of reminding anyone who needs it: storms come and boats tip over. The person beside you can as easily drag you under as pull you to shore. I hope that we all find ourselves to be—and surround ourselves with—the latter.

WADING IN

Chapter One

BLACK IN BILOXI

Back-of-Town

Before colonization, the Biloxi coastline had a natural, narrow, sandy beach. The root systems of native plants such as dune grass, sea oats, saw palmettos, oaks, and pines grew nearly to the water, protecting the sand from the erosion of wind and waves. After exploring the area in 1699, French-Canadian soldiers, led by Pierre Le Moyne d'Iberville and his younger brother, Jean-Baptiste Le Moyne de Bienville, began to build forts in "Old" and "New" Biloxi. There, the colonists had met the native Tanêks, meaning "first people" in their Siouan language. To their northern neighbors, the Choctaw, the tribe was known as the Biloxi, or "worthless," from which the names of the two colonial sites were taken, presumably unwittingly.[1]

Like other colonists on the continent, the French already used enslaved Native peoples for labor, but they wanted access to African slaves, who had been used in other American and Caribbean colonies for nearly a hundred years and were considered more profitable, better suited to labor, and less likely to successfully escape bondage.[2] At first, Bienville hoped to acquire enslaved Black persons by exchange in the Caribbean: two enslaved Indigenous individuals from the continent (primarily women and children) per one (preferably young adult male) of African descent.[3] The plan was not approved by the royal court. Instead, within the decade, the newly formed *Compagnies des Indies* was financing the French slave trade directly from West Africa to Louisiana.[4]

Agents of the slave trade did not purchase these people thoughtlessly. Ship captains were instructed to purchase healthy individuals, preferably between eight and thirty years old,[5] who knew how to cultivate rice and other imported crops, as well as possessing necessary skills for the building up of a colony, such as masonry, metal-working, carpentry, weaving, pottery, agriculture, and the maritime trades. They were often taken from specific regions in Africa that were well known for the skills in demand at any given time.[6]

While it is possible that the French may have brought a few enslaved Africans to Biloxi at an earlier date, it was first recorded that *l'Afriquian*, carrying human cargo from Juba, West Africa, arrived in Biloxi in March 1721.[7] The same month, the *Duc du Maine* landed with nearly four hundred starving enslaved Africans on board; emergency rations of corn had to be brought from Haiti to feed them. In April, *le Neride* and, in June, *le Fortune* also docked in Biloxi, each carrying hundreds of enslaved people.[8] It is unclear if any of those chained on board were sold or exchanged in Biloxi; it was still a small settlement, and few, if any, of the colonists had the hard currency typically required.[9] The ships may have only stopped on the way to New Orleans, which was soon to replace Biloxi as the capital of the French-American colonies and had a greater demand for enslaved workers to support the wealthier population. In October 1723, *l'Expedition* landed in Biloxi and traded fifteen of its ninety-three enslaved Africans to the settlers there. The same year, *le Courier de Bourbon* left five sick enslaved individuals in Biloxi on its way past. Two died, and it is uncertain if the other three remained.[10]

Drawn circa 1722, Pierre Le Blond de la Tour's map, *Carte de partie de la coste du Nouveau Biloxy avec les isles des environs*, marks a place on the Back Bay as "Habitation pour les Negroes." The nearby brickyard, established by Captain Joseph Moran, suggests those enslaved individuals were instrumental in making the bricks that enabled the construction of permanent structures all along the coast, including New Orleans.[11] The excavated clay, mixed with cured Spanish moss, may also have been used to construct the French-style *bousillage* (mud daub) houses, another durable building technique used in the era and region.[12] Furthermore, New Orleans historian and slave owner Charles Gayarreé wrote that "the whole agricultural pursuits of the country" were due to the labor of enslaved Africans, as "it was almost impossible . . . to induce Europeans to attend to the labors of the field, on account of the heat . . . and the diseases."[13]

Over the next century, as Biloxi changed hands from French, to British, to Spanish rule, finally becoming an American city in 1817, the population remained small (fewer than five hundred residents) and, according to one visitor, "primitive . . . , retaining the gaiety and politeness of the French, blended with the abstemiousness and indolence of the Indian."[14] The advent of steamboats helped in the development of Biloxi as a resort destination, nearly doubling the population in the winter and summer months. The evolution of Biloxi as a resort destination during this period is evidenced by the construction of the Magnolia Hotel and Green Oaks Hotel in the late 1840s, two of many hotels and boardinghouses to open on the coast. With its proximity to New Orleans, Harrison County by 1850 boasted more than 3,400 permanent white residents from all over Europe, as well as the northeastern and southern US states (very few heads of households had been born in Mississippi).[15] More than 1,400 enslaved Blacks made up a large, though still minority, percentage of the population. Approximately fifty freedmen and -women (mostly identifying as mulatto) also resided in the county; some of them owned enslaved persons as well.[16] In 1850, William Pease's notable surprise at seeing Black folks "[given] the sidewalk" by whites in the town of Pass Christian might suggest that the coast indeed fostered a relaxed racialized classism, in comparison to other parts of the South—an idea that was often put forth by white observers whenever racial troubles arose on the coast. The growth of such a diverse population, the large ingress and egress of tourists and seasonal residents, and the long-standing relationships (indeed, relations) between some of the white and Black families in Harrison County may all have been favorable factors for the development of such an atmosphere. However, Pease may have been observing the free and landowning class of the Black population in Pass Christian, who were treated with a social attitude that was unique to their class and not the area.[17]

Because the coastal soil of Harrison County did not support the large-scale plantations most associated with slavery, other diverse industries rose in their place.[18] Enslaved Black workers were used as domestic servants in residences or as laborers on smaller farms and small businesses. Others were made to labor in the lumber and maritime industries.[19] The largest slaveholding business in the county was the Kendall brickworks, W. G. Kendall being the fifth owner of Captain Moran's original *briqueterie*. Over a hundred of those enslaved at the brickworks were young Black men, twenty-five were young Black or mulatto women, a few elders (older than fifty), and forty-five children (twelve and younger). The facilities were damaged by fire in the early 1850s; it was subsequently foreclosed and ceased production—the enslaved laborers presumably sold away.

After emancipation (by proclamation in 1863 and then with the passing of the 13th Amendment to the US Constitution in 1865), many freedmen found the fisheries, sawmills, turpentine stills, and railway industry paid better than farm work, so they gravitated to or remained in those employments.[20] Others worked in agriculture for themselves or ran general stores, taught or administered in education, enlisted in the armed forces, and held government positions (despite protest from the white community). There were many entrepreneurs, innovators, and community and civic leaders among them.[21] Yet, however much they contributed, Black citizens continued to find their way to upward economic and social mobility obstructed.

With the extension of railroads in the 1870s, Biloxi drew ever more business, tourism, and new residents—including former Confederate president Jefferson Davis, who resided at Beauvoir plantation, writing his memoir, until his death in 1889.[22] The city had come to be advertised as a resort "without rival."[23] After the connection of the railroad lines and invention of manufactured ice for refrigeration, seafood canneries opened in Biloxi and along the coast in the 1880s, further swelling the seasonal population with thousands of itinerant workers. Although the percentage of the Black population also increased, it remained in the minority in Harrison County (although in the majority statewide). For example, Black people made up roughly 30 percent of Harrison County in 1860, which increased to roughly 45 percent in 1900. Yet, except as they were necessary to create a romanticized impression of the Old South for tourists, filling subservient and entertainment roles in hotels and restaurants, which they entered and exited by the back doors, Black citizens were expected to be all but invisible in the larger community (although, to add insult to injury, a cursory study of surnames will indicate that many of these Black and white families were related, through enslaved labor if not bloodlines).[24] The residential face of the city was divided to this end. Economic barriers, constructed through the denial of loans and other redlining techniques, joined social pressure and the threat of violence in keeping Biloxi and other coastal towns segregated. Even the descendants of the freedmen and -women who had inherited beachfront property were elbowed out.[25] In Biloxi, as in other towns, "the other side of the tracks" was not just an expression of speech: the railroad divided the beachfront from the back bays and bayous, where, at a lower elevation, the swampy lands were less suitable for farming and more prone to flood damage.[26]

Known as "Back-of-Town" (or more derogatory names[27]), the historical Black neighborhood of Biloxi was bounded, east to west, by Lee Street and Caillavet Street, Auguste Bayou to the north, and, of course, the railroad on the south.[28] One of the first public enterprises in Back-of-Town was the Colored School, opened in 1886, held in a rented house owned by the Baptist church and "poorly furnished" in comparison to the "amply provided" white school (the former was given 20 percent of the funding afforded to the latter; a larger discrepancy existed between the salaries of the principals and teachers). A few mixed-race children who could evidently "pass" were temporarily suspended in their attempts to attend the better-supplied white schools in 1905 after complaints to the City Council led to an investigation; one suspension was made permanent when the child's race was "proved," a second investigation was made obsolete when the family moved to New Orleans.[29]

In the early 1900s, Back-of-Town saw the growth of Biloxi's Black business and entertainment district of Main Street between Division Street and the railroad, including Benjamin F. Miley's The Miley Hotel, Robert Wright's barber shop (associated with the Miley Hotel), Jack Joseph's restaurant "in the quarters," and The Eagle's Nest, a "negro club or gathering place on Railroad avenue."[30] In 1908, the *Daily Herald*'s reports revealed not only the presence of a Black Business League in Biloxi but also the oppressive, dangerous atmosphere in which it functioned. The morning of November 10, 1908, a white fourteen-year-old named Elzie Hausen was attacked while walking through the woods of the Back Bay. When she made it home, she identified Henry Lidy, a young Black man who lived nearby and worked for her family, as her assailant. Lidy was arrested. While the sheriff was "at lunch," a mob of well over a hundred white men broke Lidy from the jail and took him, in handcuffs, to the corner of Lee Street and the railroad. In what the paper termed an "exciting event," the mob slowly hung Lidy with a rope purchased from a nearby hardware store. Photographs and pieces of the rope were taken as souvenirs. That evening, rumors circulated that the Black citizens planned an "indignation meeting" to discuss "bringing a suit against the city for failure to protect Lidy." The former president of the local Negro Business League, attorney and teacher James Albert Burns, was one of several Biloxians who publicly refuted the gossip that seemed poised to incite further mob violence. Burns pointed out that pamphlets advertising the "regular meeting night" of the Negro Business League had been circulated before the assault; the meeting had subsequently been postponed "for fear of being misunderstood."[31] None of Lidy's murderers or bystanders were prosecuted. (Between 1900 and 1908, at least nine Black men were tortured and hanged in Mississippi City, Biloxi, Ocean Springs, and Vancleave. Two "lynching bee" victims, Henry Askew and Ed Russell, were widely acknowledged by the public to be, without a doubt, innocent of their accused crimes at the time of their murders.) One local journalist, with a nod to the reputation of the area as well as the economic repercussions of racialized violence, observed that such "occurrence will not add to the popularity of the coast as a place of resort or residence."[32]

Denied access to the whites-only tourist attractions, including the offshore legal gambling halls of the 1920s, Back-of-Town drew Black tourists from cities like Mobile and New Orleans, offering, between police raids, its fair share of illegal gambling and sale of alcohol (aka "blind tigers")—past times for which the resorts on both sides of the color line were well known. Notably, Biloxi became the home or stopping point for several famous pioneer musicians of rhythm and blues and jazz.[33] After the construction of Keesler Air

Force Base in 1941, the consistent patronage of the Black airmen added to the diversity and economic success of Back-of-Town.[34]

Despite the redlining in the city, Black Biloxians had historically enjoyed and used the coastline as a source of livelihood, for respite in its cooling waters, and for baptisms and religious revivals.[35] In June 1943, a meeting of the chief of police (Laz Quave), the Biloxi Business Club, and the provost marshal of Keesler Air Force Base to discuss the creation of a segregated area for Black swimmers "to prevent any dissension . . . between the races" suggested that the presence of nonsouthern Blacks, in the role of military service to their country, created a unique point of contention in the issue of recreational access to the water in Biloxi, even before the construction of the human-made beach.[36] However, nothing was ever done to create such a dubious temporary solution.

From 1879 onward, the beach road had been built a little at a time, much of it paved with oyster shells.[37] The construction of the road and its attendant homes, hotels, and other businesses removed the trees, shrubs, and grasses that had, until then, protected the coastline from erosion. The beach was subsequently washed and blown away, hurried along by tropical storms and hurricanes. With the beach gone, the road was in danger of becoming compromised as well.

On September 29, 1915, the so-called New Orleans hurricane caused six feet of flooding along the coast. Leaders in Gulfport and Biloxi began a petition to build a more permanent highway and a seawall to protect the shoreline and road from damage.[38] It took years for the project to be completed. Meanwhile, all resident males between eighteen and fifty-five years of age were required to work maintaining the streets for six ten-hour days every year (or to pay the city clerk three dollars in lieu of their labor).[39] By 1923, the beach road was finally paved with bricks and asphalt.[40] The following year, the county established a 2 percent gasoline tax for building the seawall.[41] Once built, the seawall worked as planned for some time.

In 1947, another Category 4 hurricane, George, challenged the seawall.[42] A new solution was required, and a local tax would not suffice to pay for it. The City of Biloxi was granted an initial sum of nearly $1.5 million of federal money to rebuild the shoreline. In 1953, the Army Corps of Engineers, under chief engineer O. L. Adams and hydraulic engineer William L. Dolive, replenished the beach by dredging up three hundred feet of sand from the bottom of the Gulf of Mexico and recreating the scenic beaches, which increased recreation opportunities.[43] Until this point, the people who owned beachfront property owned all the way to the low tide waterline.[44] By accepting federal money, Harrison County's replenished beaches had become public property. However, rather than making the beach *more* accessible to the Black population, it had the opposite effect.

Even into the 1950s, Black citizens *did* use the beaches, although custom tried to prevent it.[45] However, as Biloxi's reputation as the American Riviera developed, segregation tightened, and the beach became increasingly restricted.[46] Biloxian Clara Watson, born in 1933, ascribed the tightening segregation particularly to the presence of tourists from the (arguably) more stridently segregated "interior" South. Black maids were able to accompany white children in their charge. Generally, Black citizens could fish for themselves. However, any attempts by Blacks to swim or otherwise enjoy the beach were subject to complaints by homeowners, leading to the former being driven away by the police.[47] Those who wished to swim or play with less harassment had to be prepared and able to travel some distance to the segregated sections set aside for the Black population, too far for many who lacked transportation. There was no such area in Biloxi itself.

One available section was an area called the Rice Fields, in Pass Christian. The Rice Fields was a double lot the length of a city block across from the Episcopal church and owned by Lucille (Kinney) Van Horn. Whenever Black bathers "spilled out on either side," neighboring property owners would call the police.[48] For a few months in 1957, Black citizens were also permitted on a three hundred-foot stretch of beach in front of Gulfport's Veterans Administration Hospital. This area was soon closed to Blacks again, due to claims of it being overcrowded and "unsanitary," with the swimmers too noisy, "clad indecently," and "interfering with recreational activities developed for patients." Later, the director of the hospital denied that anyone, including himself, had ever complained that the bathers "swam nude." He insisted that the closing of this portion of the beach had "met with complete agreement at that time by local Negro leaders."[49]

There were further threats of closures when the segregated portions of the beaches drew Black tourists, even if they came from neighboring cities. Never mind that Black entrepreneurs had as much right to tourism as white or Black citizens and as much right to the company of their family and friends: those friends, family, and tourists—being federal taxpayers—had as much right to the enjoyment of the beach as anyone.[50] The Black community was also excluded from the "nearly half a million dollars" of employment opportunities associated with annual upkeep of the beach.[51]

And so it would, in likelihood, have remained for decades longer if not for the bravery and resolution of Dr. Gilbert Mason.

Chapter Two

STILL WATERS RUN DEEP

The Beginning of a Hero's Journey

Hundreds of people contributed to the desegregation of Biloxi beach. But by far, the leader of this civil rights watershed was Dr. Gilbert Mason. In 1928, Gilbert Rutledge Mason was born at home, on Riggins Alley, in a deeply segregated Jackson, Mississippi, the great-great-grandson of both enslaved people and slave owners. Growing up, Mason, along with other Black individuals, was not welcome nor allowed in libraries, parks, pools, theaters, or other facilities that served the white community. Even as a child, Mason was subjected to little aggressions, not-so-veiled threats, and even random acts of physical violence, prompted by nothing more than his skin color.

It was also the time of the Great Depression, and Gilbert grew up poor despite his father's owning a barber shop. Although the Mason family did not have luxuries, they used their limited funds to prioritize the primary education of the three children, a value that Gilbert took up wholeheartedly.[1] Despite a dominant culture that might have challenged Mason's sense of self-worth, he credited a large, loving family and active Black community for his "dignity and self-respect . . . the starting point for respecting others."[2]

Even at a young age, Mason showed a talent for leadership and love of order. While attending Jim Hill Jr. High, he served terms as class president, editor and head of the Writer's Club, president of the Mathematics Club, and president of the Citizenship Club, which fulfilled its aim to "do unto others as you would have them do unto you" by such activities as planting victory gardens to supplement rations and boost morale during World War II. All of these positions required that Mason maintain excellent grades; he was often found on the honors list. He was popular as well, frequently featured in his school's Who's Who column as handsome, smart, stylish, and—in his own word—"smooth."[3] Tall and trim, with a naturally confident bearing and eternally youthful face throughout his life, Mason would impress even his adversaries, who could find very little negative to say about him, openly or behind closed doors.

Outside of school, Mason was a dedicated member of the Boy Scouts. Though the scouts had a problematic approach to race, categorizing Black troops as "delinquent" and "special needs," while giving them fewer resources than their white peers, participation in the organization nevertheless gave Mason and thousands of other children another opportunity to witness community activism in practice. The College Hill Baptist Church sponsored the troop, and many Black citizens of Jackson volunteered their time, energy, and skill as merit badge counselors. Rev. Robert L. T. Smith, founder of the Jackson branch of the NAACP, served on the scout committee.[4] Smith, who would go on to be one of the first two Black Mississippians to run for Congress since Reconstruction, volunteered alongside scoutmaster James A. White, not only talking to the boys about the struggle for civil rights, but demonstrating it in their daily lives, like many others in the community.[5] Another pivotal and foreshadowing experience was Mason's struggle to obtain his scout's merit badge in swimming. Prevented from using the whites-only pools, Mason and his friend Joseph Debro practiced for their badges in the local swimming hole, fed from the brickyard pond in which Mason had been baptized. They then had to wait months for permission to be evaluated by a white lifesaver, as there was none certified at the Black camp. Having obtained their final badges, Mason and Debro had earned the scouts' highest rank, becoming the first Black Eagle Scouts in Jackson, second in the state.[6] Mason took seriously the Boy Scouts' oath to "help other people at all times" and reflected often on the words of the scouts' vespers song: "As our campfire fades away / Silently, each Scout should ask / Have I done my daily task? / Have I kept my honor bright? / Can I guiltless sleep tonight?"[7]

"So it was with my life," Mason later said.[8] Going forward, he was often the first to break racial barriers in the institutions he was involved with.

In high school, Mason continued his civic roles. He helped form clubs in leadership, such as the Boys' Forum and the Social Political and Economic Club, in which he was greatly impressed by Robert's Rules of Order, the leading manual of parliamentary procedure, which he would continue to refer to throughout his life and commitment to numerous civic committees.[9] He was a well-rounded individual: social and academic, athletic and artistic, enjoying science and poetry. Having skipped the eleventh grade, Mason graduated high school at age sixteen, around 1944, and became the first in his immediate family to go to college.[10]

The local college, Tougaloo, which his parents could have afforded, offered a degree in the liberal arts—but Mason had always wanted to be a doctor. To do so, he would have to work to pay the additional expense of a medical education. Mason moved to Chicago during the summer, living with extended family and working from daybreak to dusk at a can-making company to earn his tuition.[11] In Chicago, Mason experienced a different, though not utopian, form of race relations. Neighborhoods were segregated, but public transport was not, and people of any race received service in the same restaurants and shops. During his work breaks, Mason was able to freely mingle with friends of other races, without fear of violence descending on them.

Tuition earned, Mason enrolled at what was then Tennessee Agricultural and Industrial State University, starting his journey into pre-med. Never one to do the least, Mason took a double major in chemistry and biology, with a minor in math, while continuing to work and compete on the swim team. He made straight As. In addition to excelling at all his commitments, in his freshman year, Mason found time to make a lasting connection with Natalie Lorraine Hamlar, an apple-cheeked young woman from Virginia who was majoring in social work.[12] They had a lot in common: Hamlar was also an honors student, involved in the civic life of her school, a Girl Scout, and homecoming queen, raised in a loving and active family who highly valued education.[13] The next year, Mason and Hamlar got "pinned," a symbol of pre-engagement commitment. However, equally committed to completing her program, in her sophomore year Hamlar transferred to Howard University in Washington, DC, a historically Black college that had opened soon after the Civil War. To all the usual obstacles faced by a young couple was added the challenge of maintaining their affection for each other during their time apart; as with the many challenges they faced in their lives, they were equal to it.[14]

In his autobiography, *Beaches, Blood, and Ballots: A Black Doctor's Civil Rights Struggle*, Mason later wrote, "For once, Mississippi's Jim Crow system favored me."[15] There were no medical schools that admitted Black scholars in Mississippi, but there was a great need for Black doctors. At the time of his graduation, there were only forty-seven Black doctors in the state although there were eighty-two counties. Therefore, the state offered a $5,000 stipend to Black medical students who agreed to practice in the state for five years after graduation.[16] After completing his studies in Tennessee, Mason accepted the stipend and enrolled in Howard University's medical school.

Although, to a Mississippian, Washington, DC, may have seemed like the far north, it was still a southern city. Public spaces there were as segregated as any in the Deep South. Still working to pay for his education, Mason and his Black coworkers had to keep to the back rooms and corridors of places like the Roger Smith and Omni Shoreham hotels.[17] During those years, Mason also came alongside the effects of a chilling chapter in global racism as some of his coworkers were Jewish refugees who had fled the Holocaust in Europe. Yet DC was also a pivotal place in the growing civil rights movement, and circumstances that arose with the close of World War II were major catalysts of the movement as Black soldiers, returning from war uplifted by the victory and their experiences abroad, and Black civilian workers who had aided the war effort turned their attention to the Double V Campaign, intent on defeating "the myth of racial superiority" and achieving true democracy at home as well. Beginning in 1942, Howard University students pioneered the "stool-sitting" technique of occupying stools at a local cafeteria and other stores that denied Black people service.[18] A remarkable local figure, Mary Church Terrell, one of the founders of both the National Association of Colored Women and the NAACP, was a lifelong activist. In 1950 (the year Mason was admitted to Howard), Terrell, at age eighty-six, was still winning antidiscrimination lawsuits, such as the Supreme Court victory that ended the segregation of restaurants in DC.[19] But even as one broke barriers, Black citizens were still constricted in so many ways. More than once, Mason and his peers found themselves the first Black students to extern in previously whites-only hospitals that were in the process of desegregating, allowed to go on rounds but not physically examine white patients—some of whom hardly believed Black doctors existed.[20]

All his life, Mason had experienced and witnessed the example of people who uplifted not only themselves or their own families but the larger community with their time, skill, and knowledge. At Howard, his professors reinforced this lesson by saying that a doctor is not just a healer but a teacher, and a doctor should become a part of the community. "Medicine is so close to Civil Rights," Mason would later say. "Medicine has to do with healing the soul, the heart, spirit, and the body. And so does Civil Rights." He reflected deeply on the part of the Hippocratic oath that said, "I will teach this art to my son." For Mason, this meant not only his own child, but "other sons" of the next generation.[21] And Mason *would* soon have a son to follow in his footsteps, both in medicine and community action. As well rounded as always, Mason and Natalie Hamlar married in her parents' backyard, and their son, Gilbert Jr., was born in their final semester—appearing just in time to see his parents graduate with honors.[22]

Mason took his state medical license exams in the tall brick corner building of the King Edward Hotel in Jackson. In this hotel, blues players like the Mississippi Sheiks and other Black performers were frequently applauded by the white audiences. However, Mason was not permitted to take his test break with his white peers in the lobby or hotel coffee shop, but was told to wait in the exam room.[23] Following his licensure, Mason made a connection with Dr. Felix Dunn of Gulfport, Mississippi, a Black doctor, businessman, and president of the local NAACP chapter. Dunn introduced Mason to Dr. Velma

Wesley, who was leaving her practice—and, therefore, an opening for a Black doctor—in Biloxi.[24] Natalie Mason's family, who were "used to some segregation but not the Mississippi kind of segregation," feared the reputation of the state. Nevertheless, the stipend he had received to help fund his education meant that Mason must return to the state he grew up in for at least five years.

In 1955, Dr. Mason moved to Biloxi and opened his practice as a family doctor. He bought the equipment of the outgoing doctor, and he, with his family, moved into a two-bedroom apartment on Nixon Street, where Natalie took up her full-time role as mother and homemaker.[25] One newspaper later described Mason as "a pipe-smoking man in a button-down shirt who sees flocks of patients in a cramped and old but air-conditioned office."[26] Indeed, for many years, Mason would be the only Black doctor available to a minority population of almost ten thousand in Biloxi. (Black citizens could visit white doctors if they could afford it and were willing to use a separate entrance and waiting room.) After attending all those who were able to make it to his office, Mason would depart on a round of house calls, then break for dinner and the evening news with his family before going back out again.[27] Even when he was home for the evening, enjoying television series like *Bonanza* or *The Red Skelton Show* with his wife and son, he was adept at "phone triage" with the patients who called for medical advice until they could be seen at the office the next day.[28] On Thursdays, a Black dentist from Keesler, Dr. Jerry Taylor, would moonlight in Mason's office. For many years, he was the only Black dentist to serve Biloxians, who otherwise had to rely on the undependable accessibility of white dentists.

In addition to his family practice, Mason needed staff privileges at New Biloxi Hospital on the beach in order to deliver babies and perform the minor surgeries necessary for his patients. The hospital administrator, Emma Lou Ford, who had been in the post since 1948, easily granted him staff privileges, but only as a "courtesy" member who was not allowed to vote at staff meetings for the next eleven years—a situation, his son later reflected, that worked to his advantage in some ways, helping avoid some of "the necessary hospital politics."[29] Initially, Mason encountered pushback from at least one member of the staff, who did not want to "take orders" from a Black doctor.[30] These kinds of racialized limitations also presented themselves in his membership with the Mississippi State Medical Association and Coast Counties Medical Society (which excluded women as well).[31] The medical association, for example, created the designation of "scientific member," so Mason and another Black doctor could attend those lectures but not the social or business sections of their meetings.[32] Once, Mason was excluded from the scientific lecture because the speaker, Rubel Phillips, would not speak to an integrated audience. On this occasion, several of his white colleagues found the exclusion as unacceptable as he did: Dr. Frank Gruich, Dr. Charles Floyd of Gulfport, Dr. A. K. Martinolich, and Dr. D. L. Clippinger from the naval home walked out of the conference with him. Refusing to be "embarrassed by being designated a second-rate [participant]," Mason persisted, reflecting he must "get in the door, be seen, find out what's going on," regardless of any slight.[33]

Being denied full membership and voting privileges in their state medical associations meant that Black physicians were not eligible for membership in the American Medical Association. In response, Black physicians had organized the separate National Medical Association (open to all races) and other local associations to support their peers and the timely circulation of pertinent information.[34] Because of his race, Dr. Mason was likewise excluded from the Chamber of Commerce, limiting his ability to advocate for Black businesses and entrepreneurs in the city.[35] Yet, as always, the Masons engaged in the civic life of their community through every available means. Beyond their vocations, their service included the political, economic, and spiritual; from their earliest days in Biloxi, the Masons established themselves as Scout leaders, members of the Gulfport chapter of the NAACP, and loyal congregants of the First Missionary Baptist Church, where Natalie also taught Sunday School.[36]

Within the hospital, prejudice and the effects of segregation showed themselves in some subtle and not-so-subtle ways. One of the most obvious was the banishment of Black patients to an unfinished and derelict annex of the hospital, where there were eight beds. Expectant or postnatal mothers and their infants were bedded alongside injured and infectious patients. Women in labor were not moved into the delivery rooms until the last minute, and Black babies were not put into the nursery unless they were critically ill.[37] Such conditions did not make it easy for Mason to achieve his goal of radically improving the rates of mother and infant mortality, which were (and continue to be) disproportionately high—almost double that of their white counterparts—in the Black community, even when factors such as poverty, education, limited access to and lower quality of prenatal and postnatal care, and maternal health risk factors are controlled for.[38] Given these factors, researchers try to assess what part the consequences of systemic racism play in the mortality rates of Black infants and their mothers. The cumulative or "weathering" model suggests that chronic stress damages individuals' physiological systems, suppressing immune response and increasing the risk of infections and complications in pregnancy. Some of those stressors disproportionate to the Black community were (and are, despite qualified income and credit) less access to adequate and stable housing, greater chance of exposure to environmental toxins, and jobs less likely to include benefits like paid sick days or family leave. Another factor—one that speaks to the importance of Mason's return to Mississippi—is the need for diversity among medical professionals to reflect the general population. After only three months, babies can better identify different emotions in people of the race they have the most exposure to. By adulthood, this "in-group bias," increased by cultural misinformation, may leave white doctors unable to serve other-race patients equitably (particularly women, as sexism intersects with racial bias). Even in the twenty-first century, an alarming percentage of white doctors believe such unscientific folklore as Black people having thicker skin and less sensitive nerve endings; without bias training, they may not even become aware of their prejudices or their negative effect. One consequence may be the inability to recognize, take seriously, and act quickly on Black maternal distress, pre- and postnatal.

In 1956, the new hospital administrator, S. E. Grimes, granted Mason's request for two private rooms in which to care for his mothers and their babies after labor. And indeed, throughout his career, Mason lost only one infant in over three thousand births. This was far below the US average of over forty deaths per thousand for Black infants from 1950 to 1960.[39] This same hospital administrator, however, upheld some of the subtler practices of discrimination in the hospital. Mason discovered that Grimes had directed all departments not to put "Mr." or "Mrs." in front of Black patients' names on their forms, as was done with white patients (even white children were labeled as "little master" or "little miss").[40] This absence of courtesy titles with the names of Black patients was an example of what one might call the protocol of bigotry. It was the same etiquette that dictated that Black people (as the supposedly socially inferior party) should not introduce themselves to or extend their hand to shake that of a white person (supposedly socially superior), no matter their relative education or wealth. Mason, whose parents had taught him to never accept any demeaning or subservient form of address and would not allow it among his patients, objected. Finding that a request to Grimes made no difference in this case, Mason went to the hospital board's attorney. Some of his white colleagues joined the complaint. Rather than grant the courtesy title to Black patients, Grimes finally dropped them for all—an apt analogy, perhaps, for the way an unjust culture injures everyone within it.[41]

Why, a hundred years after the end of slavery, did Dr. Mason and his peers have so much to contend against?

Chapter Three

RIPTIDES

How Black Taxpayers Were Forced to Fund Their Oppression

The 13th Amendment of the US Constitution had ended slavery, and the 14th had stated that "all persons born or naturalized in the United States" should have "equal protection of the laws." But the potential of those and the 15th Amendment, which guaranteed voting rights to all men, was quickly undermined by segregation laws, as well as unofficial exclusion practices in various states.

At first, when Black males gained the vote, registration was high across their demographic group, while many Black women joined in political activity by attending or guarding meetings, forming societies, and monitoring polling stations, not only to subvert fraud and intimidation but to ensure the men felt the weight of the gendered and racialized responsibility they bore, while also making their own allegiances known through campaign buttons and other displays.[1] In Mississippi, elected positions became well integrated. Of the sixteen Black men who served in Congress in the early twentieth century, Hiram Revels of Mississippi was the first to be elected; Blanche K. Bruce of Mississippi was the second. Black men served as policemen, sheriffs, lawyers, magistrates, mayors, senators, and more. And because jury lists were drawn from voters' lists, a Black person facing trial could expect to stand before a panel that included Black men.[2] However, even before Reconstruction ended, racial bigots mobilized to shift political control back into exclusively white (and wealthier) hands, a process they called "Redemption."[3] While these racists did what they could through grift and murder, it was also necessary to construct legal and economic obstacles to Black voting.[4]

"There has not been a full vote and a fair count in Mississippi since 1875," Judge J. J. Chrisman admitted. "We have been preserving the ascendancy of the white people by revolutionary methods . . . stuffing the ballot boxes, committing perjury, and . . . carrying the elections by fraud and violence." It was time to put the practice into law. In 1890, Mississippi was the first to write a new state constitution with the sole purpose of disenfranchising Black citizens, pooling them with the "idiots, insane persons and Indians not taxed," who were also barred from voting.[5] Judge Solomon Calhoon, president of the constitutional convention, announced clearly, "We came here to exclude the Negro. Nothing short of this will answer." They even considered passing women's suffrage as a way of mobilizing additional white votes but, perhaps realizing this would also increase Black votership, as well as undermining the hierarchy in other unpredictable ways, concluded they had enough power without resorting to such exceptional measures.[6]

The methods to exclude Black voters included grandfather and good character clauses, expanded residency requirements, poll taxes (which must be paid before candidates were announced), secret ballots, literacy and "reasonable interpretation" tests (chosen by the registrar), and publication of voters' names and addresses in the local newspapers.[7] If Black citizens could arrange time off from work without fear of reprisal, they might arrive to find a late opening at the registrar office, early closure, or prolonged lunch breaks—not to mention a patrol of armed whites.[8] Following the Mississippi convention, qualified Black votership dwindled rapidly from over fifty thousand to a few thousand voters. For a time, poor whites and Blacks were encouraged by some political parties to vote and act together based on their common class interests. As populist Tom Watson said, "The accident of color can make no difference in the interest of farmers, croppers, and laborers." Labor unions attempted to mobilize voter registration across racial lines; however, their interracial work, as well as the perception of unions as the bearers of communist ideology, brought them under attack. Other whites, like politician Marsh Cook, who did not comply with the status quo were as likely to be killed as those whose rights they sought to uphold.

In addition to cutting the feet out from under the voter base, the gatekeepers created similar obstacles for Black citizens running for elected offices, such as increased filing fees and withholding information about qualifications.[9] Most significantly, until 1944 it was not considered a violation of the 15th Amendment to bar Blacks from voting in primary elections, all but ensuring that Black representatives never made it to the final ballot and that even white candidates would be those who swore to uphold institutional segregation. In 1901, the last Black congressman from the South, George White, left Congress; it would be seventy years before the House of Representatives was reintegrated.

The steady decline of Black representation offered less and less incentive to offset the consequences of challenging the racial hierarchy in the poll booth.[10] When the 19th Amendment was passed in 1920, the same obstacles and intimidation were used against women voters, particularly those of color. (The poll tax was a special burden as most women were financially dependent and relied on the willingness and ability of their fathers or husbands to pay it.[11]) The lack of voter turnout, like other suppressed civic involvement, was framed by white supremacists as ambivalence, even contentment, within the Black community regarding the status quo and race relations.[12]

Without Black representation, it was much easier for those in power to pass legislation to maintain the status quo as well as they could through segregation. In 1896, in *Plessy v. Ferguson*, the US Supreme Court upheld the right of states to separate people for "distinctions based upon color." Justice Henry Brown, who wrote the court's decision, claimed it was faulty logic to believe "the enforced separation of the two races stamps the colored race with a badge of inferiority. If this be so, it is . . . solely because the colored race chooses to put that construction upon it."[13]

Putting aside all other sociological and moral arguments for the moment, one has only to look at a photograph of these separate but equal accommodations to see how inept the practice was. In the wake of the Supreme Court decision, many states enacted a series of laws enforcing segregation that came to be known as Jim Crow laws, after the blackface character of the name popularized in the late 1820s. Sometimes these laws were very particular: in Georgia, white and Black amateur baseball teams could not play within two blocks of each other. In Alabama, whites and Blacks could not play pool "in the company of each other." In Louisiana, any outdoor show with both races attending had to have two ticket booths, twenty-five feet apart. Sometimes the laws were broader. In Mississippi, anyone who was "guilty of printing, publishing or circulating [writing] urging or presenting for public acceptance or general information, arguments or suggestions in favor of social equality or of intermarriage between whites and negroes" was subject to a fine up to $500 and imprisonment up to six months.[14]

Particularly harmful, given literacy requirements for voting and other benefits of social advancement—and given that freedmen and -women had been emancipated from conditions under which their education had been illegal—was the appalling maintenance of dual school system. During Reconstruction, the mandate for public schooling had been called "an unmitigated outrage" against the liberty of white Mississippians, as it was believed the system was using tax dollars to primarily benefit Black children.[15] In 1904, Governor James K. Vardaman objected that "the education of a Negro only spoils a good field hand."[16] Indeed, the economic hierarchy relied on cheap, compliant, and largely minority labor.[17] As with the vote, the people in power did their best to prevent an equitable quality of education.

When visiting Biloxi as an unsuccessful candidate for governor in 1907, Judge Jeff Truly—who spoke against immigration on the grounds that white children would be influenced by families who "did not regard their racial superiority as they should"—protested that Black children, being the majority, outnumbered their white peers in school by the tens of thousands. With what newspapers deemed "not unkindly wit," Truly laughed at the need and "vogue" for higher education in the Black schools of Mississippi. He received cheers and applause when he claimed that, while a trustee at Alcorn College, he had "eliminated geology . . . and inserted bricklaying, had taken out astronomy and put in shoe-making and in place of English literature had substituted hog raising."[18] This manipulation of the curriculum to the disadvantage of Black students was mirrored in primary and secondary schools. In 1925, Mississippi's governor Henry Whitfield requested a study of the state's educational system, with an eye to suggestions for its improvement. Wisconsin professor Michael Vincent O'Shea, who conducted the study, advised not a "separate but equal" policy but an each-according-to-their-needs policy, as determined by some disturbing calculations. For the 90 percent of Blacks (and a little over 50 percent of rural whites) who were expected to become farmers, education should center on hygiene and agriculture.[19] O'Shea wrote that Black children should only be taught grammar to fifth grade, with literature not "idealistic beyond the sphere of negro life," but that would "help the negro to adjust himself most harmoniously and happily to his fellows and to the white race." There was no need for algebra or history, other than that which "will explain the status . . . of the negro" in American culture.

O'Shea admitted more than he likely intended or realized when he claimed that Black leaders agreed that the "linguistic and mathematical needs" of Black children would never be "complex or elaborate, unless social conditions greatly change." O'Shea's own attitude toward Black intelligence was ironic, given his criticism of the allegedly "unscientific, if not superstitious, attitudes towards natural phenomena" that he claimed were held by the Black community. He believed most Black people were biologically unfit for better education. Those few who were capable of leadership *of their people* he credited to the "mixture of blood" so prevalent despite miscegenation laws, which O'Shea believed resulted in "intellectual and temperamental traits which are different from those of pure blood" (emphasis mine). For those who were fit to be the "ministers, teachers, lawyers, physicians and editors" who would serve the Black community, their secondary education and training still needed only to match their proscribed needs, with a focus on hygiene, economics, psychology, and nature.[20]

The fear that the state's resources would be used to educate Black children was soon put to rest, as funds were channeled into white schools instead. In 1899, the state school superintendent, A. A. Kincannon, reported that it could be "readily admitted by every white man in Mississippi that our public school system is designed primarily for the welfare of the white children of the state, and incidentally, for the negro children."[21] By 1939, for example, money was distributed at a nearly ten-to-one ratio between the segregated white and Black schools.[22] In that period, Black teachers, whose own educational opportunities to gain official qualifications were limited, were paid less than half what their white counterparts were, resulting in fewer teachers and crowded classrooms.[23] When the state Department of Education did consider improvements for Black schools, it was framed as being "what the white people of Mississippi deserve" in the "status of their colored people"—in other words, better trained laborers and servants.[24] It was against all odds that the segregated school system and community nevertheless produced many students as dedicated and successful as Dr. Gilbert Mason.

Meanwhile, all around the country for over half a century, activists protested the Jim Crow laws by creating organizations, educating the community, filing lawsuits, boycotting businesses, and staging sit-ins and other demonstrations to bring attention to the way these "distinctions" allowed minorities to be treated as "Other" and "less than." The end of World War II in 1945 and the return of Black soldiers, determined to realize the freedom from racial discrimination at home that they had fought for abroad, coincided with a renewed determination to raise Black power, dignity, and autonomy within the larger community. Finally, thanks to the relentless effort and arguments put forth by the NAACP lawyers and scholars from Howard University, in 1954 the US Supreme Court ruled that segregation by race in public schools was unconstitutional, in the case of *Brown v. Board of Education of Topeka*. The following year, in *Brown II*, the court further ruled that public school desegregation must be completed "with all deliberate speed."[25] Unfortunately, that phrase left a lot of room for interpretation. In the case of Harrison County, Mississippi, it meant a struggle of another decade.

People who opposed the civil rights movement feared school desegregation would mean other institutions, public spaces, and facilities would eventually be opened as well. They did a lot to stop that from happening. In addition to the threat of physical violence, the white hierarchy exercised significant economic threat as they controlled huge portions of employment and housing opportunities, the judicial system, and assistance programs such as welfare and Social Security.[26] Black people who were willing to take significant risks to defend their rights also had to be prepared to take the matter to court and to appeal decisions against them, while being harassed, economically and physically abused, even killed. In Humphreys County in 1955, Rev. George Lee was murdered for refusing to remove his name from voter lists after he and Gus Courts, his partner in founding the Belzoni, Mississippi, branch of the NAACP, were the first Blacks to register since Reconstruction. The sheriff's office tried to conceal the murder, calling it a "traffic accident," and local telephone operators refused to take long distance calls from Blacks in an effort to keep the story from spreading.[27] Also in 1955, Korean War veteran Clyde Kennard tried to register at the University of Southern Mississippi to complete his political science degree. After being unable to provide the required five alumni recommendations (all previous graduates being, of course, white), he applied again in 1958 and 1959, after which he was framed for multiple charges, including the theft of twenty-five dollars of chicken feed, and was jailed for seven years. During his imprisonment, he was denied treatment for cancer and was released only to be allowed to die at home.[28]

In 1956, nineteen southern senators and eighty-two representatives let their feelings be known to Congress in "The Declaration of Constitutional Principles," also called "The Southern Manifesto." The writers said that the civil rights movement represented a dangerous "temporary popular passion," which the constitution and its amendments were designed to prevent. They called *Brown v. Board of Education* an "unwarranted decision" that substituted "naked power for established law" (apparently unconscious of the hypocrisy of such wording, given examples such as those above). Without any explanation ever given for their reasoning, they claimed—quite common among opponents of the civil rights movement—that such desegregation measures were "destroying the amicable relations between white and Negro races." They had, according to these men, "planted hatred and suspicion where there has been heretofore friendship and understanding." They vowed "to use all lawful means to bring about a reversal of this decision . . . and to prevent the use of force in its implementation." In perhaps a slight acknowledgment of the violence ever at hand, they concluded with an "appeal to our people not to be provoked by the agitators and trouble-makers invading our States, and to scrupulously refrain from . . . lawless acts."[29]

Mississippi's governor, James Coleman, created the Mississippi State Sovereignty Commission (SSC) the same year. The commission, whose office was near the governor's, was supposed to provide the nation, businesses, and tourists with the image of "friendly"—i.e., segregated—race relations in the South. Its aim was to guard against desegregation attempts and to help preserve Mississippi's traditionally segregated way of life.[30] Ostensibly, this meant advertisements, lectures, and press tours of the state. However, the SSC also hired investigators to spy and inform on over a hundred thousand suspected civil rights activists, organizations, and activities throughout the state.[31] Its goal was to keep local struggles from becoming a national issue. A public fight for rights would prove that not everyone *was* happy with the "friendly" status quo. The information gathered was used to blackmail, threaten, and harass activists and to disrupt projects intended to better the condition of Black people in Mississippi. In particular, the SSC sought to control those in leadership roles in the Black community: pastors, school principals, doctors, and journalists. They paid some of these highly influential leaders to be informants and to give interviews in the press supporting segregation (Baptist Rev. H. H. Humes and Percy Greene, both newspaper editors, were two of the first on record).[32] The SSC worked hand in hand with local law enforcement and bureaucrats, even attempting to solicit information from FBI agents.[33]

"Mississippi," wrote a columnist for the *Times Picayune*, was "the only state which has fought off racial integration successfully on all fronts" and had at its command "extensive funds earmarked for fighting desegregation suits."[34] Those funds, like those of the beach restoration, had come from taxpayers. Like their labor under slavery, Black taxpayer dollars still helped fund the very groups that suppressed and opposed them. The SSC also funneled $20,000 of this money to the private group of racial watch dogs, the White Citizens' Council (WCC), despite the protest of some Mississippians, such as newspaperman Percy "P. D." East.[35] Formed less than two months after *Brown v. Board of Education*, the WCC was considered to be the middle-to-upper-class version of the Ku Klux Klan (KKK). In addition to social and economic intimidation, the WCC extensively promoted its ideals and pseudoscience in lectures, pamphlets, radio programs, and other media, even children's books.[36] Although there was a Klan presence in Biloxi, SSC members sought to distance themselves from it. In 1960, in response to an article stating the KKK had been reactivated in Mississippi under so-called "grand dragon" Walter A. Bailey of Biloxi, SSC agents determined to find out what they could about it and otherwise "play down such an incident as it served to stir up racial agitation." Governor James Coleman claimed the KKK, banned by law, was "not active in his state." It is possible Walter A. Bailey was a Klan of one—or joined only by his wife—as newspapers do not appear to connect any other Mississippian to the organization during its dormant period, from 1944 until the 1960s. However, given that the Klan was known for secrecy, the question of its membership and activity in Harrison County during this period should, perhaps, be left open.[37]

Groups like the SSC and WCC, as Dr. Martin Luther King Jr. pointed out, demanded "absolute conformity from whites and abject submission from Negroes."[38] Enforcing segregation meant policing the white population as well as the Black. For example, in Harrison County, white beachgoers had to be removed from entering or even going too close to the segregated areas designated for the Black community. Local authorities attempted to blame these whites' apparent nonchalance toward racial separation on their being from out of state.[39] This was a far from isolated example; in fact, police and SCC agents regularly investigated and harassed whites who were suspected of integrationist, Jewish, or communist leanings (these three characteristics were considered by some practically synonymous—suspicions that were often unfounded, though members of each did reach out of the Black community for alliances based on their similar struggles and interests). SSC agent Hal DeCell compiled a list of both white and Black citizens suspected of NAACP connections and advised, "These people should be harassed as soon as possible."[40] To keep the hierarchy intact, it was imperative that Blacks not only be discouraged from seeking their own advancement but that they be cut off from any potential support, which might offer them greater visibility and security.

Chapter Four

WADING IN

Petition, Rejection, and "Operation Surf"

The Mississippi State Sovereignty Commission (SSC) left a wealth of primary source documentation of the Biloxi wade-ins and the atmosphere surrounding them. These records reveal that, even before his swim in the Gulf of Mexico, Dr. Gilbert Mason was listed as a potential agitator of civil rights.[1] At the time, Harrison County officials were apparently concerned about the growing number of local Black voters and the assumed NAACP influence behind them. The 1,400 Blacks registered were "voting in block, and ... it was apparent that someone was coaching and helping them in getting registered and showing them how to vote and who to vote for." Biloxi's chief of police, Herbert McDonnell, reported that, while there was no NAACP chapter in town, "there are, undoubtedly, members of the NAACP in Biloxi who attend meetings of this organization elsewhere." Mason was listed among these potential agitators, along with his home and office addresses.[2] Gulfport's chief of police, George E. Mullens, expressed suspicion that one of the two Black deputies on the force was a member of the NAACP. Mullens wanted to fire the man but felt it was impossible, as the deputy had lately been wounded in the line of duty.

There was significant pressure not to be, or to not let it be known if one was, a member of the NAACP.[3] One technique of subverting detection and harassment was the use of other Black action groups, social clubs, lodges, and associations that vicariously supported the NAACP. The SSC listed the local "fronts" as including the Regional Council of Negro Leadership, the Negro Ministerial Association, the Negro Elks, the Black fraternities Kappa Alpha Psi and Omega Psi Phi, and the Negro Youth Council—perhaps "the most potentially dangerous," it noted, "because it is dealing with Negro teenagers."[4] On the other hand, obtusely or with genuine delusion, segregationists sometimes concluded, by the scarcity of visible NAACP activity, that Black people did not want equal rights. In his report of December 4, 1958, SSC agent Hal DeCell wrote that not everyone listed as a local member was truly "sympathetic to the NAACP"; some—he claimed—were becoming "disillusioned" and would, like others, "drop their memberships and get in step with the majority of the Negroes."[5] While DeCell smugly believed the Black community had "absolutely no knowledge of the existence of this list and . . . are thereby easier to keep track of," Harrison County Sheriff J. J. Wittman's assessment that the active NAACP in Gulfport "kept their movements and activities secret" seems more clear-sighted.[6]

Dr. Mason never felt the need for secrecy, however. He often talked with family and friends about the need and opportunities for desegregation in Harrison County and was, as suspected, already working with the Gulfport NAACP to grow the local minority vote. Looking ahead to his son's education, he was troubled by the significant inequality of the segregated school system in Biloxi, and he was disturbed by the so-called "traditional" segregation of the beach.[7] Like anyone who wishes to live on the coast, Mason was drawn to the area, in part, because of the warm water of the Gulf of Mexico.[8] He had, after all, loved swimming and excelled in the sport since his childhood. As exemplified by the historical seaside revivals, not only is water necessary for survival and beneficial to our physical and mental health, but it carries great symbolic meaning. It represents our origins, furthest horizons, and unexplored depths. To be denied its use and enjoyment sends a clear message of one's status or lack thereof.

There were places Mason could take his family to swim. A section of the beach, twenty miles down the highway, in Pass Christian was where Black swimmers were met with varying degrees of tolerance and harassment. The two-acre human-made lake at Camp Attawah, the Colored Boy Scout camp, located forty miles north near Wiggins, Mississippi, was advertised for its "significance" as the only "place where negro youth in South Mississippi can learn swimming and life saving and other aquatic skills."[9] Other options were the segregated pool next to Nichols High and—after they had befriended some of the Keesler Air Force Base officers—the desegregated pool on the base, which the Mason family enjoyed in addition to its desegregated movie theaters and other amenities.[10] However, none of these was a substitute for the wide open splendor of the groomed white sand and calm, silty waters of the Gulf, just a few blocks away. The county-owned garbage cans and maintenance equipment kept on the beach were a constant reminder that it was public property, which tax dollars from both Black and white citizens had paid for and continued to be required for its upkeep.

In the afternoon of May 14, 1959, with the weather a sunny, 85 degrees,[11] Mason approached his neighbors. This was the day. He was ready, as he said, to get "into trouble": he was going to swim.[12] He invited his neighbors, Murray Saucier, whose family owned the funeral parlor across the street,[13] and James Hoze, who lived in neighboring apartments and whose sons were in Mason's Boy Scout troop. Accompanying them, Mason brought his own five-year-old son. Hoze brought his children, Jimmie, Gloria, and Jackie.[14] Thirteen-year-old Adell Lott (who was also in the scouts and had been spending the afternoon at the Mason apartment, as he often did) and Otha Lee Floyd came as well.[15]

The nine drove down—Dr. Mason behind the wheel of his "treasured" Banner Blue Ford—choosing a spot south of Biloxi's old cemetery to unpack.[16] It must have been like any fine day: feet sinking into the hot white sand until one reaches the cool, damp, compact shoreline. The salty, slightly sulfurous scent of the water. The cry of gulls circling overhead, above the lulling sound of low, easy waves. Beyond the tall, long piers, the white silhouettes of sailboats or the outrigging of shrimp trawlers on the horizon. Mason, his friends, and the children had only been in the water a short time when, responding to a car accident on the road nearby, a policeman came and ordered them out.[17]

"Take your time," Mason said, encouraging the children not to be afraid. To the officer, he asked what law they were breaking.[18]

"Negroes don't come to the sand beach" was all the policeman could tell them. He threatened them with arrest if they would not leave.[19]

Hoze took the children home in one of the vehicles. Mason and Saucier, however, followed the officer to the police station to get exact information about the problem.[20] At that time, the police station was on the first floor of Biloxi City Hall, a building like a small brick castle with twin, square turrets.[21] Inside, Mason demanded to see the law that they had broken.

The police could not show them one. They claimed, inexplicably, that the book was locked up. They insisted, however, that the beach and even 1,500 feet into the water (more than the length of four football fields) was the private property of the white homeowners.[22] To Mason's insistence that—from the county equipment routinely on the beach and the gasoline tax—it was clear the beach was public property, the police simply said he could return the following day to see the law.[23] It was a common technique: simply put people off. Put the onus of finding the time, energy, and resources of pursuing the matter, of insisting on proof and accountability, onto the shoulders of the oppressed. The officials did not count on Mason's endurance.

The doctor and Saucier *did* return the next day. They were somewhat surprised to be met by the Biloxi mayor, Laz Quave. He had been chief of police, then sheriff of Harrison County, before being elected to his current position.

One would assume he knew the current laws very well. In fact, Mayor Quave told the men the beach *was* for the "public," but "If you go back down there, we're going to arrest you."[24] (This kind of logic, often repeated in records throughout the wade-ins, revealed many whites' attitude about who constituted the "public" or, in other words, true and full citizenship.) Ironically, and setting aside the danger of physical harm, it was more in the doctor's interest than it was in the mayor's for that threatened arrest to take place: doing so would create a record of members of the Black public being denied entry to the beach. However—for now—Mason did not pursue that avenue.

It is unclear whether Dr. Mason had picked up on a thread of community action already taking place or his trip to the beach was the stone thrown in that created all the ripples that followed. It is clear, however: following his first wade-in of May 14, 1959, the beach was on the minds of many. On May 22, Dr. Dunn wrote to the Harrison County Board of Supervisors to ask about the law concerning beach property, only to be told there were plans to provide a segregated area for the Black community.[25] SSC records show that, to the dismay of the Gulfport chief of police, George E. Mullens, Black citizens were "beginning to assert themselves" by calling in and citing their payment of taxes as proof of their entitlement to use the beaches freely. Efforts at beach desegregation, said Chief Mullens, had become his "greatest problem."[26] He cited a complaint that a busload of Black children had been brought to the beach by two white nuns, which led to the Gulfport police coming to stop the field trip and remove them.[27]

In Biloxi, Curtis Dedeaux was campaigning to be elected county sheriff. In Black neighborhoods, Dedeaux was asked how he would address beach segregation, and he reportedly said that he would support the public's right to the beach, even appointing armed Black deputies to guard them if necessary. In response, an editorial in the *Gulfport Pictorial Review* compared Dedeaux's alleged promise to "radioactive fallout from . . . atom bombs" and threatened that "if that were ever to be tried, the people of Harrison County . . . would make *the Till and Parker case[s] look like kid stuff*" (emphasis added).[28]

Five years earlier, fourteen-year-old Emmett Till had been beaten, mutilated, shot, tied with barbed wire, and thrown into the Tallahatchie River for allegedly speaking flirtatiously to a white woman. Only weeks before Mason's first wade-in and only sixty miles away, Mack Charles Parker—already beaten severely at the time of his arrest—was abducted from jail, beaten again, shot, and thrown into the Pearl River for the alleged rape of a white woman. Despite the public nature of these murders, no one was ever convicted— surely, a worse and truer example of "naked power over law" than efforts to desegregate public schools. White women as victims and targets of racialized lust was an oft-given reason to stop steps toward equality and interaction between the races. The same *Gulfport Pictorial Review* editorial cited the undefined "difference in family and sex training between most white women and negro men" as the key danger of allowing desegregated use of the beach.

Nevertheless, by June 1959, Dr. Mason and other community leaders had organized around the issue. Mason, Dunn, and Joseph Austin joined the recently formed Harrison County Civic Action Committee, with Dunn as chairman, and made beach integration its primary aim.[29]

The formation of the Harrison County Civic Action Committee perhaps begs the question: why wasn't the Gulfport branch of the NAACP, of which Dunn was president and Mason a member, the organization to address the issue? Traditionally, the NAACP had preferred the battle of the court to "direct action," but they were at a turning point.[30] Later, Dunn told SSC agents that the NAACP had wanted to be involved at the time of the petition "but that he alone prevented" it. Mason always maintained that Dunn had been code-switching when he spoke to white officials, who also "tried to twist his words." Although the context in which Dunn gave his statements must be considered, his agency must also be allowed.[31]

Dunn has been somewhat criticized for his involvement, or lack of it, at key moments in the beach desegregation movement. He had grown up in the county and had a different level of connection to the community than did Mason. Aside from his medical practice, he had businesses that tied him to local law enforcement and may have represented a conflict of interest. His relationship with SSC agents was far more conciliatory than that of Mason, who had no voluntary contact with them. Dunn often expressed little interest in going to the beach and disavowed any leadership role in the wade-ins, although he always maintained the legal right of Black citizens to enjoy the fruits of their taxpayer dollars as much as any white person.[32] His actions and comments surrounding the beach issue are, indeed, difficult to define.

There are a several points worth remembering about the context of this situation. There were other members of the Gulfport NAACP to whom Dunn was answerable. Perhaps some were off-put by Mason's willingness for direct action, or their focus was on other priorities, such as increasing votership and addressing poverty and infrastructure issues. Perhaps some members did not believe in desegregation at all; some people, Black and white, ostensibly believed that the problem was not separation of the races but the unfair implementation of the "separate but equal" policy. Others, like the members of the Republic of New Afrika, based in Mississippi, wanted to live as a separate nation.[33] To some degree, desegregation was as much a threat to the maintenance of distinctive minority cultures as it was to the hegemonic status quo, resulting, for example, in the breakup of historical Black townships.[34] In the short term, a disruption in tourism due to any perceived racial inharmony was also a concern for Black business owners.[35] Perhaps it is not so simple as saying the local NAACP was or was not involved in the petition since membership in the NAACP was already under intense scrutiny by local officials. Forming other organizations (many of whom supported the NAACP) such as the local Progressive Baptist State Convention, Mutual Association of Colored People South, Negro Peace Conference, and Christian Association was one way of flying under the radar.[36] Whatever the factors involved, it was determined that the best course of action was to form a separate committee to address the issue.

The Civic Action Committee met twice monthly, speaking to religious organizations and in social clubs and urging others to get involved.[37] In early September 1959, committee members decided to present a petition to the Harrison County Board of Supervisors, asking that all people be allowed to use the beach freely. Four signers were elected to represent the Black communities: Dunn for Gulfport, Eulice White for Turkey Creek, Joseph Austin, director of the Colored Division of the Gulfport Recreation Department, for Handsboro, and Mason for Biloxi. (Dunn missed the presentation of the petition; he had traveled to Los Angeles to see the Dodgers play the White Sox in the World Series.[38])

When the chosen day, October 5, came, the board's attorney, Harrison County state senator Stanford Morse Jr., tried to shift responsibility for the beaches away from the county and onto the private landowners.[39] "You have addressed your petition to the wrong body," he claimed.[40]

But Dr. Mason was well prepared. He knew about property law and litigation and was able to cite the precedent of local cases. As usual, he made a strong, positive impression even upon his adversaries, although it was not enough to persuade them to act. Only Biloxi Police Chief McDonnell (perhaps the most vehemently racist and violent of the recorded speakers) denigrated Mason's poise by calling him a "smart aleck" behind closed doors.[41]

The board president, Dewey Lawrence, responded with another common tactic of the time: veiled dismay and concern, under which lurked a threat. Lawrence began by saying the relationships "between colored folks and white folks on the Mississippi Coast have always been very good." It was said that the "town boys" and airmen from Keesler generally had more problems than existed between the races in the local area.[42] However, Lawrence continued, "If we integrate that sand beach, we're going to have some riots down there and someone is going to get hurt or killed."[43]

Such statements ignored some facts and implied others. "Good relations" had always, and obviously, been contingent on Black citizens being controlled by white, as demonstrated by interviews with Black citizens, their actions in pursuit of civil rights, or a review of the demeaning and threatening columns published in white-run newspapers as well as other sources. To maintain the status quo, Black citizens must be content with verbal and physical violence, degradation, and the leftovers or nothing at all. In addition, Lawrence's words illuminated the fact that Black citizens had no hope of equal protection under the law, despite their constitutional and moral rights. *Who* exactly was going to get hurt or killed, and by whom? Why would that be the end of the story, rather than a court trial in which the assailants would be held accountable by a jury of their peers? As in the cases of Till and Parker, the absence of justice further implied that the Black people who were harmed deserved what they got.

Switching gears, board president Lawrence assured those assembled that he was "in sympathy" with the need for more swimming areas for the Black community and that something—segregated and suitable—would be provided.[44] Until that time, the Black community of Biloxi could use the fifty-foot pool at Nichols High School.[45] Foreseeing that further pursuing the issue would involve a legal battle, Dr. Mason—who insisted from the beginning that he would not be satisfied with anything less than full desegregation—sought legal counsel. Dunn introduced him to the attorney Knox Walker, who had been working with unions and other labor associations and in assault and injury cases since passing the bar in 1951.[46] Mason also communicated the facts of the case to Dr. James Nabrit, dean of Howard University School of Law, who had been an attorney on *Brown v. Board of Education*, and received confirmation that the facts of the case were in his favor.[47]

The Daily Herald reported that the Board of Supervisors did nothing else with the petition.[48] But that wasn't entirely true. On October 7, 1959, Morse, the board's attorney, drove to the SSC office and asked the agents to investigate and discredit the four signatories. Morse said he could "handle Joseph N. Austin who is a City employee" and also Eulice White, who was a general repairman for a white family. As he also "had considerable information" on Dunn, it was Mason who was to be the primary target of the investigation. Morse believed he could put pressure on Dunn by alleging that the doctor was "splitting fees" with lawyers and reporting this "grievance" to the medical association, possibly putting his medical license at risk.[49]

On October 14, SSC (and former FBI) agent Zack J. Van Landingham came to Harrison County. Although a large part of SSC investigations seemed to involve numerous phone calls and memos, mostly repeating information gathered from local newspaper articles, Van Landingham did a thorough background check on Mason. It included details about his wife, his car, his parents' address and telephone number, a credit check on him and his father (both exemplary), and even his high school disciplinary record (or lack thereof). Van Landingham also went to Dunn's and Mason's offices, but found, essentially, that neither had any interest in interrupting their professional day to speak to him.[50]

By the time Van Landingham visited Biloxi and Gulfport, the petition had already had several effects. The very day it was presented, "Negroes Seek Use of Harrison Beach" was the headline in the *Daily Herald*. The paper called it the "first significant test of Mississippi segregation laws."[51] (To the contrary, there was, as Mason pointed out, no law being tested, but rather the unlawful enforcement of racist custom. It must also be noted that civil rights activities were often suppressed and hushed up to the best of local authorities' ability, resulting in the probability that many peaceful demonstrations throughout Mississippi were never publicized and that framing Mason's action as the "first" of its kind discounted previous challenges to the status quo, such as boycotts and attempts to desegregate the universities.) Also, the response from the white community was immediate. All four Black men involved received threatening phone calls.[52] Eulice White and his wife, Alice, were fired from their employment with a private Gulfport family; White was "temporarily relieved of his job for a cooling off period" as Dunn put it.[53] Joseph Austin was also suspended from his job at the Gulfport Recreation Department and was told he could return to work if he convinced the others to withdraw the petition.[54] This economic fallout was, presumably, what Morse had meant when he said they could be "handled."

In addition, a cross was burned in Austin's yard, and another cross was burned on the beach. (This menacing message was almost forty years away from being outlawed as a hate crime.) The next day in interviews, Austin said that the petition was not a move toward integration, but only of desegregation.[55] It was a common line used throughout the Biloxi wade-ins. Even Mason, the only person to consistently insist that full desegregation was the goal, occasionally pointed out that it did not mean people would *have to* mingle socially.[56] Dunn put it this way: if, when driving his car, "I happen to be in the midst of 11 or 12 cars having white occupants, I would not be integrated with them."[57] Referring back to the gasoline tax that maintained the seawall, he said, "I have two cars. If the beach isn't public, then I'm paying to keep up somebody's front yard. The issue is purely economic. It has nothing to do with social trends."[58]

Eulice White, who had several school-age children to support, asked for his name to be withdrawn from the petition and issued a statement that he "did not want anything to come to breach the good relations between the races," wording that sounds suspiciously like the language used by the Board of Supervisors or the SSC.[59] The Civic Action Committee took donations to relieve the financial burden for the White and Austin families, while they tried to recover from the repercussions of their civil challenge of the status quo. Austin was eventually rehired.[60]

It was more difficult to pressure Dr. Mason or Dr. Dunn, who were economically independent by contrast. But it was not impossible. In addition to cancellation of some of their insurance, subtle pressure from their landlords, and whatever leverage the SSC felt they had on Dunn, which may or may not have influenced him, the specter of more damaging effects was always before them.[61] Two physicians engaged in the civil rights struggle had already been harassed into leaving the state. In 1956, Dr. T. R. M. Howard, of Taborian Hospital in the historic freedmen's town of Mound Bayou, had been outspoken in his fight against the White Citizens' Council (WCC) and in his criticism of the investigation of Emmett Till's murder. He received so many death threats that he slept with a machine gun at the foot of his bed and later moved his family to Chicago when the stress became overwhelming. Dr. Clinton Battle, president of the NAACP in Indianola, Mississippi (and so skilled that white patients visited him under the cover of darkness), also relocated after the owners of local plantations told their Black sharecroppers they would not pay medical bills owed to him and the police confiscated his car for false drinking charges, leaving him without a way of making house calls.[62]

One of Mason's colleagues, Dr. Clay Easterly, warned him that those who took the pursuit of beach access as a challenge to white supremacy would surely harm Mason any way they could and stressed that he must be careful.[63] Attorney Knox informed Mason and Dunn that KKK assassination lists had already begun to include their names. Mason became careful to keep his windows covered to guard against drive-by shootings. Although the Masons had only lived in Biloxi four years, the family had made such an impression on the local Black community that over a dozen residents—many of whom were veterans, with service weapons from their time in the armed forces—formed a security detail to watch his house and office.[64]

From SSC records, it is clear the governing bodies and law enforcement were well aware that residents no longer owned the land to the waterfront. Behind closed doors, they acknowledged it would be "quite a problem if the negroes should go through with their stated plans of bringing suit in

Federal Court."⁶⁵ Now elected sheriff, Curtis Dedeaux reported to the SSC that he was also "expecting trouble from the NAACP and the negroes," especially "with reference to" the beach. Perhaps with some remembrance of his alleged campaign promises to the Black community, Sheriff Dedeaux said if the Board of Supervisors were "dragging their feet" arranging the segregated area they had proposed, he wasn't going to remove anyone from the beach when complaints were inevitably made. He, too, was sure a suit would be won if taken to court. It was his "opinion that the negroes are becoming well educated" and cautioned that "we are not going to be able to control them . . . like we have in the past."⁶⁶

The chief of police of Gulfport, George E. Mullens, who knew about Sheriff Dedeaux's campaign promises, said he only wanted Dedeaux to "not interfere in any way with him or his force in controlling the negroes and preventing them" from going to the beach.⁶⁷ The Biloxi chief of police, Herbert McDonnell, felt likewise. The assistant chief of Biloxi, Walter Williams, thought they ought to just "beat hell out of any Negro found on the beach."⁶⁸ These men evidently knew the power they wished to exercise depended on under-the-table deals and brute force, far beyond the limit of legal jurisdiction not to mention civil morality. The favorite suggestion of the officials was to circumvent the problem by providing a fenced, segregated portion of the beach for the Black population. Budgets, locations, and naming it "for some outstanding negro without calling it a negro or colored beach" were discussed although no action was ever taken. Dunn was recorded by the SSC and reported in the *Jackson Daily News* as being prepared to accept the proposal for a segregated portion of the beach and to convince others to favor it; he later refuted this claim.⁶⁹

In January 1960, Mississippi's new governor, Ross Barnett, inherited the situation. Barnett was a flagrant racist. As a lawyer campaigning for the governorship, he had claimed to be able to expose the forces behind integration as "advocated largely by the mulatto or mongrels" and argued that "no right thinking Negro desires that the blood of his race shall be contaminated or destroyed by the comingling of his blood with either the white or yellow races."⁷⁰ Clearly, his seat in power would not benefit Black Mississippians, much less aid in Dr. Mason's "significant test" of segregation.

Soon, another summer was heating up. As nothing had happened with the petition, the Civic Action Committed formed a plan called "Operation Surf." Getting arrested was the next logical step. This would create evidence that Black citizens were prevented from using the beach and lay the groundwork for a lawsuit. Mason and his colleagues had little expectation that a local judge would issue a verdict in their favor. They had to be prepared to work up through the Court of Appeals. Mason and Dunn wrote to anyone they could, from individuals to associations, trying to raise the $10,000 needed to retain attorney Knox Walker for a potential fight all the way to the Supreme Court. After all the donations offered were counted and it was still short of the total, the doctors contributed the remainder of Walker's fee themselves.[71]

In the weeks approaching the date chosen for Operation Surf, the doctors spoke to the Black community, encouraging people to join the peaceful demonstration. Sundays were always the day chosen for the Biloxi demonstrations. In addition to taking advantage of what Mason called "reverence for the Almighty," Sundays made sense logistically: in the morning, the community was gathered together, and it was the day of the week most likely to be free of employment, available for boycotts and other protests.[72] That Easter Sunday, Mason made his final appeal at church, where the congregation expressed interest and support, though surely the possible repercussions of merely petitioning for use of the beach were on their minds. The single mother of Adell Lott, who had joined the first wade-in, asked him not to participate again, for fear of losing her job as a maid.[73] Others shared her fears. Even those who were self-employed and of good and independent standing in the community, Mason recalled, were not "an island; they had wives and extended family (even parents) that were domestics" or otherwise more vulnerable to harmful repercussions.[74]

On April 17, 1960, another warm and beautiful day, Dr. Mason drove down between the lighthouse and the Buena Vista Hotel and found no one there to join him. After the first, spontaneous wade-in, his wife kept their son home for safety this time, remaining behind herself to be available for posting bail.[75] Disappointed but undeterred, Mason went swimming alone.[76] He was determined to bring the matter before the courts.[77]

"It was very tranquil," he later told reporters. He was floating about a hundred yards from shore when the police arrived.[78] To make the point of the demonstration, Mason refused to leave the water until he was arrested for what was said to be "disorderly conduct."

Mason drove behind the police to the Biloxi station, where the arresting officers remained cordial enough. Chief McDonnell, however, loudly swearing, threatened bodily harm to Mason if he returned to the beach again and asserted that Mason's "own people" or medical colleagues might "get him" as well.[79] Ironically, prosecuting attorney John Sekul later told reporters the arrest had been due to police's intention to "prevent someone from getting hurt."[80] Natalie Mason, who was active in her husband's litigation throughout the struggle to desegregate the beach, arrived, still in her Sunday dress, to pay his bond of twenty-five dollars.[81] Because she did not drive and perhaps also for protection, she was always accompanied by a male acquaintance, this time Wilmer McDaniels. Gilbert Jr., her son, was likely left in the care of one of his sitters from the community.[82]

Six months earlier, Dr. Dunn had told the press, "Personally, I don't want to [go to the beach] but a lot of my people do."[83] However, that Easter Sunday, Dunn, his wife, and three children went swimming in Gulfport.[84] Their daughter, Felicia, recalled that morning the children had received pails and shovels instead of Easter baskets. While they were picnicking, the police arrived and escorted the doctor to the Gulfport jail, although no charges were filed or formal arrest made. A few days later, in a meeting with SSC agents, Dunn alleged that, during the encounter, the Gulfport chief of police, George Mullens, Mayor Billy Meadows, and Sheriff Dedeaux had "told him they did not want to have any trouble at Gulfport," but that he could return to the outing. The family did, indeed, return to finish their picnic, without being harassed.

The next day, the SCC agent called Mayor Meadows, who was angry to hear about the meeting and claimed that he "had run Dr. Dunn and his family off the beach." Whatever the tenor of the event, Dunn's status as a doctor and his business links with Sheriff Dedeaux may have protected him from the same degree of harassment other Black citizens experienced and affected his sense of urgency in the matter. (Just as Mason always maintained that Dunn was simply telling officials whatever they wanted to hear, it is worth noting that Mayor Meadows and other whites may have engaged in code-switching as well; as late as June 1964, Meadows's "conspicuous" absence from an SCC meeting was thought to be due to the "severe criticism" he had received for giving "a group of Negroes permission to have a picnic on one of the beaches" the previous week. According to Wilson Evans II, a leader of the longshoremen's union in Gulfport, Meadows was known by some as "the n----r mayor," presumably for his fraternization with Blacks and lack of preventing civil rights activity.[85]) Later, Dunn said Mason's beach trip had been an "individual matter . . . not sanctioned" by the Gulfport chapter of the NAACP. That comment is an example of the mixed signals that Dunn gave in regard to beach desegregation.

Mason's arrest got the attention of the press. City officials were not happy with the attention and tried to minimize the event. Under the headline "Negro Doctor Breaks Color Line at Biloxi," the *Clarion Ledger* of Jackson quoted Mayor Quave's response: "They're trying to make a national issue out of it but we're trying to handle it locally and I'd rather not comment."

Chief McDonnell would not even confirm the arrest, saying, "it would take too much time to look it up."[86]

The next evening, April 18, 1960, Mason returned to court for sentencing. This time, he was not alone: people had gathered to both oppose and support him. Some of the white crowd waiting outside shoved Mason and his attorney, Knox Walker, as they walked into the courthouse. Two days later, Walker was further harassed when he was arrested for failure to signal and an improper tag.[87] At the court that evening, about a hundred Black community members and a few whites supporting the demonstration attended. The right side of the segregated courtroom was filled to standing-room only—an unusual arrangement as traditionally minority spectators were confined to a balcony. There were complaints by at least one member of the white community that the courthouse did not provide such a space.[88] Judge Jules A. Schwan, the municipal judge hearing Mason's disorderly conduct case, acquiesced to Chief McDonnell's attempt to minimize publicity and forbade pictures of the trial.[89]

The assistant police chief, Walter Williams, testified that Mason was a repeat offender. Rather than disagree, Mason declared he would return to the beach and continue his demonstrations.[90] "We intend to secure for ourselves the rights of all citizens," he insisted.[91] Yet, at the end of the testimony, Judge Schwan delayed making a ruling. This was a strategy developed in collaboration with Governor Ross Barnett, the Biloxi mayor, Laz Quave, and SSC officials. Records show that they believed they could wait out Mason and pressure anyone else involved into silence.[92] Mayor Quave and Governor Barnett had determined to continue "putting off Mason's trial until they wore it out." They knew a ruling (inevitably against him) would be appealed and that he "would surely beat it in the long run."[93]

Rumors had circulated that some of the Black community were already planning further demonstrations. It is difficult to determine whether the rumors were just that or whether they were real proposals that did not materialize.[94] The following night, at a meeting of the SSC, the Board of Supervisors, county mayors, and law enforcement, Sheriff Dedeaux was "reluctant to speak until he knew everyone in the crowd." Once he was satisfied, he did most of the talking. It is possible not all of the local officials were interested in the SSC's agenda or that there were other fractures among them. Gatha Ladner, the board supervisor of Beat Four, was said to avoid "most of these important issues." The mayor of Pass Christian, Francis Hursey, seldom spoke.[95]

Rebuffing Mayor Quave's reminder that Mason wanted total desegregation (and seeming to have forgotten his previous opinion that educated people like Mason would not be controlled), Sheriff Dedeaux now claimed he could still handle the situation and that Dr. Dunn (with whom he—and other significant figures—were in business via the Negro Juke Box and Cigarette Machine company) was the main leader.[96] Dedeaux seemed to feel that he had particular weight with the county's Black population as he claimed to have "given the Negroes special privileges since his election" (apparently without noticing the irony that any "privilege" he could grant only represented an exclusion from basic rights in the first place). Asserting that he was in favor of separate but equal accommodations, Dedeaux returned to the suggestion of spending half a million to a million dollars for a segregated beach in front of Moody's Tourist Court, with bath houses and concession stands.[97] Mayor Quave responded that he did not want to "spend too much money." Quave claimed for himself a "very firm policy" regarding the Black community and said he didn't "want to pet them." Instead, he thought they could get "Negroes off the beach by a sanitation provision," watching for when they "throw beer cans" or used the beach for bath or toilet facilities and then arresting them. Acknowledging the necessity of some pretense of equal protection under the law, Quave admitted that "they might have to arrest some whites at the same time, but that would just have to be done."[98] Herbert McDonnell, again perhaps the most threatening voice in the room, said ominously that "the Citizens Council was badly needed . . . in and around Biloxi" as "there was really no one down there besides the police who could coordinate the activities of the citizens against this particular type of trouble." At no time in this meeting was there any mention of the rights of the so-called landowners. The men left the meeting without any plan for how to handle future "disturbances" other than Dedeaux's offer to speak with Dunn.

Happily, none of the intimidation nor evasion had the effect the segregationists hoped for; in fact, it was quite the opposite. Dr. Mason's arrest convinced others to join him.

Chapter Five

BLOOD ON THE SAND, CAUSE OF INJURY: "INTEGRATIONAL"

There must have been a lot of conversation in living rooms, across store counters, and on street corners in both the Black and white parts of town that week in April 1960. The Monday following Dr. Mason's arrest, teenagers James Black, Clemon Jimerson, Ethel Rainey, and others came to his office to offer support. Ethel Rainey, a high school junior and one of thirteen children of parents who worked in the local fisheries and seafood factories, was a leader among her peers at Nichols High.[1] She and the others were well aware and excited by the organization around civil rights across the country. They were eager to be a part of the movement taking part in their own town, and Ethel told Mason she and quite a few of her classmates wanted to help.[2]

Over the next week, other community members began to voice their intentions to show up the next time Mason organized a demonstration. In preparation, he and Dr. Dunn held meetings to develop their plans and review the procedure of nonviolent protest: no one should bring anything that could be thought of as a weapon, and if attacked, they should cover their heads and duck, not respond with more violence.[3] It was, however, important that they not leave the beach when asked but that they require the police to arrest them for the purposes of bringing the issue before the courts.[4]

On Wednesday, April 20, at the meeting of the Civic Action Committee, Mason said he would be going to the beach the following Sunday. He informed Biloxi police chief Herbert McDonnell of the plan, and Dunn reported the planned time and location to Sheriff Dedeaux.[5] Although the demonstrators at this event were expecting a greater pushback than previously from the white population—including being yelled at and enduring obscenities, threats, and economic reprisals, with some of this harassment coming from the police force itself—they nevertheless expected law enforcement's protection from any greater violence that day. They were wrong.

In their meetings with SSC agents, Chief McDonnell and Assistant Chief Walter Williams reported, "a lot of people had notified them that they would be around the beach in case Mason showed up."[6] Other witness statements alleged it was not only the public notifying the police of their intentions but the other way around as well. Rev. Richard Ellerbrake, the white pastor of Back Bay Mission, wrote that it was "generally known" that "several policemen made the rounds of the bars, getting up a mob" for Sunday, and a particular rumor placed the police in the pool halls on Point Cadet, encouraging others to join.[7] The *Daily Herald* later confirmed that local whites "said they were asked Saturday to join the group that assaulted the Negroes."[8] However it transpired, the police decided it would be best to let the public "take care of this situation." The police chief said that both he and Sheriff Dedeaux planned not to be on duty and to send a bare minimum of officers to monitor the beach situation.[9]

On Saturday night, a cross was burned by the lighthouse in a final effort to intimidate the would-be Black swimmers. Nevertheless, on Sunday, April 24, over a hundred Black men, women, and children gathered in Back-of-Town in front of Dr. Mason's office.[10] They were mostly the younger and older members of the community; those who were breadwinners of their families may have feared the economic reprisals of participating too much.[11] Some of the elders were old enough to have remembered the lynchings in Mississippi City and Biloxi in 1900 and 1908.[12]

It was hotter than the week before, bright, and sunny. The protestors had chosen three locations that were not in front of private residences: the Biloxi MacArthur Hotel (previously the Hotel Biloxi at 1300 W Beach Blvd.); the lighthouse, which still stands at 1050 Beach Blvd.; and the New Biloxi Hospital at 648 Beach Blvd., near the Small Craft Harbor, a stretch of a few miles.[13] The plan was to occupy the beach for approximately three hours and reconvene in Back-of Town.[14] As they moved toward the beach, down the final slope of asphalt to cross the four-lane highway bordering the sand, some by foot and some by car, the participants were playing and joking with each other in high spirits. Mason observed several whites watching them, a few with two-way radios in their hands.[15] Other Black citizens had come to watch from the seawall or other side of the highway. As even being in the area after the riot began was a danger to anyone there, observers may be on wade-in participant lists.

"To feel that sand between my toes was something to experience, that I had not known," Ethel Rainey later reported.[16]

Photographs of the day show white swimmers pausing to stand by with hands on their hips or sitting on the seawall.[17] Black participants set up their picnic baskets and casual ball games.[18] Mason drove among the three areas, overseeing the demonstration.[19] Ethel Rainey's father, Jesse James, had borrowed a boat; he and his wife, Ruby Hawkins Rainey, patrolled the shoreline from the water. On his second pass, Mason saw that more than just casual observers had arrived. Newspapers would later report that several hundred whites, "a large percentage of them teenagers and some young women," had come, some armed with sections of pool sticks, clubs, chains, and other homemade weapons.[20] Although the legal dispute centered on ownership of the sand, it was when some of the Black demonstrators stepped into the water that the mob seemed to take it as their signal to attack. The armed whites began to chase and strike the protestors, destroy their belongings, and vandalize their cars. Photos show the attackers almost gleeful, grinning as they chased the demonstrators across the sand.[21] Mason abandoned his car on the road near the lighthouse when he saw five white men beating two Black youths, Joe Lonberger and Gilmore Fielder, with weighted pool sticks.[22]

"Look what we have here," the assailants said when they saw Mason, according to the *Daily Herald* report. They turned to attack him as well, striking him in the forehead. Mason wrestled a pool stick away and began to fight back. When the deputy sheriff (Claude Miller, in 1959) approached, he grabbed the doctor, allowing the whites to run away.[23] Mason heard another officer say they were getting "what they deserved."[24] Later, Sandy Daniels would say the officers had backed away before the mob attack.[25] Others reported that, throughout the attack, the police were focused on directing traffic on the highway.[26] Sheriff Dedeaux had said "he did not want any arrests on the beach," in an attempt to subvert the protestors' grounds for litigation.[27] As the attack began by the Biloxi MacArthur Hotel—led by Marvin Dickey and said to be made up of the oldest participants—Bernell Burney Fletcher, who was pregnant and accompanied by a friend and the friend's three children, heard police telling some of the white civilians to "get the n-----s off" the sand.[28]

The group of demonstrators who had gathered in front of the New Biloxi Hospital was the largest. Charles Ellis, eighteen at the time, later testified about his and his friend's experience being hit with sticks.[29] Marzine Thames was beaten with chains, in the words of his attackers, to "teach him a lesson, to go places he's not supposed to go."[30] His seventeen-year-old brother, Kenneth Thames, was beaten by ten to twelve men, sustaining a deep cut above his eye. Luzell Bullock, Le'Roy Carney, and Sanford Williams were also listed among the injured.³¹ Ellis Brown, in his early thirties and the owner of a cleaner's shop, had been beaten in the head.³²

In the section of the beach near the lighthouse, Delores Steward Sheely saw the police stop a group of about fifty white men approaching. But then, letting the mob go on, the police returned to their cars. Some of the men confronted Dorothy Galloway, a disabled veteran and the leader of that portion of the protest group, which contained many of older students, such as Ethel Rainey and Gloria Fleeton. The white mob alleged they had been "ordered" to remove the Blacks from the beach. In the ensuing violence, someone punched Sheely in the mouth with brass knuckles, breaking her teeth and blackening her eye, and kicked her when she had fallen to the ground. She saw them beating another woman with chains.³³ Galloway was hit repeatedly in the knees, fracturing them. A white airman who tried to help him up was also attacked.³⁴ When the police finally interceded, it was to put the wounded protestors in the back of a car with the windows up and no air-conditioning, leaving them confined for forty-five minutes before taking them to the hospital.³⁵

Nine-year-old G. W. Carney had ridden to the beach with his older brother in Wilmer McDaniels's car to the area near the New Biloxi Hospital and Small Craft Harbor.³⁶ He had stripped off his shirt and was playing volleyball when he noticed that several drivers passing by had pulled into the parking bays and the white crowd was growing. One of the adult protestors told the children to run. Carney abandoned his belongings as he rushed for safety.³⁷ Clemon Jimerson and his friend James Black had come with Jimerson's mother, Myrtle Jeanette (McSwain) Fleeton, and his stepfather, Walter James Fleeton, half-sister Gloria Fleeton, and aunt, Willie Jean McSwain.³⁸

Clemon Jimerson had been born on Keesler Air Force Base. Like Dr. Mason's son, he had been able to swim in a desegregated pool on the base. At fourteen, in addition to his school life, he had begun to play drums in a local jazz and swing band, performing at desegregated military clubs as well as all-white clubs in town.³⁹ He washed dishes at Baricev's restaurant on the beach, had bagged groceries at one of the oceanfront stores, and had grown up hearing his mother's childhood stories about freer access to the beaches before the improvements. "I had been waiting all my life to go down there on that beach," he later reflected.⁴⁰ Jimerson was so happy and proud to participate that he had purchased an ensemble for the occasion: beach shoes, bright shirt, and an Elgin watch. His uncle, Nolan McSwain—who had worked in many of the best-known white-owned Biloxi businesses, including the Buena Vista Hotel, Longfellow House, and Mary Mahoney restaurant—had arrived in Jesse Rainey's boat and got out to join the family. As he and the boys began swimming, they could see the parking bays by the seawall beginning to fill up. When the white men began to get out and talk to each other, Jimerson "didn't think anything of it." They had expected curious bystanders, jeers, even an arrest. Then the attack began.

Wilmer B. McDaniels (who owned a funeral home across the street from Dr. Mason's office, was a pianist at his church, and a significant figure in the local civil rights movement) was interrupted playing softball with the children. A large white man—reportedly the owner of Trahan's Hardware—took the bat out of his hands. "Alright, let's go," the man said. When McDaniels, a much smaller man than his assailant, began to reply, the white man began to beat him as his wife, Dorothy Holley McDaniels, tried to shield his body with hers, crying, "Please don't kill my husband!"[41] Wilmer McDaniels later confirmed that he had recognized the first man who struck him.[42] When some members of the mob turned toward Clemon Jimerson, he sprinted toward the road as did Gary Rainey, running through the sand as fast as they could. As the mob pursued Jimerson across the hot asphalt of highway, where traffic had all but halted, he heard a white adult urge his assailants, "You better catch that n----r. You better not let him get away."[43] One of Jimerson's classmates, Richard Dryden, was caught on the beach and struck in the forehead.[44] Lee Owens Jr., a World War II veteran who had worked in the construction of Keesler Air Force Base, saw his friend Mack, though not a good swimmer, choose the other direction and strike out to the Raineys' boat for safety.[45]

McDaniels was not the only one who recognized his assailants. Ethel Rainey saw one of her coworkers from the Buena Vista Hotel among the attackers.[46] Bobby C. Hope, who had come to the beach with his friends James F. Davis and Willie C. James and some older cousins, was caught playing softball and struck hard in the head before he escaped. He recognized some in the white crowd as people "I had been knowing all my life," whose parents had been "raised by black" maids.[47] Even so, the identity of these white assailants was not reported in the press.

Some of the demonstrators fought back. Eleanora Hayes reported that she and a friend, Ann Shirley, both pregnant, had snuck in a "little knife," with which—in addition to their fists—they fought off the men beating McDaniels and the others, "just as fast as [they were] coming."[48] Just as Dr. Mason's arrest had provoked others to join in the demonstration, the onslaught of the white mob drew more of the Black community to the beach. Janice Kennedy, whose father was part of the group that guarded the Masons' home, was with her godmother, Alteese McGee, when word of the violence reached

Back-of-Town.⁴⁹ Her godmother loaded her own brass knuckles, Janice, and her cousins into the car, hurrying down to the beach where the children watched as she "snatched the white men off the Black men."⁵⁰

Despite the chaos and violence, there was some impromptu help from some of the white onlookers. In a newspaper article with the disturbing title "Racial Battle Enlivens Beach," Mason was reported saying, "None of the white swimmers joined in the fight. In fact, some tried to help us."⁵¹ Five Keesler airmen—race unmentioned—were caught in the violence. A large group of white teens assaulted them, robbed them of their watches, and ransacked their car. As one of the airmen was beaten unconscious, a white woman from one of the beachfront properties rushed out with a gun to scare the attackers away, and the policemen finally approached to help.⁵² Some white people prevented their families from getting involved; in Back-of-Town, Clara Watson saw a truck of men pull up and try to summon the sons of a white family who lived across the street to "beat up on these n-----s on the beach." Their mother came onto the porch and said the demonstrators on the beach had not done anything and that if the agitators did not leave, she would get her shotgun and make them.⁵³

Rev. Richard Ellerbrake of the St. Paul's United Church of Christ and Back Bay Mission at 424 Chartres Street heard about the assault on the radio as he was driving back from a seminary event in St. Louis and visit to the home of Clarence Jordan, founder of the integrated cooperative Koinonia Farm in Americus, Georgia, where Ellerbrake had examined the "bullet holes in [Jordan's] wall where they had tried to shoot him."⁵⁴ Ellerbrake drove straight to the beach to help where he could and witnessed approximately three hundred white Biloxians—in the words of one—"waiting for the n-----s to come back," under the watchful gaze of the police and SSC agents (the latter recording the license plate numbers of the Black demonstrators' cars).⁵⁵ The police were not helping the injured. Instead, with obscenities and threats of further violence, they were ordering the wounded off the beach and barring others from returning to help.⁵⁶ The ambulance that had been called for an injured Black airman had still not arrived. Reverend Ellerbrake then drove to the hospital, "opposite the second of the riot scenes," where he spoke to some of the victims in the parking lot. According to Ellerbrake, Mason had a "pretty rough cut above his left eye which was bloody."⁵⁷ Despite being under arrest, Mason had not been put into custody. He moved through the crowd, treating the injured. Burnell Fletcher called him over to James McGowan Sr., who, like Delores Sheely, had had teeth knocked out in the violence.⁵⁸

In the immediate aftermath, Jimerson and his stepfather returned to search for his clothes, which had been left behind as the young man ran for safety. Perhaps in hindsight, "it might have been crazy," Jimerson reflected later to a journalist, "but they say God protects old folks and fools." At fourteen, he was still young enough to be focused on the loss of his new watch. As the two approached on the north side of the highway, a white man elbowed Walter Fleeton as he passed. When Fleeton said, "Excuse me, sir," the man snapped back, "You better say 'Excuse me,' n----r." On the beach, they could see a smoking pyre in the area where they thought the clothes had been left behind.[59] Fleeton looked down at his stepson. "You can get another watch, you can get some more clothes, but you can't get another life," he said. They returned home to take shelter for the rest of the evening.[60]

Reverend Ellerbrake reported the "great discouragement and heartbreak" of the Black demonstrators, who were reeling with shock from the assault, as well as the emotional exhaustion it caused him even to "relive these days" for the purposes of the letter.[61] At least thirteen people had been injured, although it is likely others treated at the veteran's hospital or at home were not included in official reports.[62] Eight injured airmen, between the ages of seventeen and twenty-four, were admitted at Keesler medical facilities and hospitalized for injuries in fights and "rock-throwing incidents."[63] Sixteen-year-old David Hamilton (whose mother had asked him not to attend the beach protest, but who was nevertheless arrested later in the evening), along with Marvin Dickey, an embalmer at Brown Funeral Home, who had been present with his wife, Ruby, drove Dorothy Galloway, James McGowan, and Dr. Mason to the hospital.[64] Five others were admitted (two driven in by white airmen), including Wilmer McDaniels, who was treated for head and eye injuries. A white nurse wrote "integrational" as the cause of the injuries.[65] Others waited at Mason's office for stitches and tetanus shots. Dr. Dunn (who had not participated in the protest) arrived at the office as well.

It was only now, after efforts had been met with mob violence, that the doctors fulfilled the longtime suspicions of the local officials and SSC and called in the "outside agitators," as the white authorities called them: the top officials of the NAACP, who happened at that time to be in Meridian, Mississippi.[66] After he had finished helping everyone who needed his services, Mason drove to the station and turned himself in. He was charged with fighting and obstructing traffic. Natalie Mason and a friend, Christopher Rosado, quickly arrived with bail, which had been planned in advance.[67]

As soon as he was released, Mason proceeded with Dunn to a meeting at the New Bethel Church, where four or five hundred members of the Black community had gathered to vent their frustrations and rally their hearts and minds for the next step.[68] Later, in meetings with the SSC, Dunn would take "full credit . . . for the fact that the negroes did not push their attempts any further" that evening.⁶⁹ At some point, he and Mason were questioned by FBI agents.⁷⁰ Afterward, the Masons returned with the Dunns to their home in Gulfport, where they often shared Sunday night dinners and where they slept that evening, while the police fielded calls warning that Mason's office was "to be blown up that night."⁷¹

Ethel Rainey later reflected that the traumatic events on the beach left a blank in her memory, so that she did not remember how she got away.⁷² Near-riot conditions continued that night throughout town. The tension was like a wire that could snap any moment. People feared that it could escalate, and they prepared for the worst. Three hardware stores sold out of guns and ammunition. A man from the Sears Roebuck informed the sheriff that Black people "in droves" were asking about firearms. Sheriff Dedeaux said the staff should send anyone asking to "get permission . . . and register this stuff before they bought it," which sounds like a clear discouragement from doing so. Soon, the mayor put a curfew in place, the sale of firearms without a permit was prohibited, and guns already in possession were required to be registered.⁷³ Yet, within the Black community, there was still the unofficial distribution of guns to some of the unprotected households. When Clemon Jimerson's uncle Nolan McSwain discovered that evening that the family did not have any weapons, he went out and brought back a .22 rifle.⁷⁴

That evening, approximately two hundred police officers from the city, county, and highway divisions were out, carrying riot gear and trying to break up groups on the street. They closed bars in the main area of the white part of town (side street bars remained open) and all bars in Back-of-Town. On bullhorns, they announced that Mason would be held responsible for any trouble that occurred.⁷⁵ The air force pulled its personnel in.⁷⁶ Before they could do so, there were several other assaults, including on two Black airmen who intervened near the corner of Howard Avenue and Lemuese, when they saw a group of whites attacking a car "occupied by two elderly or middle aged colored people," and were struck with a lead pipe for their trouble. Three more airmen walking through town were beaten "virtually unconscious," until assisted by a "civilian passerby" who drove them back to the base. Two Black staff sergeants were attacked on their way back to the base and another airman while walking between the police station and bus terminal. Three white airmen in the student squadron, Edward G. McClocky Jr., Robert H. Rock, and Arnold W. Green, were on the beach near Porter Avenue at 3 am when they were attacked. Keesler officials called in extra air police to be on standby.⁷⁷

Despite the curfew, for several hours groups of white citizens congregated outside the police and bus stations (possibly because they suspected out-of-town reinforcements would arrive as they persisted in believing outsiders were orchestrating, encouraging, or exacerbating the situation). Taxis and cars driving through the "wrong side" of town (depending on the race of their drivers or occupants) were chased, rocked, or hit with bricks, rocks, and bottles. Pedestrians risked being followed by vehicles and harassed. The police station was swamped with calls from Black citizens asking for protection of their homes or to be escorted from their places of work. Some simply stayed where they were for the night. Some turned off their lights and told their children to stay away from the windows.[78] Walter Cook remembered the evening for the unusual occurrence of his father coming home early from his "two or three jobs," and the family listening to the radio for reports of shots fired while sirens wailed in the background.[79]

Violence continued through the evening. Some young white men stopped Rev. John Ferdinand as he was walking down the street and slapped him. L. J. Derouen and Leo Rolkosky, who were white, said a bottle was thrown at them from a car driven by Gifford Eatman, who was black, in which Albert Moore and Robert Andrews were riding. Derouen and Rolkosky followed Eatman and attempted, they later said, to have Eatman arrested. There was an altercation, and the window of the Coquet Furniture Company (on Howard near Lameuse) was broken.[80] Other accounts describe a man being thrown through a store window, and Robert Andrews was accused of destroying city property, though it is not clear if all of these referenced the same incident. The Black-owned businesses The Twilight Grill, Little Apple Bar, and the Standard Station were shot up. An eyewitness alleged that a police officer was among those who had fired on the Little Apple.[81] Several other Black people and one white teenage boy, Andrew Taylor, were shot. Fortunately, none were seriously injured or died from their injuries. The youngest victim was thirteen-year-old Elnora Mary McNair, who was standing with her mother and aunt, Roma Mae Patterson and Levanie Rankin, in front of Jordan's Grocery, at 460 Magnolia Street, when the three were fired on.[82]

Myrtle (Bridges) Davis, who had not been at the beach, was at home when she heard the shots fired. Knowing that her sister's four children were home alone next door, she and her son, Johnny Chapman, started out to check on them. Another car went by, with the occupants firing at the Kitty-Cat Cafe. Johnny caught the license plate of the shooter's vehicle. Davis's pregnant sister, Alethea (Bridges) McGowan, who was working at the Southern Kitchen across the street, rushed out to meet them.[83] She had just witnessed Oscar Jones and George Riley struck and slightly wounded by the shotgun blast of buckshot fired through the café window. When the police arrived, Chapman told them he had taken down a license number. The police insisted he and McGowan come to the jailhouse to give their witness statements. Davis demanded to go with her son. Another white mob was waiting in front of the station; as she was quoted saying in the *Daily Herald*, they "rushed into [Chapman] and started hitting him" as he got out of the car, leaving him with a severely bloodied nose. Rather than intervene, the police arrested Davis, Chapman, and McGowan for "disorderly conduct."[84] The police threatened to have the women fired and evicted and said they were lucky to be in the jail, as the mob outside would "put y'all under" it. The women had to send messages out of the cell window to have their brother Frank Bridges attend to the children who had been left at home and bring back food for the women. The police never took down the license number Johnny had recorded.[85]

The police made several more arrests, with the charges of resisting arrest, drunk and disorderly conduct, and destruction of property. By the end of the night, the police had reportedly taken knives, an eighteen-inch homemade whip of braided wire, sawed-off table legs, lead pipes wrapped in tape, baseball bats, rubber hoses, and sawed-off broom sticks.[86] The *Jackson Daily News* called it the "worst race riot" in Mississippi. (Tom Ethridge wrote an editorial for the *Clarion-Ledger* pointing out that several post-Reconstruction race riots had led to deaths;[87] it is perhaps truer to say the Biloxi beach attack was the worst riot in nearly a hundred years.) Later, the day would come to be known as "Bloody Sunday."

"I'm cautious," Dr. Mason later said to the *Commercial Appeal* regarding the dangers inherent in continuing to pursue his civil rights goals. "But death is a static state and I'm concerned with living." However, the Masons did send their son to stay with family in New Orleans or to neighbors like the Elzys or the Dunn family in Gulfport to be what Gilbert Jr. called "hidden in plain sight" during times when trouble was more anticipated than usual.[88]

Chapter Six

FROM RIPPLES TO WAVES

Shifting Blame, Calls for Peace, and the National Campaign

Monday evening, as the night court prepared for session, nearly two hundred white people gathered in front of the police station to hear the verdicts against those who had been arrested.[1] Police officers were photographed escorting Dr. Mason into the building.[2] This time, the protest had made national news, in print and broadcast.[3] Almost two dozen people had been arrested—mostly Black, as were most of the injured. Reverend Ellerbrake reported that "several white boys [had been] taken to the jail to cool off," but few charges were filed.[4] When spoken to about the violence and evident bias in the arrests, Mayor Laz Quave "expressed concern" over the "unequal law protection." However, as Reverend Ellerbrake responded, "it is hard to believe he was not aware of this" previously. Meanwhile, Medgar Evers of the NAACP confronted Governor Barnett regarding the "barbarous actions against Negro Citizens of Biloxi by white hoodlums," in the face of the "apparent breakdown of law enforcement"; but Barnett's response was not recorded.[5]

Many white-run newspaper reports reflected a similar racial bias, framing the story with descriptions such as "officers arrested three Negros for fighting with whites in battles stemming from Negro invasions of the all-white beach front" in the May 21 *Jackson Advocate*. Most press coverage, under Black or white leadership, largely repeated the same information and quotes found elsewhere, with only a comparison of headlines revealing a divergence in the framing of events; for example, the *Jackson Advocate*'s "Federal Suit for Negroes Right to Swim on Gulf Coast" on May 21 versus the *Daily Herald*'s "Coast Officials Prepare Legal Fight for Beach" on May 18.[6] Officials did nothing to correct the impression in the newspapers that the Black participants were responsible for the violence. One desk sergeant said he was not sure if white persons had been arrested and that, to his understanding, "the [negroes arrested] were fighting among themselves."[7] Mayor Quave insisted that reports of the violence were "greatly exaggerated," keen to deflect any question over whether or not he should call in the National Guard.[8]

The names and street addresses of the detainees were published in the *Daily Herald*. In addition to Mason, Joe Lonberger, and Gilmore Fielder, the list of those arrested for disorderly conduct included A. J. Parker, Althea McGowan, Myrtle Davis, Johnny Chapman, Vernon R. Owens (AFB), Spencer Hanshaw, and Sam Jones. Six others in custody were charged with concealed weapons: Paul Brown, George Seall, Ernest Fair, Zeb Lowe, James Francis, and Malcolm Jackson, a recent graduate of Nichols High.[9] Although not listed in the papers, Eleanora Hayes reported that she and Ann Shirley were also jailed overnight; Mason came to examine them before they were released, through the assistance of the Elks Club leadership.[10] Minors such as David Hamilton were also unlisted although, faced with interrogation before he was released, Hamilton told authorities, under obvious duress, that "he would be satisfied to use the Nichols pool now."[11]

Judge Anthony Anglado oversaw the cases of Mason and the two young men he had saved from being beaten, Lonberger and Fielder. Perhaps wanting to minimize the publicity of the trial, Judge Anglado took the three defendants into his private office, where he ruled all three had been guilty of disturbing the peace. He fined Mason for the additional charge of obstructing traffic. In his concluding remarks, Anglado said that if the violence continued, "innocent people not even interested in this [issue] will be hurt. It's one of the means not to get what you want."[12] Unsurprisingly, he suggested no alternative means and left the vague pronouncement hanging in the air, sounding like nothing so much as a threat. Judge Francis Guidry ruled in the remaining trials. He fined Gifford Eatman and Albert Moore in the case of the bottles thrown from Eatman's car and the fight afterward; the charges against the others, Derouen, Rolkosy (both white), and Andrews, were dropped. The other nearly two dozen defendants were fined amounts ranging from ten dollars to one hundred dollars, but appeals were immediately filed on behalf of all.[13]

On April 26, 1960, Governor Ross Barnett signed a bill into law to, as Mason described it, "nip in the bud" any more demonstrations.[14] The new bill would allow the sentencing of up to ten years in prison for anyone inciting a riot in which a person was injured. One can imagine how broadly those terms might be applied. Nicknamed the "Mason Bill," this bill "originally was proposed to combat Negro sit-ins at any lunch counter" or "any other lawful business" (including "store, restaurant, sandwich shop, hotel, motel, lunch counter, bowling alley, moving picture theatre or drive-in theatre, barber shop or beauty parlor"), but it was now amended to specify that any "breach of peace *on a coastal beach*" would be a felony (italics added in Mason's book when he quoted the original newspaper article). Lesser disorderly conduct such as "crowds on a sidewalk [that] fail to disperse" or "anyone acting or speaking obscenely toward another" could be fined $200 and subjected to four months in jail. In a deeply troubling explanation of the necessity of such a measure, District Attorney Boyce Holleman stated, "even the peaceful exercise of a constitutional right can, at certain times and under certain circumstances, interfere with public safety and must yield."[15] Three other bills were also approved, that were according to the *Daily Herald* "designed to discourage Negroes from making complaints to the civil rights commission or its state advisory council and any other federal or state agency in order to start an investigation." Under these measures, a person could be "convicted of giving false statements to a federal or state agency if the falsity is corroborated by a single witness" and subjected to up to five years in jail and a fine of $1,000.[16]

During the week following Biloxi's "Bloody Sunday," as it came to be called years later, the beaches and sidewalks remained all but deserted.[17] The rumor mill churned continuously with allegations of plans for further demonstrations or acts of violent intimidation. Rev. Richard Ellerbrake received calls warning that the Back Bay Mission would be bombed or set on fire, as there were rumors that he had been "the leader of the beach mobs" (by which, it seems, they meant the Black protestors) and that he used the mission as NAACP headquarters (rumors that were false but perhaps prompted by the reputation the mission had for offering some community services on a desegregated basis).[18] Reverend Ellerbrake reported that the mission's "'fan mail'... was about 60% threatening and 40% encouraging," with substantially more of the phone calls "anonymous and hateful, threatening even the life of [his] wife and infant son."[19] Mayor Laz Quave's office had received "15 or 20 letters" from citizens; some "condoned the handling of [the] Negroes and others protested."[20] A meeting was arranged between the mayor and Keesler Air Force Base's commanding general, Major General John R. Sutherland, Commissioner Roy Elder, Colonel Walter C. Barrett, Major C. W. Rusch, Captain Robert Harris, and Ray Butterfield, in the presence of newspaper and radio representatives. Chief of the Office of Information from Air Training Command, Colonel Willis L. Helmantoler, had even flown in for the meeting.

On Wednesday afternoon, white youth Alvin Arnold Flowers told police he had been jumped by five Black people. Mayor Quave cautioned "people on both sides" not to "get panicky" and advised that there were "discrepancies" to the story (indicating that perhaps Flowers was taking advantage of the current racial tension as a cover for whatever truly happened, though Quave certainly may have had motivation to downplay or divert escalating violence).[21] Seemingly in response to what he called this "alleged incident," the editor of the *Daily Herald*, Cosman Eisendrath, asked for "calmness and clear thinking on the part of the better elements," without recourse to "retaliation." In somewhat ambiguous language, the editorial continued by saying "the better elements of both races deplore the incidents," which would "take a long time to erase from the good name of the community." It furthermore urged officers "to put down any further trouble" by a "lookout for any gatherings" of either race and for citizens of both races to "cooperate."[22]

The police and churches continued to receive calls from both Black and white individuals who were scared to leave home.[23] Some children were kept home from school and were advised to "stay away from trouble areas."[24] Dr. Mason donated his time, driving people to and from their jobs, when they could not afford to miss a day.[25] Downtown saw a steep decline in profits. One department store reported a 45 percent reduction in business, and a "luxury hotel had plummeted from $1,700 to $97 a day." The Harlem Theatre simply closed. Alex Poinsett of *Jet* magazine, who had traveled to Biloxi to cover the event, wrote that "the violence . . . washed away more than $1 million worth of resort trade."[26] As the following Sunday approached and further demonstrations were expected, city and county patrolmen drove along the beach highway, among those who were out cruising, waiting to see what would happen next.

Law enforcement was less than reassuring. "If those Negroes continue to go down to the beaches," police chief McDonnell told the press, "I'm not going to be a baby-sitter for them. This thing could get serious."[27]

The reaction of the white community is only captured spottily through public sources. Apart from the actions of the mob, statements by officials, and Eisendrath's editorial, the most vocal of the white community on record were a few religious leaders. While they were clear on the call for an immediate and complete end to physical violence, they tended to also use ambiguous language when defining the issue at hand, who was at fault on either side, or possible solutions moving forward.

Rev. Maxie D. Dunnam, minister of Trinity Methodist Church in Gulfport, wrote a column in the *Daily Herald* urging "prayerful consideration" following the "outburst of racial strife." While some of Dunnam's language may be interpreted as equivocal, such as when he asserts that "following our own way we accomplish our ruin," which could be taken to apply to either the white attackers or the Black demonstrators, his list of inexcusable behaviors—"shootings, bombings, beach fights, mob action, terrorizing"—appears more clear and pointed. In the most cosmic and poetic appeal to humanity, Dunnam wrote, "When we commune with God, not when we fling ourselves violently at each other in hate and bitterness, we link ourselves to the power that spins the universe."[28]

Leggett Memorial Methodist Church in Biloxi was situated on beachfront property, about a mile from the lighthouse demonstration. The church's pastor, R. Inman Moore Jr., wrote in the *Daily Herald* that while "I do not feel that Dr. Mason was wise in leading the group of colored citizens to one of the most populous areas on the beach" where it was "certain to arouse animosity and ill will," nevertheless, "law enforcement officials could have capably handled the situation without any assistance." Reverend Moore urged white citizens "to consider . . . the underlying causes of this attempt," particularly the use of Black taxpayer dollars in the construction and maintenance of the beach. "Even within the framework of our Southern customs," wrote Moore, "there must be justice." Drawing on the religious affiliations of the coastal community, he added that the "Christian majority must always maintain a concern for the minority."[29] Whereas his letter in the newspaper spoke largely of secular concerns, from his pulpit he sermonized more emphatically on the Christian perspective, stating that one of the core causes of the civil rights movement was Christianity itself, which preached that all people were the "sons and daughters of God." Mindful that Christian scripture had historically been used to justify slavery, segregation and bigotry, Reverend Moore attacked these problematic interpretations, particularly the curse of Ham by his father.[30] Although this was a moderate stance, spoken in terms well within the purview of his vocation, there were well-respected and well-known people, even within the church, who never spoke to him again.[31]

A third article was penned by a biracial coalition between the white Gulf Coast Ministerial Association, represented by its vice president, Rev. Howard T. Lips, and the Black Interdenominational Ministerial Alliance of Gulfport, represented by its president, Rev. Famous McElhaney. Accompanied by other ministers of their organizations, Lips and McElhaney had met to discuss and write for the *Daily Herald* the "call for [sanity] and goodwill," an end to the violence, and "justice and mercy for all." "Men can and do differ in their opinions in regard to segregation, desegregation, and integration" ran the statement, yet "we can still be vitally concerned with justice." Like the other individual writers, this united front of pastors summoned the professed morality of their Christian colleagues, asking that the community "apply Christian motives" to the solution of the racialized issues arising.[32]

As a matter of public record, the issue of morality and race relations in Harrison County came primarily from the religious leadership of the Gulf Coast. For the governing body, there were other concerns than moral imperatives or even legal rights. The impact on the economy was a real source of apprehension. The money companies had been willing to invest in Arkansas had dropped more than two-thirds after the violent response to school desegregation in Little Rock in 1957. At face value, the economy was a primary reason the SSC had formed: to paint a positive picture of race relations in Mississippi, encouraging businesses, tourists, and new residents to come to the state. Sales tax from tourism contributed millions of dollars to the state budget annually. In Biloxi, a huge amount of money flowed into the community from the $15 million yearly pay roll of the Keesler airmen, who were now ordered not to leave the base.[33] Weighing in on the beach issue as it intersected with tourism, publicist C. C. Hamill pointed out that winter and spring resort tourism particularly relied on visitors from farther away than Mississippi and its neighboring states. He suggested the sand beach, the main attraction of the coast, should be "preserve[d]," i.e., segregated, for the sake of the local economy (without mention of the rights of the homeowners). However, he continued, "somewhere" beach facilities should be provided for Black beachgoers.[34]

On Friday, April 29, Mayor Laz Quave paced the floor of the hastily arranged SSC meeting. In one of several attempts to place blame elsewhere, Quave snapped that the Board of Supervisors were the ones avoiding the issue: it was for them to designate beach areas for the segregated populace. Publicly, Quave expressed the fear that the violence was just beginning. There were (according to him) Black agitators in Biloxi from "everywhere else," infiltrating the coast in "an organized move." To explain the fact that only one of those arrested the night of the wade-in had an out-of-state address, Quave claimed others had given fictitious addresses in Biloxi. Reverend Ellerbrake disputed these rumors in his letter to the *Petal Paper*, detailing the events of the week.[35] Nevertheless, Quave instructed the highway patrol to be on the lookout for any group from New Orleans or Mobile so "we can be ready for them." Although much effort was made to publicly blame outside agitators for racial unrest in the South, this narrative was belied not only by witnesses, but by the constant monitoring of local groups and individuals suspected of civil rights activities by the SSC and other officials. Dr. Mason went on to attribute the acceptance of this narrative to the "strange psychology" of even "well-meaning whites," who combined negative and (so-called) positive stereotypes, believing local Blacks did not have the strength or wit to organize and challenge the hierarchy, nor the desire or necessity, given the image of well-contented southern Black persons.[36]

Further trying to frame the violent white mob as not quite culpable, Quave described the participants as "either teenagers or young adult hot-heads, who lost all responsibility in groups." Likewise, focusing on the alleged youth of the Black beach demonstrators undermined both, casting them as neither organized and sensible protestors nor premeditated, culpable antagonists. Furthermore, it was not the attack on the peacefully assembled Black families, Boy Scouts, and community leaders that Mayor Quave considered proof of the hot-heads' irresponsibility. "For instance," Quave explained, "one white group beat two unidentified white officers from Keesler."[37] Essentially, the press blamed the Black community for the need to protest at all, bringing back up the alleged reasons of sanitation and decency for which use of the beach in front of the Gulfport veterans' hospital had been withdrawn from them several years prior.[38]

Sheriff Dedeaux, who had previously agreed to let the public "handle" the demonstrators, now blamed Clayton Rand, publisher of and columnist for Gulfport's *Dixie Press* and the *Dixie Guide*, for being "Daddy of the whole situation." Rand had seemingly "raised so much fuss with Negroes in front of his home on the beach that the people had to do something."[39] Rand, a frequent local speaker and leader of the States' Rights party in 1948, had once done a remarkable job of white-washing the history of slavery when he spoke at a Gulfport Rotary Club meeting, saying the invention of the cotton gin had begun the "optimistic period . . . of individual liberty and free enterprise," which was coming to an end only because of the "deadly enemy" of Communism.[40]

The intersections, real or imagined, among civil rights activity, Communism, and Jewish interests were another target of blame for the civil rights movement in general and now of the wade-in. The general manager of the Biloxi Chamber of Commerce, Anthony Ragusin, accused the NAACP of having plotted the demonstration, adding that the organization was financed "with overseas money from enemies of the United States."[41] The *Shreveport Times* blamed the "white-directed" college group, the Congress of Racial Equality (CORE), for coaching masses of Black citizens to "intrude illegally" anywhere.[42] Some simply claimed it was the mishandling of the separate-but-equal policy that was causing the rebellion of Black citizens nationwide. Percy Greene, the editor and founder of the *Jackson Advocate*, though critical of Mason's actions, wrote that "the race rioting [is] the result of the purely negative attitude, or do-nothin' approach" of institutional bodies like the

Board of Supervisors. "The great mass of Negro citizens," Greene declared, were not against maintaining separate facilities for every aspect of life, so much as "the stark discrimination practiced in the name of segregation."[43]

Of course, no attempt to shift blame took the focus entirely away from Mason. Chief Herbert McDonnell told reporters that Mason had "this town in an uproar" and was "responsible for the riot."[44] "All of us," McDonnell concluded, "got along good with colored people down here until he stirred up some of the younger ones."[45] Senator Stanford Morse of Gulfport said Mason was the "most dangerous agitator in Harrison County" and that any racial or subversive activities occurring locally had been orchestrated with the doctor "behind the screen or actually in front directing the agitation."[46]

Criticism took the shape of questioning Dr. Mason's professionalism and ethics as well. The *Jackson Advocate*, under the leadership of Percy Greene, who was on the payroll of the SSC, wrote that the desire and time needed to find cures for such things as "crippling children's diseases . . . would give little time to the really dedicated doctor for leadership in political action."[47] James M. Ward, editor of the *Jackson Daily News*, accused Mason of neglecting his patients to gain notoriety.[48] Such criticism was more than just lip service. The New Biloxi Hospital staff committee threatened to remove him from the hospital but, meeting with resistance from Mason's white colleagues—particularly Dr. Frank Gruich—did not move forward.[49] The Coast Medical Association, which had denied him membership, strangely found it within their purview to send a letter reprimanding him for "conduct unbecoming of a physician."[50] Rumors circulated that white employers pressured their employees not to receive treatment from Mason any longer—the same methods that had been used to drive Dr. Clinton Battle and Dr. T. R. M. Howard from the state in previous years.[51] To this end, the theme of white womanhood was mobilized to covertly threaten the poorest Black population with a potential loss of free medical service from the Harrison County Health Department in Gulfport (and, likely, to enflame the paper's white readership). James M. Ward wrote that "Negroes . . . taking full advantage of the free service" would "participate in no movement that would pose any threat to visitations by the trained white nurses," who might be "afraid to enter Negro communities" if racial agitation continued.[52]

There were other social consequences. The Pine Burr Council, which oversaw the Boy Scouts of Southern Mississippi, canceled Mason's invitation to the 1960 national jamboree, an integrated event, leaving him to attend at his own cost.[53] There were the usual phone calls and letters, swearing and threatening violence against the family, which the Masons would continue to receive for nearly forty years, sometimes frightening enough that they sent their son to sleep at a friend's house. Their property was vandalized and crosses burned in the yard. One of several drive-by shootings at their home left bullet holes in the brick beside the front door frame.[54] But Sheriff Dedeaux could not have been more wrong when, behind closed doors, he voiced the thought that Mason "would mouth-off quite a bit . . . but after he got knocked in the head Sunday, he wouldn't attempt to go back on the beach any more."[55]

On April 25, 1960, the field secretary of the NAACP in Mississippi, Medgar Evers, drove from Jackson to meet with Mason and Dunn. He collected seventy-two affidavits and photographs detailing the events of the wade-ins and the subsequent violence and filed them with the Justice Department.[56] Arrangements were made for attorney Robert Carter, assistant to Thurgood Marshall, to assess the situation as well.[57] With the advice and organizational assistance of Evers, a Biloxi chapter of the NAACP was formed. Mason would serve as president of the chapter for over thirty years.[58] Ethel Rainey became the first president of the youth branch and James Black the vice president.[59] The very thing the SSC most wanted to avoid had come to fruition: from this point forward, Mason and his colleagues would have the legal assistance, resources, and media power of the NAACP behind them.

In a belated, misguided, and *totally* ineffectual attempt to resolve the beach issue, the Board of Supervisors responded by creating a special nine-man committee to address the matter. Rather than, as suggested by local religious leaders, forming a diverse, representative panel, the nine were all men and all white. It hardly mattered, however; faced with Mason's ongoing assertion that he would accept nothing less than full integration of the beach, the committee never did anything beyond forming. When Mason heard about this attempt, he simply replied that he had a nine-man committee as well: the US Supreme Court.

On Sunday, May 1, 1960, Mason and Dunn spoke at the Elks Hall to inform the Black community about developments with the NAACP and make plans for the future. Medgar Evers was in the audience, as were SSC agent Bob Thomas, District Attorney Boyce Hollemen, and Sheriff Dedeaux.[60] A dozen policemen were stationed outside, "only to direct traffic," as the doctors advised attendees to continue protesting peacefully and to bear their scars proudly.[61] They suggested a boycott of several businesses that had fired Black employees following the protest, as well as white-owned businesses in the Black portion of town, if their owners were known to have taken part in the mob or had sold the pipes and chains used to beat protestors. The only business publicly named was Trahan's Hardware, but others included a "laundromat, variety store, grocery store and insurance companies."[62] Boycotting went both ways. The local KKK advised whites to boycott any establishment "employing more than one person of African descent," as well as any goods coming from southern cities that showed "any inclination toward racial integration."[63] The KKK also organized "buy-ins" of businesses under protest by civil rights groups; business owners seem not to have appreciated the attention, as it resulted in the loss of more Black patrons.[64]

The magnitude of the wade-in was felt across the nation, as Roy Wilkins of the NAACP began to use the Biloxi demonstrations as the model for events in eleven other states, expanding the movement to desegregate beaches from "Cape May, NJ to Brownsville, Texas." Biloxi's KKK grand dragon, Walter Bailey, wrote to Chicago's mayor, offering his help "in every way possible" after the demonstration to desegregate Rainbow Beach in April 1961; the offer was ignored.[65] The press dubbed these demonstrators "Freedom Waders."[66] Although the brutal confrontation in Biloxi had been so traumatic and some may have been frightened away from future protest, many others were determined to see the fight through. "We talked about [going back] and some of us cried about it," Ethel Rainey recalled of conversations with her classmates in the ensuing weeks. "We didn't want nobody to get killed or hurt or nothing like that, but still we were so fervent."[67]

Later that May, the US Justice Department sued the city of Biloxi (which included the mayor, the chief of police, the county sheriff, and the Harrison County Board of Supervisors) on the grounds that since well over a million dollars in national funds had been used to rebuild the beach, it could not be treated as private property.[68] This was the first lawsuit of its kind in the nation. The suit included a charge against the police for complicity with the violence of the riot. The federal government said Harrison County officials had "aided and abetted" the white mob in forcing Black people off the beach, "deliberately [refusing] to assure" their right to its use.[69]

"Providence has ways and means of salvation for all people," Dr. Mason told the press, triumphantly. "We are happy to see this action."[70]

Chapter Seven

WHITE SAND, WHITE SOLIDARITY

The Continued Policing of Harrison County Beaches and *United States v. Harrison County*

On May 18, 1960, Governor Ross Barnett announced he would aid the county "in every way possible" in keeping the beach segregated (again, with no mention of the alleged rights of the homeowners). His authority in saying so was perhaps undermined by his having been "reached at his vacation hideaway" where he didn't "have a copy of the alleged contract." He claimed he had not "had an opportunity to talk with [the] officials of Harrison county" about the federal contract, although he had been aware of the issue for nearly a month, at least since the signing of "The Mason Bill."[1] Most of the men named in the suit objected to being called to account: Mayor Laz Quave and Chief Herbert McDonnell because they were officers of the city, not the county, and Sheriff Curtis Dedeaux and the Board of Supervisors because they claimed to have never "asserted any power or authority" over who was permitted to enjoy the beach. They insisted use of the property was determined solely by the homeowners. "Public use" in the government contract was asserted by the defendants to refer only to the maintenance of the beach.[2]

"I'm not interested in questioning who owns the property," Sheriff Dedeaux told the newspapers. "I'm a law enforcement officer."[3]

US Senators James Eastland and John Stennis of Mississippi (signatories of the Southern Manifesto) said the Department of Justice was "dreaming up the grounds for its suit" and that there were "no specific charges against any of the specific individuals named." According to the senators, when the government could not find a "basis for desegregation action in any civil rights legislation," they had been "forced to examine an obscure contract." Eastland and Stennis said they believed when the "heat of the current [presidential election] year dies down" the suit would be dropped, certainly a motivation to continue the strategy of delaying the trial indefinitely. In the meantime, Eastland and Stennis pronounced it a "travesty of justice" for the US government to use the courts "for such a nefarious purpose."[4]

Harrison County had one thing primarily in favor of its argument that the beach was private property. The biggest problem in proving the legitimacy and intent of the beach contract was that the county had not conducted an eminent domain process—the right of the government to take private land and convert it to public use—which included paying compensation for the land taken. (The county had given public notice of the intention to replenish the beach using federal funds, however.[5]) Homeowners quickly assumed the offensive position, hoping to circumvent the federal government's claim. Lee Dicks Guice and the newly formed Biloxi Beach Property Owners Protective Association took initiative on behalf of the beachfront landowners, represented by Guice's husband, attorney William L. Guice.[6] She brought a suit against Harrison County in chancery court to ensure her rights to the land south of the seawall, "including especially the beach . . . and all other littoral privileges" in front of their residence and other beachfront lots they owned, excepting only "the right of the state of Mississippi to . . . control US Hwy 90" and the county to maintain the seawall.

In June, real estate broker Paul M. Skrmetti also filed a motion to his claim of land ownership in west Biloxi, claiming the Board of Supervisors and US government were "trespassers" (likely as an extension of this suit, he filed a letter asking not to have the beach replenished by the Army Corps of Engineers again in July 1962). Winifred Green filed a similar suit against the county Board of Supervisors in August 1960.[7] But it was the case put forward by the Guices that was at the forefront in the press. Attorney William Guice said that taking the land "without compensation [would be] an attempt to deprive Mrs. Guice of due process of law," in violation of the state and US constitutions.[8] The property association requested the county remove maintenance equipment from the beach in order to bolster the impression of it as private property.[9] The second, smaller argument on behalf of Harrison County was that the federal government, by having prevented free use of the beach by Black citizens in front of the Veterans Hospital (through the staff of the hospital), did not "come into court with clean hands" and so did not have a right to pursue the case in a "court of equity."[10] This objection was quickly dismissed.

Judge Sidney Mize was set to preside over *United States v. Harrison County*. Just a few months before, Mize had overseen the grand jury that failed to indict the murderers of Mack Charles Parker. Mize had refused to admit FBI evidence, narrowed the kidnapping statutes under which the men might have been found guilty, and ruled that all the accused or none must be indicted—all but ensuring the impossibility of the case.[11] It was one of several examples in the courtroom that demonstrated Mize was not sympathetic to the struggle for civil rights. No doubt Dr. Mason knew there was a long and arduous trial ahead, with the likelihood of appeals to the higher courts.

The federal government, as plaintiff, filed an intervention to open the beaches that summer, so the Black community would not have to wait for a verdict to enjoy their civil liberties. In June 1960, Judge Mize stifled that possibility when he extended the usual time defendants had to answer the suit's allegations by an additional sixty days.[12] He then delayed the hearing by requiring the government to clarify what he found to be the "vague" accusations of the suit.[13] After these requests were met and depositions were in hand, Mize said he would not be ready to start trying the case for several months, as his court docket was full (including the Guice chancery suit).[14] In fact, the judge decided to leave the federal case pending to allow for the resolution of the latter. By prioritizing the homeowners, the interested parties hoped that a ruling in Lee Guice's favor would strengthen the defendants' position in *United States v. Harrison County*.[15] The government's complaint that these delays were "causing the United States injury in that it makes the United States participate, against its will, in a violation of the fifth amendment" was to no avail.[16]

It hardly seems coincidental that, in June 1960, the Mississippi State Sovereignty Commission (SSC) apportioned over $20,000 of its taxpayer funds to support the White Citizens' Council (WCC). Albert Jones, director of the SSC, tried to rationalize this appropriation by claiming it "offered the best possible means of presenting the case for state sovereignty . . . to the nation."[17] Rev. Richard Ellerbrake wrote to Jones, forwarding a copy of his letter to the editor of the *Daily Herald*, Cosman Eisendrath, stating that the SSC's "flagrant violation of the democratic principle that public funds are to be used for . . . the best interest of the public" was "not only extra-constitutional but immoral as well."[18] The SSC engaged in its usual investigative phone calls. Mayor Laz Quave was not complimentary when he described Reverend Ellerbrake as "persistent in his efforts to bring about equality among the races." At least one member of Biloxi's St. Paul congregation reported "very little respect for Ellerbrake's ideas regarding segregation."[19]

Although Ellerbrake's advocacy exposed him to other heavy-handed criticism, he received support as well. An anonymous letter to the *Petal Paper* praised his "intestinal fortitude" in confronting Mississippi's government for "such high handed misuse of the public funds. Especially where it will be used to promote bitterness, hatred and anger over the racial issue. . . . Incidentally," the writer continued, "I happen to be a white man and also from the deep south. BUT I owe my allegiance first to my GOD. . . . And Christian justice is something that the minority groups of this nation have not received."[20] Rev. Murray Cox of Gulfport, chairman of the Mississippi Advisory Committee to the US Civil Rights Commission (which had been formed in 1957), asked Ellerbrake to become secretary of the committee.[21]

Regardless, the WCC formed new branches in Biloxi and Gulfport, determined to socially police the community by their means. In mid-June 1960, Clayton Rand was among those speaking at a WCC banquet held at the Edgewater Gulf Hotel. For twenty-five dollars a plate, participants would listen to speeches on the theme "White Solidarity Means White Beaches." The former lieutenant governor, Cayton Bidwell Adam of Gulfport, was master of ceremonies. The proceeds would enable the WCC to intensify its activities along the coast, including surveillance of civil rights activists and attempts at economic pressure. Aware of such methods, civil rights activists resorted to hand-delivering more sensitive messages.[22] The Mississippi Advisory Committee's subsequent assertion that "an exposure of the files" of the SSC and WCC "would reveal that these organizations are engaged in activities of a secret police nature, aimed at the suppression of Mississippi's Negro citizens" would go unanswered for over thirty years.[23]

While the federal suit of *United States v. Harrison County* was stalled, nothing had stopped the policing of the beaches. As each rebellion against Jim Crow traditions occurred, the police walked a fine line between discouraging and breaking up the gatherings while avoiding further arrests, which could have led to further court cases.[24] On high alert and taking the offensive, the SSC reached out to the various heads of local law enforcement to determine if other coastal cities were experiencing civil rights demonstrations. Sheriff Gerald V. Price of Bay St. Louis reported that he "always controlled the Negros" and that there were two segregated sections of the beach for them to use, one "between Clement Harbor and Lake Shore known as Jackson ridge" and another "at the north end where the sea wall ends." He said the only recent incident had been when a Black woman, Ms. Zinglind, brought her six children to an area reserved for whites. When his deputies ordered the family to leave, Zinglind responded that she paid taxes and had a right to the beach but ultimately moved on. Sheriff Price said he had more trouble with white people from out of town going to the Black sections of the beach and getting "too close" or even mingling. Allegedly, the whites "didn't know where they were going" although they didn't seem to object to "swimming along with" the Black bathers once they had arrived, demonstrating again that maintaining segregation involved subjugating people of both races.[25]

In Pass Christian, there were complaints of "abnormal use of the beach facilities," by which the authorities meant greater numbers of Black citizens enjoying the segregated area set aside for their use. Most, the report claimed, were from Biloxi and Gulfport (who had not even a segregated area to use in their own towns). They would "get off limits to the East," according to the report, but would cooperate willingly by returning to the designated space when asked. Local law enforcement threatened to revoke Black use of the beach if these conditions persisted, never mind that even if the bathers had driven from Maine, the replenished beach had been paid for by national tax dollars and Black tourists had as much right to it as anyone.[26]

The wade-ins may have sparked more conviction regarding the use of all federal land, as a similar type of desegregation event was policed on the Fourth of July at Desoto National Park, sixty miles north of the coast. Apparently the consistent rumor mill had predicted Black demonstrators would again try to desegregate the beaches that weekend; officials later defined these rumors as a "smoke screen," distracting from the real "well-planned effort" to spend the day in a public park "historically ... used by whites."[27] The event began when a few dozen Black citizens arrived, determined to enjoy the facilities like the many white families picnicking, playing baseball, and enjoying the summer weather. One onlooker, C. W. Craft, heard some white men planning to retrieve their guns and "clean out" the newcomers.[28] Craft called the police, citing his concern for the women and children present, saying, "if these white men got started, it would be plenty of trouble." Highway Patrol inspector J. W. Warren was in the process of sending up to twenty of his men, armed with tear gas and other "emergency gear," to the park when Sheriff Dedeaux called and said everything was under control. Five of the sheriff's deputies—including Chief George Rosetti, Doug Thompson, Glen Wright, and Milton Cuevas—had already responded to the scene.

As the sheriff's deputies surveyed the situation, Black youths and families kept arriving, including two busloads of young people from the Black high school, Nichols High of Biloxi, and two airmen from Keesler.[29] For several hours, approximately eighty Black participants celebrated the holiday, using picnic tables and benches, the swimming area in the river, and all of the convenience facilities. A disagreement arose about the use of the baseball diamond: according to one report, Black youths were engaged in a game when white teens attempted to take the field and the "Negroes ... declined to yield"; but according to a second version, the white teens were playing when the Black group approached and the former group quit the field, complaining they had been "deprived" of their game. Either way, "tension was gradually building up," Sheriff Dedeaux later told the press.[30] The other "dissatisfied" white picnickers were demanding action as well.[31] The sheriff's deputies replied that "they would like to do something," but since the site was a national park, it was public property.³² The deputies contacted the county and district attorneys for advice. In the end, they waited until most of the three hundred or so picnickers of both races had finished eating and then asked them to leave. By that time, the sheriff and several more regular and auxiliary deputies had arrived to oversee the process.

Local journalist Tom Cook aided the SSC in minimizing the publicity in his coverage of the event.³³ The SSC claimed that no discrimination had been shown by the sheriff's department and that the action taken "was for public safety only." However, although the perceived threat had been due to white men saying they would bring out guns, Sheriff Dedeaux informed the press he would have "arrested the Negroes" if they had not left willingly, under the authority of "a new Mississippi anti-riot law" passed in the wake of racial conflict (i.e., "The Mason Bill").³⁴ It was the first time the bill had been cited to support law enforcement officials' claim to jurisdiction. The police had also taken down a list of car tags belonging only to the Black participants. (Although the cars may have been borrowed from relatives or friends, they were registered to Leroy Word Johnson, George Johnson, Howard B. Wheatley, Willie Burkett, Haywood Knight Jr., and Lucille Currie of Gulfport, Robert Harris and Clarence Addison of Biloxi, William Gaddis Jr. from Keesler, and Gene A. Cherry of Moss Point, as well as three cars from Alabama and Louisiana.³⁵) W. C. Craft had not want to give the names of those white men who had made the threats (though he said he would do so if a case came to court), so those names were not recorded.³⁶ Although neither Dr. Gilbert Mason or Dr. Felix Dunn had been present, the SSC nevertheless maintained suspicions that the event had been planned by them. It is possible that the Mason family, who attended scouting events and also traveled during summers to visit family in Virginia, Jackson, and New Orleans, was not even in town.³⁷

The Desoto incident also drew national attention. Michigan's first Black congressman, Charles L. Diggs Jr., who had previously spoken out about the political situation in Mississippi—and was the only congressman to attend the trial of Emmett Till's murderers—called for an investigation by the secretary of agriculture. In response to the press coverage, the supervisor of Mississippi's national forests, L. S. Newcomb, only said he supported law enforcement's "full authority" within the national parks in their jurisdiction.³⁸

As to the legal cases concerning the beach, in August 1960, engineer William Dolive, who had worked on the beach erosion study in Harrison County in the late 1940s, testified that, prior to the replenishment, little beach land "of any appreciable size" had existed between Point Cadet in Biloxi and Henderson Point in Pass Christian, and he provided four aerial photographs to that effect. Depositions from county engineer Arthur McArthur and his former assistant H. A. Campbell were also taken.[39] The argument was that Lee Guice and other property owners had "lost title to lands that had eroded [and] had not acquired title to lands made."[40] Guice, however, contended that her property had included up to 250 feet of high ground used as a lawn, above a beach of a width of forty feet, and that construction of the seawall (in a concave, rather than in the "authorized" step formation) had caused an "artificial action of the waves" that eroded the natural sand. It was confirmed that the greatest erosion had occurred after the building of the seawall (however, it is unclear if this assessment was made before or after the Category 4 hurricane of 1947). The subsequent replenishment of the beach by the Corps of Engineers had filled in some of the shallows, "resulting in an extension of the Guice uplands," a benefit the homeowners had not looked for but which they claimed a right to nonetheless.[41] The littoral rights, defined as "the enjoyment of ... the water in connection with the land" were said to be "the most valuable attribute of such property." By annexing this borderland, the county would, supposedly, dramatically reduce the value of coastal residences and businesses without compensation.

It is interesting to note that, while the chancery suit was brought in Lee Guice's name, her husband's testimony was quoted in the press, saying he had made no objection to the replenishment "because I thought nature would destroy it." (Somewhat contradictorily, Mr. Guice testified that the replenishment might have worked if it had been "allowed to impact," instead of being groomed by the maintenance tractors.) The centering of the husband or wife in two separate situations raises the question of who had primary ownership of the property. Most of the chancery suits and subsequent trespassing charges were brought under the names of women. (Paul Skrmetti appears to have been a widower.) Using women's names in this way makes one wonder whether this was an odd coincidence or a tactical deployment of gender meant to sway the judge and the public, in another manifestation of the oft-mobilized stereotype of white women in need of protection.

It would be difficult to determine how the highway, seawall, and replenished beach had affected property values, for good or ill, particularly keeping in mind that, as members of the public themselves, homeowners were not, in fact, denied access to the water in any case. What was clearly at risk of being taken from them was the power of exclusivity.[42] Harrison County Board supervisor Dewey Lawrence contended that he had "never authorized members of the general public to use the beach" and that any reference he had made to it as "a public beach" had meant only that the county had the right to use "public funds" to protect the seawall; this was regardless of the fact that constant aesthetic grooming of the beaches implied the county intended the beach as a public tourist attraction as much if not more than road protection.[43] Lee Guice did not live to see the conclusion of her case. Her illness and subsequent death in March 1961 resulted in further delays in the proceedings and left her husband to take the place of plaintiff in May of the same year.[44]

It took a year longer for Judge Sidney Mize to submit his ruling. In May 1962, he ruled in favor of the plaintiffs, due to the fact that there had been no eminent domain proceedings prior to the county's signing the contract with the federal government. Asked for his comment, Biloxi mayor Laz Quave told the press that the ruling was "very gratifying" and that the ramifications were likely to be "far reaching." "It has been my contention all along that it is private property," Quave added.[45]

But Dr. Mason still held hope for the federal case, which was still to be heard.[46]

Chapter Eight

MANY OARS

The Other Avenues of Civil Rights Progress in Harrison County

Bigotry had not stopped to await the results of the beach trials. Neither had activism. Alex Poinsett of *Jet* magazine wrote that the "tempo has quickened" throughout the state, with read-ins, boycotts, and voter registration drives.¹ More than one oar was needed to steer the boat forward, and two of the most significant oars in the water were the efforts to increase Black representation in the government and to desegregate the schools in pursuit of quality education.

By the 1940s in Mississippi, less than 1 percent of eligible Black citizens succeeded in registering, and even fewer succeeded in casting their vote. In 1946, Harrison County officials had turned away all Black voters and some whites from participating in the white primary, threatening at least one of the Black citizens with death.²

The end of World War II and the return of Black soldiers from abroad inspired increased efforts in the political arena. But even in the 1960s, in a state with as large a Black population as Mississippi, voter registration had only increased to 4 percent, and some counties had no Black voters registered at all.³ In 1963, an alliance formed by the major civil rights organizations in Mississippi, the Council of Federated Organizations, conducted mock elections to demonstrate the discrepancy between the willingness of Black citizens to vote and their official turnout. Particularly in urban areas, a staggering four times the number of Black citizens registered to cast their ballots in the mock election.⁴ Although in both 1961 and 1964 successive chiefs of police of Biloxi (E. F. Witzel and Edward McDonnell) told Mississippi State Sovereignty Commission (SSC) inspector Virgil Downing that the NAACP had not started Black voters schools in the city (Witzel said he would "not tolerate any trouble"), the Biloxi and Gulfport branches of the NAACP were forging ahead, offering education on voter qualifications and other assistance.⁵ After 1955, Mississippi registrars were no longer required to visit each precinct, and applicants had to travel to the county courthouse in Gulfport. NAACP members like Dr. Gilbert Mason coordinated and provided transportation where needed. The newly formed Biloxi NAACP Youth Branch enthusiastically aided in the registration drives, trained by members of the Student Nonviolent Coordinating Committee (SNCC) and Congress of Racial Equality (CORE).[6]

SSC records again demonstrate that white conformity was not absolute. On January 15, 1961, the grand dragon of the Mississippi Ku Klux Klan, Walter A. Bailey, wrote to Governor Ross Barnett that the "sorry-so-called white man" Nick Guidry, who was employed by the city of Gulfport, had registered four "n-----s" to vote. Bailey implied the SSC should do something about it. In April, SSC agent Bob Thomas attempted to coordinate a redistricting of the voting precincts, "so as to be able to tell where the strong Negro vote would go."[7] But, regardless of bigots like Bailey, hundreds of new Black voters were registered yearly in Biloxi and Gulfport.[8] By 1961, Black voters in Harrison County were approximately 20 percent of registered voters, the third highest percentage in the state.[9] Thankfully, despite the vehemence, threats, and pressure of bigots like Bailey, Black voters on the coast experienced substantially fewer shootings, arsons, and arrests than did activists in other parts of the state.[10] Governor Barnett called the mass registration drives taking place throughout the state "as dangerous to the community as a loaded bomb" and claimed voter registration was being orchestrated by "hired outside agitators [marching] falsely under the banner of freedom" in a "masquerade of privilege and iniquity." Qualified voters, he claimed, need "no crowd," despite all evidence to the contrary.[11]

In his autobiography, *Beaches, Blood, and Ballots*, Mason wrote that the most disturbing markers of the backlash to increased civil rights activity on the coast were the deaths of Malcomb "Papa" Hoyd Jackson and Willie "Bud" Strong, both of whom Mason and others believed were murdered.[12] Most publications on the Biloxi wade-ins relied on Mason's recollections, stating the deaths occurred the week of the riot although that was not the case.[13] Malcomb Jackson, a former member of Mason's Boy Scout troop, was first arrested the night of the bloody wade-in. Then, in March 1975, during a traffic stop in Pascagoula, Jackson allegedly attacked the officer and was arrested again, now at the age of thirty-three and the father of nine children. On May 30, he was charged with aggravated assault against three other prisoners. On June 3, Jackson was found alone in his cell, allegedly having cut his wrists; it "took several men to subdue him," so he could be taken to the hospital, where he died. Some in the Black community did not believe the death had occurred as reported. Jackson's online memorial suggests the family never accepted the official version and still hope to find out more about his death.[14]

Willie "Bud" Strong, also known as "Hatchett," died around January 26, 1961, a little over eight months after the wade-in. Strong was a mentally challenged, illiterate, elderly man born between 1878 and 1883.[15] In all likelihood, his father, George, was born enslaved. Willie Strong, who worked at the local lumber mill in the early 1900s, was old enough to remember the lynchings in Back-of-Town and the adjacent cities. In 1961, he lived in a small house near the railroad, behind his younger sister, Myrtle Corrinne Strong Williams, a public school teacher at Nichols, who supported him.[16] He was known to collect bottles and cans for extra money. It was later reported that Strong was last seen about noon, January 25, at the Little Apple Cafe, holding a broom and chasing some children who had called him names. His sister didn't hear him come home that night.

At 2:30 am, with the weather rainy, Strong's body was hit by a car on Highway 90, in the mile and a half stretch between the old Jefferson Davis home, Beauvoir, and the Edgewater Gulf Hotel. Two male taxi drivers and a woman later reported they had almost hit a Black man matching his description near the beach early that morning.[17] The impact was thought to have broken Strong's legs, but according to the coroner, the cause of death was a deep cut on his throat. The coroner determined that the cut had come "at the hands of person or persons unknown," and he said he believed Strong had been killed at a separate location and then brought to the beach highway. Strong's body had been left there propped up in a standing position by three broomsticks. Wade-in participant Bobby C. Hope later recalled that, as a boy, he had seen an old, gray-bearded man "hung up on a cross in the middle of Highway 90." For some reason, Sheriff Dedeaux was not notified about the body by Highway Patrol until noon. Dedeaux was angry, saying he should always be immediately told about a case "where murder is apparent." By the next day, however, a pathologist, Dr. Henry Haberyan, explained away the lack of blood at the scene by saying Strong had bled internally and said that the car was the cause of death and near decapitation. Following this pivot, Dedeaux would only refer questions to the chief detective, Lt. Eddie Vann, who said the office "found no indications of foul play."

While the amount of time following the wade-in makes it unlikely Strong's death was a direct consequence of that event, the manner and location in which the body were displayed, as well as the officials' cover-up, certainly indicate a racial element. Had Strong been walking the beach that night and been murdered for supposedly trespassing? Or had his killers abducted the old man elsewhere and left him on the neutral ground of the main thoroughfare to discourage the general movement toward civil rights—including the surge in voter registration?

For years, Strong's sister, Myrtle Williams, bought "in memoriam" space in the local paper, lamenting the life "snatched away. No one knows how or why." But of course, that is not entirely true. It is possible that someone today knows the answer to these questions. Under Dr. Mason, the Biloxi branch of the NAACP pressed for investigation of Strong's death, but no one was ever named or charged.[18] The cold case is still being investigated by private researchers.

While there had been a time when white political candidates would hardly have bothered to appear in Back-of-Town, this was no longer the case in 1961. When elections came around then, the Black votes of Biloxi were not likely to go to incumbent mayor Laz Quave. Going into the election, newspapers detailing the "showdown" between Quave and the "determined" Dr. Mason almost made it seem as though Mason was Quave's real competition; at least, it certainly indicated the political pull Mason had in Biloxi.[19] Quave had no sufficient answers for his response to the mob violence at the wade-in, Willie Strong's death, or the poor condition of the streets, drainage, and other infrastructure problems in Back-of-Town.[20] Instead, the election was won by the younger candidate, Daniel Guice (son of the Guices of the beachfront property owners' chancery suit), who had run on the promise to "promote the best welfare of all the citizens."[21] Mayor Quave and the other incumbent commissioners' promise to continue with "full devotion to our duties" may not have sounded so reassuring to those who had reason to question exactly what those duties were perceived to be. While Daniel Guice, who had joined the White Citizens' Council in December 1960, was not free of problematic racial rhetoric, his election did coincide with a shift in the local tide toward equality.[22] Mason credited Mayor Guice with being more progressive and respectful to the Black community than his predecessor, and Guice became the first mayor to appoint Black citizens to city boards and commissions, as well as hiring the first Black police officers in Biloxi (Bernard Seymour and Florian Tichell), making it the only the sixth city in Mississippi with such representation.[23] Whether this initial Black participation in the city's administration and law enforcement resulted in more equitable treatment of the Black population is a subject for further study.

The other priority of the civil rights vanguard in Biloxi was school desegregation. The conditions of Black educational facilities had always been far below the standard of so-called "separate-but-equal." In 1908, with the efforts of principal Archie E. Perkins, funds had been raised by the city, the Black community, and William Gorenflo, a businessman and pillar of the local white community, to replace the "crowded . . . unfit" house on Main, across from the Miley Hotel, that had been rented from the Black Baptist church for use as the Black school since 1886; there, at recess children had "to play in the street as there [was] no yard."[24] The new ten-room wooden frame Biloxi Colored School, after being twice delayed, was constructed on the corner of Nixon and Division streets. In 1916, Professor Marshall F. Nichols of Ocean Springs was asked by Biloxi's Black parents to relocate and take the position of principal. He increased the number of grades to nine (taught by four teachers) and started extracurricular clubs, such as gardening, fishing, and cooking, later expanding to the full twelve grades. In 1919, a Black night school was also approved for adults and children.[25] The Biloxi Colored School was condemned—but still in use—by 1945, when the largely white voter base of the city refused to pass a bond to construct another building. Nichols had passed away that year, and his wife, educator Fannie L. Nichols, had taken the role of principal. "We wish for our children everything possible that they should . . . grow to be strong, healthy and stalwart citizens," she wrote in a letter to the *Daily Herald*, calling for funding in a manner that hinted at the sentiment that better Black schools were what the white community deserved as much as anybody else. "Good schools and good teachings," she wrote, "are requisites to good citizenship."[26]

Well-meaning (but problematically paternalistic from a modern point of view) cannery heiress Irma Dukate Gorenflo appealed for another vote for funding in order to give the "well-behaved" Black population their due, writing that "the very floors are unsafe to walk on, the steps are falling down . . . and if a fire occurred there would be an appalling tragedy."[27] At that time, the school enrolled 392 students, one of the highest enrollment levels in the city, matched only by that at Biloxi High School.[28] In white schools, the student-to-teacher ratio was "27–38 per teacher," but at the Black school there were "as many as 72 pupils" in each classroom.[29] Even more egregious, less than half of the Black children of school age in Biloxi were attending the school.[30]

It should not be construed that Black educators did little with little resources. They contributed to charity drives, enrichment activities, and extracurricular efforts to supplement, as best they could, the disparities in education and materials. As part of her community education during "Negro Health Week" in 1945, Principal Fannie Nichols made suggestions for improving the health and independence of the neighborhood in Back-of-Town, including the growth of "little care" plants in home gardens, such as "okra, corn, beans, peanuts, and potatoes," as well as sanitary care of outhouses and "pit toilets," the elimination of stagnant water, which bred mosquitoes, and application of whitewash, which reflected heat and repelled some pests. In 1947, one second-grade teacher and her fifty-four pupils raised fifty dollars to start a library of books bought from "five and 10-cent stores," in the effort "to get at least three library books for each child in the primary and elementary grades."[31] In an attempt to prevent Black educators from joining civil rights activity, Black teachers were required, under the Subversive Activities Act of 1950, to sign an Employee's Statement and Affidavit, listing their organization memberships—a list that the SSC continued to keep abreast of.[32]

Those who may not have been concerned about Black education from a moral point of view could be worked upon in other ways. Superintendent A. E. Scruggs noted that the struggle of the Black schools kept the educational records of Mississippi low nationally. Dr. P. H. Easom, state supervisor of Black education, argued that Mississippi's economic progress was crippled by only half its population being properly "educated and trained."[33] The first federal funds were received in 1945, but it took a further four years to construct the concrete and steel fifteen-room building, south of Division Street, that included a cafeteria, auditorium, clinic, washrooms, and gas space heaters; it was named M. F. Nichols as a tribute to its first principal. The quality of the new facility led to a significant increase in registration. Only built for four hundred students, by 1952 it had six hundred enrolled, forcing extra classes to be held in the auditorium and balconies.[34] The *Daily Herald* reported, "In the first through third grades there were above 60 [students] to a class," but again this overcrowding did not meet the real need of Biloxi's Black population. Older students still "dropped out in the higher grades because they were not being given certain instruction desired." The junior class had only nine students, and the senior class, seven.[35] The steep decline in attendance as students aged meant that the average education for Black students in Mississippi was six years, nearly half the average of their white counterparts.[36] In 1952, plans began to be made for an adjacent six-room elementary school, built on reclaimed marshland. In 1954, the A. E. Perkins Elementary School (named for another early Black principal of Biloxi, Archie E. Perkins) opened with an enrollment of 240 students.[37] That same year, the US Supreme Court issued its ruling in *Brown v. Board of Education* to desegregate schools, but it had no effect on educating the Mississippi population. In fact, in 1955, the Mississippi legislature enacted an illegal statute (number 6220.5) making it a criminal offense for a white person to attend primary or secondary school with any Black person, another instance of the necessity of policing both races to maintain segregation.[38]

Throughout all these years in Harrison County, as in other parts of the state, Black schools were run on the basis designed decades before by Judge

Jeff Truly, Professor Michael O'Shea, and others, placing emphasis on training in the manual arts (not including office skills or other white-collar work). Materials and equipment were secondhand from the white schools and were of poor quality in both condition and content.[39] Higher academic courses and arts that were offered at the white Biloxi schools were absent from the curriculum. However, because all the schools used the same report card, Black students were given a "C/Satisfactory" in the classes that had not been offered to them. On average, Black students ran a year and half behind their white peers.[40] In addition, students at Nichols received no counseling in continuing education opportunities for graduates.[41]

The first efforts at desegregation focused on higher education institutions. In 1956, Clyde Kennard began applying and reapplying to Mississippi Southern College, until in 1959 he was framed for theft and incarcerated.[42] In 1958, a former Alcorn College professor, Clennon King (after being fired following student protests over his anti-NAACP editorials), attempted to register at the University of Mississippi to pursue a doctorate in history and to raise interest in a petition to desegregate Gulfport's elementary schools, which his children attended; later, King left the state in an ongoing cloud of controversy.[43] In 1961, James Meredith—who became friendly with the Masons through the local civil rights network—attempted to register at the University of Mississippi, with proceedings delaying his entrance for more than a year.[44]

In fall 1960, Gilbert Mason Jr. was starting school at A. E. Perkins Elementary, skipping kindergarten and moving directly into the first grade.[45] In Harrison County, the budget gap had closed to a four-to-one discrepancy between white and Black schools, and the Mason family was quick to notice the consequences.[46] When his mother received a report card with a C for an art class that didn't exist, Natalie Mason "went down there with her hair on fire."[47] For parents like the Masons, who prized education and had pursued their own educational advancement at the best-quality institutions, these conditions were simply unacceptable. Since the school district did not or could not budget any more money to provide all the children with art supplies, Gilbert Jr. was given time during the school day when he was "the only pupil taking art," while the others were told to do homework or "keep their head down."[48] Appeals to the school board for changes to the curriculum were exhausted with no result.

On October 4, 1960, Mississippi NAACP field secretary Medgar Evers appears to have been in Biloxi to meet with the local chapters and discuss, among other issues, whether Black voters would be invited to the coffee party for President Kennedy's mother, Rose Fitzgerald Kennedy. The event, planned for the upcoming weekend, was ultimately canceled, leaving the issue undecided, although the organizer of the event, Rose Flemming, said she "hadn't given any thought to the segregation or integration of any of the [Democratic women's] parties."[49] In an interview, Clemon Jimerson recalled that Medgar Evers had become "like a brother" to the Masons and that Gilbert Jr. remembered him as a man who was "easy to admire . . . affable and quiet but articulate about what needed to happen."[50]

Gilbert Mason Jr. said in an interview that these meetings at the Elks Clubs, association halls, and Baptist churches were a "very emotional" and "important" time to him and others in the community, and he was proud to see his father speak "really well, very clearly," though without "the soaring oratory" of preachers like Dr. Martin Luther King Jr. It was during these meetings that Clemon Jimerson remembered Dr. Mason reciting the US Constitution by heart. As the meetings started to wind down, one of the speakers would instruct those in the crowd to put their arms over each other's shoulders to sing an uplifting song, such as the one beginning to become emblematic of the civil rights movement, "We Shall Overcome." Gilbert Jr. remembered that, by the third verse, he would be in tears. Seeing his parents upset or his family friends, he recalled, "made me . . . angry in a way I didn't understand."[51] The others in the audience, feeling the same emotional stirrings and determination, were moved to act together.

Medgar Evers and Dr. Mason discussed the issue of school desegregation, and the following week, Evers wrote to several important leaders of the NAACP to seek legal advice and representation on the issue.[52] He had decided he had to live and lead as he preached, and on October 18, he wrote to Mason with encouragement and support in the doctor's determination to desegregate the schools as well as the beaches in Biloxi.[53] On August 17, 1962, Evers and nine other parents petitioned to register fifteen Black students from various neighborhoods across Jackson in grades two through twelve of the white schools there, intending to integrate all schools in the city.[54]

In September, the Supreme Court ruled to allow James Meredith to be enrolled at the University of Mississippi. On October 1, Meredith's first day on campus, a showdown between federal marshals and a mob of over two thousand white protestors resulted in three deaths and hundreds of injuries. Meredith spent a year being harassed at the university before graduating in August.[55] Meanwhile, the shockwaves were felt throughout the state. Larry Still of *Jet* magazine reported that bigots, "resorting to the old slave technique of 'channelized aggression,'" were attacking Black leaders across the state, including a bomb thrown into the home of Dr. J. L. Allen in Columbus and drive-by shootings in the neighborhood in Carthage where the Meredith family lived, and, in Jackson, Medgar Evers received the usual threatening calls.[56] In Biloxi, on the evening of October 1, a cross was burned in front of Nichols High. Molotov cocktails were thrown at Dr. Mason's clinic and a gas station on the same corner, owned by Dr. Dunn and Emmett Clark. The bottle that hit the exterior of Mason's clinic burned out with little damage, while the other homemade bomb broke the gas station window and burned several items, but neighbor A. Taylor arrived in time to put out the fire before more damage was done. It was, apparently, not enough of a reaction for some: Biloxi's KKK "grand dragon" Walter Bailey announced he was disbanding the Mississippi Klan as there had been no response to a call for a council of war following an unnamed "emergency." Nevertheless, Bailey continued to harass local civil rights workers and to be known as a leader of the KKK, which saw a resurgence in Mississippi in the years shortly to follow.[57]

In January 1963, the Mississippi Advisory Committee made its report to the Civil Rights Commission, with the conclusion that "in all important areas of citizenship, a Negro in Mississippi receives substantially less than his due," from birth "to the day he dies." The disparity between Black citizens' social and political treatment and that of white citizens was found to be "incompatible with Christian ideals about the dignity of man and with the principles of Anglo-Saxon criminal law."[58] The grassroots movements in Biloxi were beginning to find more recognition and assistance coming from the national level.

That same month, the Department of Justice under Attorney General Robert Kennedy filed four suits to desegregate the schools around federal military bases in Alabama, Louisiana, and Mississippi, including those in Biloxi and Gulfport. This tactic was just one in a five-pronged approach the federal government was taking in efforts to hurry along the decade of "all deliberate speed." These "impact areas" around military bases received additional federal funding to offset the burden on the district. As though *Brown v. Board of Education* had not already ruled school segregation was unconstitutional, the federal government argued that "children of federal employees or servicemen" must be schooled on "the same terms" as local children (and in a constitutional manner). To do otherwise would not only violate "contractual and statutory obligations" of having accepted additional federal funding for the schools; it could deprive military families "of the opportunities for education and advancement which they would enjoy in civilian life," where they could choose to live in less segregated areas. This would lead to either a crippling of "the efficiency and morale of the Negro serviceman" or "limit his assignability by geography," which, in turn, interfered with the unencumbered "exercise of war power." It was an appeal to the pride of a militarized and powerful country: maintaining its position in the global hierarchy superseded the hierarchy of nationalized white supremacy.[59]

Dr. Mason refused to be intimidated by the firebombing of his clinic, as he had been by every other show of force. In March 1963, he and twenty-two parents whose work (many associated with Keesler) allowed them relative freedom from financial consequences signed petitions to desegregate Biloxi schools across age groups.[60] Perhaps not so coincidentally, in April, US congressman Charles Diggs Jr. returned to Mississippi on a fact-finding mission. After staying with Aaron Henry in Clarksdale, Mississippi, where the home was attacked with Molotov cocktails during the night, Diggs continued south and stopped in Biloxi to hear from Black businessmen who "had received threats of economic reprisals from the WCC."[61] The school board took no apparent action regarding the petition. In May, parents sent a telegram, demanding an answer from the board, again with no response.[62]

On June 4, 1963, thirteen families represented by NAACP attorney Derrick Bell filed a motion for a preliminary injunction to desegregate the schools. Dr. Mason's son, Gilbert Mason Jr., was the lead plaintiff named in the suit. Most of the children's suits were brought by their fathers. The children named were Gary, Jerry, and Diane Black, children of World War II veteran Lewis Black and Adele Mingo Black; Daryl Boglin, son of Keesler instructor Harold Boglin and Myrtle Shirley Boglin; Linda, Jessica, and Henry Lee Davis, children of Rev. Thomas Davis; Glorhea Diane Edwards, stepdaughter of Samuel Edwards; Janice and John Elzy Jr., children of John Elzy Sr. and Blanche Avery Elzy; Rehofus Jr., John, Michael, and LaValeria Esters, children of World War II veteran and Keesler employee Rehofus Esters Sr. and Barbara Carter Esters; Barbara Harris, daughter of Rev. Oscar Harris; Sylvia and James McKinley Jr., children of Korean War veteran James McKinley Sr. and Maude Brown McKinley; Adrienne Martin, daughter of Jack Martin; Gretchen and Clifton Nunley Jr., children of World War II veteran and Keesler employee Clifton Nunley Sr. and Doretha Pitts-Hall Nunley; and Bernard and Ernest Rosado, sons of World War II veteran and Keesler employee Christopher Rosado and Ruth Elmer Rosado. One mother, Johnnie Mae Collins Brown, brought the suit for her daughters, Patsy and Rosa Mumford.[63]

The suit was countered by requests for dismissal from the school board. The familiar figure of Judge Sidney Mize deferred the hearing about the injunction, which—if granted—would prevent schools from reopening on a segregated basis while the case was tried, saying he would first consider the defendants' motion to dismiss.[64] Unsurprisingly, Mize ruled in favor of the defendants, dismissing the petition to desegregate Biloxi schools without trial (as he did Medgar Evers's petition in Jackson and a similar suit in Leake County), claiming "the parents had not used all their administrative remedies" with the school boards.[65]

Chapter Nine

TIDES TURNING

Resuming the Federal Trial and the Final Wade-In

Although, in May 1962, the Guices' suit had concluded in favor of the property owners, it was still necessary to resume the federal case of *United States v. Harrison County*. So much time had passed that the government had to amend its complaint to address the current members of the Board of Supervisors and county officials.[1] In July 1963, Judge Sidney Mize denied a motion for immediate judgment and instead ruled that "every person who owns property fronting the sand beach" must be made litigants.[2] This would involve over two thousand entities, including home owners, mortgagees and trustees, private individuals, banks and other lending institutions, religious institutions, and the federal government itself (regarding the property of the VA hospital) and would mean an enormous increase in time and money required to try the case. First, however, the thousands of litigants were sent waivers of process, so that the number might be cut down to only those who wished to proceed; this mailing alone cost the county over $4,000.[3] Judge Mize predicted that the case was certain to be lengthy and complicated as the title history of some beach properties stretched back to the eras of French or Spanish governance. The federal government's objections were dismissed.

It could take years to open the beaches to the public, and longer if the plaintiffs were forced to appeal to the higher courts as seemed likely. The civil rights activists of Harrison County were no longer willing to idly wait. They had to keep the issue alive in the court of public opinion and demonstrate that they would not allow the courts to drag the case out forever. As others before them, they believed justice too long delayed is justice denied. Dr. Mason began to form plans for another demonstration. He was open with the local authorities. Mayor Daniel Guice, unable to head off the protest, asked Mason to delay the next wade-in until after the Blessing of the Shrimp Fleet, when, the mayor said, all possible police protection would be available.[4] This time, there was no scramble to involve the Mississippi State

Sovereignty Commission (SSC). Although Mayor Guice had been a member of the White Citizens' Council (WCC) only a few years before, he and local law enforcement quietly rebuffed the repeated visits of SSC agents, saying they were "glad to know" the services were available and they would "call when necessary"—a necessity that never seemed to arise.[5] The SSC received similarly vague responses from the new Biloxi chief of police, Louis Rossotti, Sheriff Luther Patton, Gulfport mayor Reginald "Billy" Meadows, and others. Often, SSC agents would arrive and find the officials they were seeking were "not in."

On June 10, 1963, Medgar Evers spent the night with the Masons, as he often had when events brought them to work together. In the morning, Evers got up and shaved before his drive back to Jackson, promising to return for the wade-in the next weekend. That evening at 8 pm, President Kennedy gave his civil rights address on national television, announcing that he has arranged for a congressional vote on a civil rights bill that would desegregate all public facilities. He said, in part:

> The rights of every man are diminished when the rights of one man are threatened. . . . Legislation, I repeat, cannot solve this problem alone. It must be solved in the homes of every American. . . . In this respect I want to pay tribute to those citizens North and South who've been working in their communities to make life better for all . . . and I salute them for their honor and their courage.[6]

Evers had always declined a protective detail, despite numerous threats on his life. Just after midnight on June 12, he was shot on his doorstep, returning home from a civil rights meeting, with T-shirts reading "Jim Crow Must Go" in his arms. He was shot with a scoped rifle, just as President Kennedy would be, five months later. The bullet passed through his body and a window into his house. Evers's wife, Myrlie, and young children found him bleeding on the porch. He was taken to the nearest hospital, which, being whites-only, at first refused to treat him. Evers died less than an hour later.[7] His killer, Byron De La Beckwith, a white supremacist who had once wished to work for the SSC, had systematically stalked Evers in the days before his murder. The WCC raised funds for Beckwith's legal defense, listing his memberships with various churches and organizations—though omitting his membership in its own. De La Beckwith went free until he was retried for his crime thirty years later, at which time he was convicted and sentenced to life in prison.[8]

In St. Louis, Missouri, Rev. Richard Ellerbrake was driving home from Deaconess Hospital before dawn as the news came over the radio that Medgar

Evers had been shot. Arriving home, Ellerbrake called the chairperson of the Mississippi Civil Rights Advisory Committee, Jane Schutt of Jackson, to break the news. Fearing that Evers's assassination was part of or would touch off a chain of violence, the committee planned to contact its every member, so they could get to a safe location, such as the gates of Keesler.[9] In Biloxi, Dr. Mason was out on his medical rounds. His son, Gilbert Jr., was with his mother when they saw the news on the local station, WLOX. Arthur Bousqueto, their neighbor and a member of the Black Angry Men protective watch, "climbed out onto his roof and stayed there all night," Dr. Mason remembered. His wife and son were tensely waiting for Dr. Mason's return for the evening when the power to their apartment went out. Stepping outside, they realized it was only their residence that was affected. Natalie Mason noticed a bag hanging on her front gate. Taking precautions, she called the police, who discovered the ominous corpse of a dead cat inside.[10]

When Mason arrived home, he had already heard the terrible news. The family spent a somber evening at home, "very quiet," Gilbert Jr. remembered, except for the calls that came through the night: those unidentified, sometimes silent, sometimes threatening calls that regularly harassed activists throughout the movement. In her high-pitched voice, Natalie Mason informed callers that she kept a military rifle (given to the family by one of its veteran guards) ready for anyone who came to harm her family. Dr. Mason said the Black Angry Men (and Women) protective detail, which had wound down over the years, came back "in full force."[11]

It was likely with frustration and dismay, but less surprise, that Dr. Mason and his peers heard that the federal suit to desegregate schools around military bases was unsuccessful.[12] The defendants' rebuttal that the federal government did not have the proper jurisdiction nor "the requisite interest in the subject matter" to qualify as a plaintiff in the case was accepted by Judge Mize, who dismissed the suit on June 17, 1963.[13] On June 19, Mason and Dr. Dunn were among those who served as pallbearers at Evers's funeral. Dr. Martin Luther King Jr. walked in the procession behind them.[14] Gilbert Jr. was also in attendance, feeling self-conscious about the scruffy Keds he had to wear with his suit as his parents had forgotten to pack his dress shoes.[15]

The final Biloxi wade-in was postponed a week and half, as the community grieved. President John F. Kennedy had asked for a stop to public demonstrations as the civil rights bill was progressing through Congress, urging votes instead of demonstrations but ignoring the fact that many Black citizens needed a demonstration just to reach the voter registration office. The *Jackson Advocate* urged that demonstrations be "prayerfully suspended in favor of silent and prayerful mourning for Medgar W. Evers," but Black Biloxians were just some of those who were prepared to prayerfully mourn in a different way.[16] As June 23, the Sunday then chosen for the demonstration, approached, Clara Bradley Ramsey and other women in the community sewed black flags to be planted in a double row on the beach, creating a path of mourning and hope, to be walked in remembrance of Medgar Evers, the friend and advocate who would no longer walk with them.[17] On June 23, seventy-one protestors (mostly males but with sixteen women) gathered on Division Street and walked or drove down the hot asphalt to the beach.[18]

It was a perfect 82 degrees and sunny. The group was integrated, having been joined by four white members of the Back Bay United Mission Church: Rev. John M. Aregood, Rev. Roger G. Gallagher, George Wright, a student interning for the summer, and an unidentified seventeen-year-old male. The other church staff was to remain available for bail purposes or to pick up the pieces of whatever followed (Reverend Ellerbrake had been called to serve in St. Louis, Illinois). That very morning, three Black citizens (including E. L. Jackson and perhaps Rosa Martin) attended a service at St. Paul's, a white church. None of the white congregants walked out, but, afterward, a white woman—who had once invited the pastor to her home to meet her daughter in hopes they would make a couple—stopped and said, "Well, Reverend Aregood, I'll see you around but not around here." Aregood later described himself as reluctant to attend the "beach party," fearing a "great tragedy," and said Reverend Gallagher—a recent transplant to the South—was an "impetuous man" who "jumped in with both feet" without fully understanding the dangers.[19] James Black, vice president of the Biloxi NAACP youth branch, again joined the demonstrators who had not been frightened away by the previous episodes of violence and economic manipulations. Myrtle Davis was one of the sixteen women in the crowd, now a devoted member of the Biloxi NAACP.[20]

As the group approached the waterfront properties, Dr. Eldon L. Bolton, who was chief of staff at the newly constructed Howard Memorial Hospital, warned them away from the area in front of his yard.[21] Dr. Mason had been advised by the Department of Justice not to go onto clearly marked private property, so the demonstrators moved down the beach.[22] As they had done before, some began to play ball, while others waded into the water or simply enjoyed the weather, under the gaze of over two thousand white people, law enforcement armed with riot gear, and the press. The FBI, at the request of the department, had agents present, watching from the lighthouse with cameras and binoculars. According to the *Daily Herald*, Mayor Guice and two city commissioners were "at city hall and on the beach, directing the police action."[23]

The police had cordoned off the area to prevent assault. One white man ran forward with a gun but was apprehended and arrested (this may have been John H. Giannoutses, reportedly arrested by Detective Elvin P. Vincent for "carrying a gun concealed in a magazine").[24] Other white men slashed the tires on Dr. Mason's Buick, scratched the n-word on the side, tried to set the seats on fire, and, when unsuccessful, turned it and two other cars over on their hoods, including one belonging to Floyd Braxton.[25] Real estate agent William Allen, representing the Desporte Agency, and Eurilda Seal Lopez, owner of a home at 1132 West Beach Blvd., announced on a bullhorn that the demonstrators were trespassing. Allen and a second property owner, Mrs. James Moore Parker (who owned 1128 West Beach Blvd.), signed a sworn statement to that effect, and the police arrested all seventy-one demonstrators.

The Black demonstrators formed a calm procession, some smiling, some carrying the black flags of mourning, escorted by helmeted policemen and led by Dr. Mason, unusually casual in his button-up, floral shirt. Previously, law enforcement had allegedly arranged for school buses to transport the demonstrators to jail, but the change of date had not been accounted for.[26] Instead, the demonstrators were directed into the back of a hired van with no ventilation or light for their trip to the police station. As the van moved through the crowd, the mob rocked the vehicle, knocking some of the people inside to the floor. Reverend Aregood reported that one man locked in the van beside him struck the walls, saying, "I hate whites!"[27] But at the station, the protestors came out of the van singing.[28]

Mason was soon bailed out and working on bail for others. The court was allegedly requiring property bonds instead of cash. Dr. Joel Overton Tate, a Black dentist in Gulfport, Robert Nance, bishop of the Church of God, and Dr. George Powers, a white dentist and member of the Civil Rights Advisory Commission, offered to put up their properties as security, but the paperwork could not be processed until the following business day.[29] About thirty of the protestors were minors, so after being interrogated, they were released to their parents.[30] There was not enough cell space at the Biloxi jail for all those arrested, so the remaining demonstrators were loaded back into the van for a further thirty-minute drive to the non-air-conditioned county jail in Gulfport, where they were kept without food: women in one cell, men in the other.[31] The three arrested white participants (the seventeen-year-old minor likely having been released) were kept in the cafeteria area, as the police evidently did not want to house them with either the Black jail inmates nor the white inmates already there, who jeered through the bars that they wanted to show the white demonstrators "what life is really like in jail," according to Reverend Aregood.[32]

The jailed demonstrators sang through the dark, until the morning.[33] This time, the police took care to avoid a repeat of the violence from three years earlier. They guarded Back-of-Town and made the crowds of whites who gathered throughout the city disperse. According to the *Daily Herald*, they arrested "a dozen young men" for carrying weapons in their cars, including "revolvers, chains, crow bars, wire cutters, shotguns and cue sticks"; they had also searched the cars belonging to the demonstrators and found "one pistol, brass knuckles, chains and sticks."[34] The next day, at the wrecker service lot where Dr. Mason's car had been towed, someone tried to make good on the attempt to incinerate his car. The seats were lit on fire from what the responding firemen called a "cause unknown" for the second time, and someone had also broken into the trunk. As Mason had previously removed his equipment, he suffered no further loss.[35]

Reverend Aregood was dismayed that no other clergy from the area arrived to offer support to him and Reverend Gallagher. Instead, a local dog catcher and a plumbing supply driver, who were members of the mission, tried to bail out the pastors. But because they were not property owners, they were not able to offer enough collateral for a bond. The protestors were not released until noon, after which Reverend Aregood, who had spent the night thinking over the matter, proposed to his future wife, Joy Hartman.[36]

As part of the milieu attempting to get a handle on race relations in the wake of these activities, Gulfport's mayor, Reginald "Billy" Meadows, met with leaders of the Mt. Olive Baptist Church, a Black church, on June 24, 1963. Afterward, Meadows appointed a biracial (though majority white) Community Relations Committee to "report to the city administration on any [inequitable] situation . . . which may adversely affect its citizens." He suggested, however, that no public report be made of the "meetings, recommendations, or other actions."[37] Meadows and Dr. Dunn, who had been named to the committee, immediately received threatening phone calls. On the night of June 24, a small explosive was thrown onto Dunn's lawn. On June 26, what the *Daily Herald* called an "aerial flashbomb" was thrown through the window of his medical office nearby. The FBI assisted in the investigation, but the incident passed as another unsolved crime.[38]

John Sekul, the prosecuting attorney during Mason's first trespassing trial, sat on the bench now. Judge Sekul conducted the new trial over the alleged trespass. On the day the Biloxi court convened, the Black half of the gallery was full, with another fifty people left standing. Sekul denied a request to let the standing members sit in the unoccupied seats on the white side, saying his decision was due to "the policy of the court and in the interest of peace."[39] The eight highest-profile protestors were sentenced to the maximum penalty of a hundred-dollar fine and thirty days in jail. Besides Mason and the two white pastors, Aregood and Gallagher, this included Marshall White, Harry Cannon, Cornelius Kemp, and brothers Alvin and Clarence Schneckenburg.[40] Although it is not clear why the latter five were deemed to be leaders of the demonstration, Gilbert Mason Jr. and Clemon Jimerson later remembered the men as being mature, "able to reason in a challenging situation" in Mason's words, and not quick—but well able—to fight.[41] The other protestors were given a suspended fine of fifty dollars and no jail time. Judge Sekul said he believed the five men had been "led" into the demonstration.[42] Twenty-nine of the demonstrators appealed their sentences, and a new court date was set for November.

Judge Luther Maples, who was set to try the case of the juvenile demonstrators for the youth court, told the press that the "parents of children who were among the group . . . may be subject to charges of contributing to the delinquency or neglect of minors." The National Council of Juvenile Court Judges, Maples said, "deplored the use of children in demonstrations of a public nature where they might be in danger of being injured." Dr. Mason Sr.'s testimony that the children at the beach had been "panicked" when the arrest order was announced was an indication, according to Maples, that the situation had been inappropriate for minors to be involved in.[43] It is unclear what the result of the youth court trials was, as greater care for the privacy of minors was observed.

Besides the committee appointed by Gulfport mayor Meadows, the greatest supportive response from the white community regarding the year's civil rights struggle was from a group of Methodist ministers. In mid-October 1963, Rev. Maxie Dunnam of Gulfport was one of four pastors who, based on their moral conviction and Methodist doctrine, authored the "Born of Conviction" statement, which denounced racial discrimination and reprisals against ministers who spoke against injustice and said desegregated public schools should be kept open.[44] A total of twenty-eight southern Mississippi Methodist pastors signed the statement, including Reverends Inman Moore Jr. of Leggett Memorial in Biloxi, Jim Waits of Epworth United Methodist in Biloxi, Keith Tonkel of Guinn Memorial in Gulfport, John Ed Thomas of

First Methodist in Gulfport, and Harold Ryker of Beauvoir United Methodist in Biloxi.[45]

Not only did Reverend Gallagher sign the Born of Conviction statement, but on Halloween night in 1963, he helped to host the annual ministerial banquet of the Mississippi State Conference of the NAACP at the Back Bay Mission. Before that evening, word of the meeting got out, and the mission began receiving threatening phone calls. On Halloween, police were stationed outside the integrated gathering but could not, or did not, stop a mob of over two hundred neighbors and ex-members of the church who said they felt they had been "'pushed out' by the Negroes" from attacking the mission before the banquet began, according to an unnamed ex-member quoted in the *Daily Herald*. The white crowd began throwing vegetables and fruits from neighborhood gardens, until a young man began selling chunks of concrete from a road construction project on Caillavet Street for fifty cents each. At least one person was injured as the attendees were evacuated out the back, while the building's plate glass windows were smashed in the front—some said with the approbation of the police. However, in response to the attack on the mission, Mayor Guice said, "Certainly we regret this incident, but . . . the leadership of the NAACP could have expected nothing but trouble by having this integrated function in a white residential area and more especially on Halloween night." Reverend Aregood recalled Guice was the only elected official to "totally shut [him] out."[46]

The Gulf Coast culture was changing, though the changes were resisted and criticized every step of the way. Over the next three months, as the Back Bay Mission's windows were replaced, they were broken four more times, and the mission was robbed, though no one was apprehended for the crimes. Throughout the summer, volunteers at the mission found their cars keyed or turned over. Crosses were burned in the yard. Some of the white people resistant to change showed their displeasure in other ways, such as refusing to speak to community members they'd known for years and an incident in which a crossing guard spit on Reverend Aregood's shoe as he walked by. Attendance at St. Paul dropped from over a hundred to thirty-five members and stayed that way "for the rest of the time till it closed all together," according to Aregood.[47]

Judge Luther Maples was assigned to the appeal of the trespassing convictions and began the hearing on November 21 in Gulfport. The two prospective jurors who were Black were excused by the prosecutors. Maples denied civil rights defense attorney Richard Jess Brown's request to annul the jury and call a new one, with the hope of better peer representation for the defendants. "What we are trying here is a simple case of trespass," claimed Maples (as though such sentencing was immune to racial prejudice). "It's not an integration [issue]."[48]

By the time of the trespassing appeal, the US civil rights bill in the House of Representatives had passed from the Judiciary to the Rules Committee. As the Biloxi court recessed for lunch, some defendants went across the street and sat in two booths and at the counter of the white section of the Greyhound bus station restaurant. They were served coffee in the presence of the police. Afterward the owner closed the white section and what the *Daily Herald* called the "smaller restaurant which normally caters to Negroes" for the duration of the trial.[49] The next day, the final day of the appeal, was November 22; shortly after noon, President John Kennedy was shot and killed. Returning from lunch, the Black defendants reentered the courtroom and stood for a minute in silent prayer.[50] The appeal had reduced, but not overturned, their sentences. The defendants appealed again, unsuccessfully, to the 5th Circuit Court of Appeals in New Orleans and, finally, to the Supreme Court, which ruled in their favor with no dissent on December 12, 1966.[51]

Gilbert Mason Jr. was in his fifth-grade class at A. E. Perkins Elementary School when a woman teacher came into the classroom and called all the girls to the auditorium, while Percy Allen came to be with the boys. "I thought that maybe there's something we had done as boys that was untoward, that they wanted to talk to the girls about it," he reflected later. Instead, the teachers broke the news of the presidential assassination. Parents were called to pick up their children for an early dismissal, and the community, said Mason, "spent the weekend praying about it." The children remained home on Monday, watching the funeral service on television.[52]

Chapter Ten

HIGH TIDE, LOW TIDE

Progress, Pushback, and Desegregation

The fight for school desegregation was the next issue to rotate back into the limelight. After Judge Sidney Mize's initial dismissal in July 1963, the court of appeals refused a plea for an injunction that would prevent the schools from reopening on a segregated basis while the case was ongoing, meaning the 1963 Mississippi school year went on as it had for a century.[1] However, all three cases were remanded by the high court around February 20, 1964, for "prompt [re]consideration," stating the parents concerned had indeed done all they could by their administrative appeals to the school boards. Whereas the Biloxi, Jackson, and Leake County petitions had first come before the court separately, they were now combined into one case.

While Judge Mize reluctantly set a trial date, newspapers reported no obvious pushback from white parents in Biloxi—though the school board said it would "continue to resist and oppose" orders for desegregation.[2] In Jackson, however, white fathers Alec Primos and James Goodman submitted a petition to the courts, claiming to represent the students "who desire not to be forcibly compelled to associate with ... Negroes" and citing the "wide divergences" between the abilities of Black and white students, including "cranial capacity and brain size." They also alleged that segregation was a natural state that "arises primarily from a ... biological selection mechanism."[3] The White Citizens' Council (WCC) issued a statement in support of leaders like Jackson's mayor Allen Thompson, who blustered that he would not "permit the evils of race mixing to wreck our public schools" by recreating the "blackboard jungles" of the North. During a Jackson hearing, reflecting the old argument of the differences between desegregation and integration, NAACP attorney Derek Bell and defense attorney George Leonard clashed over the latter's term "mix." Judge Mize "ruled against usage of the word." The editor of the *Delta Democrat-Times*, Hodding Carter II, called Mayor Thompson's statements of defiance against desegregation "legislature's usual ... buffoonery."[4]

Despite Attorney General Robert Kennedy's unsuccessful suit, the presence of Keesler Air Force Base was instrumental in advancing the argument for desegregation.[5] White and Black Keesler airmen had been taking segregated extension courses offered by the University of Southern Mississippi, University of Mississippi, and Alcorn College (a historically Black university), held in classrooms in the Biloxi schools.[6] In February 1964, Keesler requested the classes be moved onto the base, where they would be integrated. The universities temporarily suspended the courses while they decided what to do. What happened on base could be more or less ignored by segregationists, but leaders at the two white universities feared that Black airmen who were discharged would be allowed to complete courses they had enrolled in, even if the courses were only available at the all-white campuses. On the other hand, county officials and business owners feared the entire base would transfer away from Biloxi if the request was denied, taking millions in annual payroll with it. Airmen, who depended on the courses to facilitate their promotions, were anxious about the pause, and State Sovereignty Commission (SSC) members said they thought it would not be long until there was an official protest. Although resolution of this dispute does not appear to have been publicized, given the trajectory of desegregation it seems likely the airmen's request was eventually granted.

In late February, as reported in the *Daily Herald*, Biloxi attorney Victor Pringle asked that his report to the school board on the desegregation suits be conducted behind closed doors as "there were some things he wanted to say that he didn't want in the paper." It seems likely that the board's acceptance of the plan to start summer school at Nichols High and Biloxi High was one of several last-ditch efforts to show that the schools were offering quality, equitable education through the segregated system (or perhaps to close the gap that neglect had caused between Black and white students in the case desegregation did occur).[7] In early March 1964—stating that previous legal decisions had made it "compulsory that I proceed"—Judge Mize ordered a temporary injunction: while the case was still being heard, schools in Biloxi, Jackson, and Leake County could not reopen on a segregated basis. They must submit plans for integration of at least one grade per year by July 15, 1964.[8] The court of appeals refused to hear any arguments against this ruling.[9]

Yet, as Judge Mize continued his "reconsideration," the press reported little of the merits of the NAACP's argument and far more of the defendants'. The attorneys for the defense continued to claim "disparities" between white children and the "ethnic group *allegedly* represented by [the] plaintiffs" were the "rational basis for separation" into "specially adapted schools" that created "equal opportunity for the development *of the differing capacities*" (emphasis mine).¹⁰ This latter phrasing reveals much about the covert interpretation that legislation and the white majority had acted on ever since the ruling of *Plessy v. Ferguson* in 1896.

One white community leader who opposed this language was the editor of the *Delta Democrat-Times*, Hodding Carter II, who wrote that the defense's argument was an "attempt to reverse history," not based on the usual "pretense that [the] schools are not segregated by race" but an effort to force the repeal of the supreme court's ruling in *Brown v. Board of Education*. The defense argued that *Brown v. Board of Education* had been decided using the "insufficient evidence" of Dr. Kenneth B. Clark's study of sixteen Black children in Clarendon County, South Carolina, which showed that segregation—or perhaps, more conclusively, racial hierarchy—was psychologically harmful to them. The defense claimed that the study (conducted with Clark's wife, Mamie Clark) was refuted by the Clarks' similar study of 250 Black students from segregated schools in Arkansas and nonsegregated schools in Massachusetts, which showed that while a majority of the children had preference for white dolls over Black, it was the children from nonsegregated northern schools who showed significantly more dislike of the Black dolls.¹¹ The defense also called educators, administrators, and psychologists to give testimony concerning the "aptitudes of white or Negro children," the difference which, they insisted, increased "at a relatively constant rate'" as the children grew, increasing by a one year "lag" in the primary grades "to three years plus by the end of the secondary grades."¹²

According to newspaper reports, the defense also claimed desegregation of schools in other states had led to a lowering of school standards, difficulty in keeping "a good faculty," and a decrease in matriculation to college (although the defense simultaneously asserted Black teachers were "better prepared" than their white counterparts; it is unclear if this latter argument only spoke to the qualifications of teaching Black students).¹³ The defense's lawyers even called upon James Gooden, the retired Black educator and director of Jackson's Black schools, to testify, and he agreed separate schools were best for both races "unless the attitude of white persons toward Negroes could be changed."¹⁴ *Delta Democrat-Times* editor Carter found these arguments so outrageous that he theorized "since no defense would prove to be successful" in the fight against desegregation, it was "being staged only for Mississippi's benefit," as a show of token resistance.¹⁵

In perhaps a more effective strategy of resistance, in early June the Mississippi legislature, with the support of Governor Paul Johnson, created a special committee to develop a parallel, supposed "freedom of choice" plan, with the intention of opening private schools as a means of circumventing what it called the "threat" of desegregation.[16] In dizzying double-speak, Governor Johnson emphasized that public schools would not be abolished, yet warned that he had "the power to close, by a stroke of the pen, all the public schools, colleges and universities of the state," and hoped only that others would "join" with him "to enact legislation that will make such action unnecessary." The committee began discussions about whether to grant tuition supplements to children who transferred to private school and whether these funds would extend to church-run schools or only secular; its meetings cost taxpayers $30,000 in salaries and $10,00 in expenses per week.[17]

It was a year of so much change that it is difficult to untangle the threads and present them in a linear fashion. Of course, in reality there was no detangling; each vibration in the web was felt throughout, affecting and being affected by the whole. On June 15, 1964, civil rights volunteers began to arrive in Mississippi from around the US to organize voter drives for the Black community in what would be called Freedom Summer. Less than a week later, newspaper columns covering the issue of local school desegregation wrapped ominously around a headline in the *Hattiesburg American* that was soon to dominate national news: "Mystery Surrounds Disappearance of Three Civil Rights Missionaries." The disappearance of civil rights workers James Chaney, Michael Schwerner, and Andrew Goodman in Neshoba County, Mississippi—which Senator James Eastland initially called a "publicity stunt"—was soon to rock the economy and reputation of the Magnolia State, especially in tourism-driven areas like Harrison County's "American Rivera."[18]

On July 2, the Civil Rights Act of 1964 was signed into law, desegregating public accommodations. Dr. Mason joined Black Biloxians, including members of the Youth NAACP branch and Freedom School (opened July 8), in forming the Food and Restaurant Committee, Entertainment Committee, and Public Accommodations Committee to test local compliance with the federal requirements. Fact-finding delegations came from out of state, accompanied by Charles Evers of Jackson, to register at the Edgewater Gulf Hotel, Sun 'n' Sand restaurant, and Hotel Markham in Biloxi and Gulfport; registrations were completed without incident, though under the surveillance of the SSC and the new Harrison County sheriff, Edward E. McDonnell.[19] Owners generally complied gracefully although white patrons were sometimes a source of harassment as when Mason's new yellow Mustang was keyed outside the Sun 'n Sand restaurant or food was thrown at Black moviegoers during the Saenger Theatre's showing of the Rat Pack musical movie, *Robin and the Seven Hoods*.[20]

A Freedom School had opened in Biloxi, with teachers Steve Blum and Gren Whitman and students including Carolyn Smith, Carolyn Weathersby, Janice Thomas, Janice Huggar, Lodie Robinson, Mary Brown, Linda Davis, Cheryl Davis, Linda Whitsun, Reuben Brown, and Elaine Davis. When students Lester Smith, Tommy Jackson, Candy Robinson, Donna McNair, and Inez Rozetta tested the Edgewater Plaza's compliance, they were served the sodas and sandwiches they ordered but were told some would "lose their jobs."[21]

Another small group from the Council of Federated Organizations (COFO) piloted its "White Community Project" in Biloxi during Freedom Summer. A small group of workers, mostly from the South, moved into the Hotel Riviera, at the corner of Lemuse and Beach Boulevard, with the goal of convincing the poor white fishermen on Point Cadet that they had more in common and more to gain politically and economically from allying themselves with their Black peers than with wealthier whites and the elected leadership. The COFO volunteers (and the Riviera hotel-keeper) were harassed by KKK leader Walter Bailey, blocked from employment and residential opportunities, arrested for minor infractions, and endured other forms of harassment by law enforcement and civilians. One Biloxian working with the group, Robert Williams, was shot at by a car full of local youths. Williams also reported being reprimanded and threatened by Mayor Daniel Guice for being a "local white getting mixed up . . . with those civil rights people, causing trouble." Twelve-year-old Lodie Robinson of the Freedom School, who worked with the White Community Project to canvas neighborhoods in integrated pairs, reported a bomb thrown at a car of Black youths including herself, Melinda White, Jerry Black, Pat Money, Mary Money, Herbert Robinson, Earnest Rogers, and the driver, William Griffin. The project was fairly short-lived and unsuccessful due to infighting, hesitancy on the part of the workers, and reported fear in the white community that the poor whites would lose what little they had to the promotion of Blacks.[22]

On July 7, 1964, Judge Mize reluctantly ruled that the school injunction was permanent. Again he proclaimed that previous rulings required him to do so "although it is contrary to the facts" that begged for a "complete reconsideration of *Brown v. Board of Education*."[23] "The evidence as to racial differences," he claimed, with obtuseness that seems shocking in even a dyed-in-the-wool racist of his education, access, and position, "is overwhelming, undisputed and unchallenged," and he said there had been no "effort to show that the separate schools were unequal."[24] (It seems impossible that Judge Mize meant those statements to apply to all of legislative and cultural history. Perhaps he only meant the plaintiffs had found it beneath them and beside the point to even bother to address those issues during the course of the case.) The court of appeals, however, responded by ruling that ongoing arguments over school desegregation "tax the patience of the court," particularly any argument that involved a judge who "abused his discretion" by allowing evidence attempting "to show that the Supreme Court's decision in *Brown* was wrong," guided "by the popular myth that *Brown* was decided for sociological reasons untested in a trial."[25]

The Jackson and Biloxi school districts filed their (identical) plans a day early.[26] NAACP attorney Bell and local parents eyed the "vague" phrasing in the plans, such as "where adequate facilities are not available" and "for justifiable administrative reasons," with all-too-familiar skepticism and petitioned to expand the grade-a-year plan to something more efficacious—not surprisingly, without success for the 1964–65 school year.[27] Meanwhile, in addition to attempting to pass tuition grants that would enable white children to transfer to private schools, the Mississippi Senate Education Committee scrambled to write measures that would soften the blow to the status quo, such as standardized tests to determine the grade of transferring students or division of the sexes, under the long-standing premise that, above all, white females must be segregated for their protection. "The less said about the measure, the better," said Representative J. P. Love of Holmes County, chairman of the committee, as the bill passed with "no explanation" (though the plans never came to fruition).[28]

Yet, in his article "Changes in Mississippi," Hodding Carter II was able to write hopefully that "the attitude in Mississippi about . . . desegregation is slowly but perceptibly beginning to alter for the better . . . despite the desperate acts of brutal and unthinking men." Carter pointed to the Jackson Chamber of Commerce's "forthright stand" of compliance with the ruling, despite "coercion and legislative censure."[29] Two white women's organizations began speaking out against the segregationist legislation being designed to divert funding into private schools. Both the League of Women Voters and the newly formed Mississippians for Public Education officially opposed desegregation but nonetheless asserted that the time for debating the issue had passed. Now they said, according to the *Delta Democrat-Times*, that the focus must be to ensure "a peaceful atmosphere" for the transition and that children were not "penalized or disrupted" by school closures or budget cuts.[30] Their formation "smacks of the daring," wrote Carter in "Changes in Mississippi." "Can anyone conceive of a similar group making a public appeal two years ago?"

These women recognized that taxpayers would be funding the estimated $185 per student in tuition grants awarded to those transferring to private schools, while the drop in attendance at public schools would decrease the state budget, leaving students who did not transfer "without proper facilities or accreditation" (without expressing any sense of empathy or irony that Black students had suffered under these circumstances for decades).[31] Given that white women were often defined as being in most need of protection from desegregation, as well as the guardians of their children's education, these groups' position on this issue seems especially important—and especially ironic when the WCC accused the women of "evasion and doubletalk," whose real goal was to "support the integration" of the races. Anyone who would "place a price tag on the future of our children," stated the WCC, "should be deplored."[32]

But regardless of some continuing attempts at suppression, Carter wrote that "Decent people . . . are tired of abdicating leadership to the demagogues and the haters." Although Carter was perhaps skimming over economic motivations at play, he nevertheless pointed to the subjugation and terrorizing of every demographic group that had been part of maintaining white supremacy, when he wrote, "the shackles of fear which have for so long bound white as well as Negro can be removed once and for all" if "every Mississippian who has held his council and bided his time . . . who has let the forces of conformity go unchecked through a sense of futility, should make himself heard now."[33]

One who made himself heard was a self-proclaimed moderate, Clay Thompson Jr., who wrote to the *Delta Democrat-Times* that "whites who are apprehensive" about desegregation "as it may affect their own welfare have no reason to be so, any more than they fear the superiority of their white contemporaries." Furthermore, Thompson dismissed the fear that desegregation would lead to a change in curriculums to pander to "the aptitude of the slower students," as bigots persisted in calling Black students. If this had ever been true, Thompson pointed out "there wouldn't have been as much 'flunking'" of students throughout the ages. Although segregationist propaganda generally tied the fight for racial equity to the perceived threat of communism, Thompson countered that the ability of the races to compete on equal footing was "directly opposed to communism." He also tuned in to the common argument that desegregation did not necessitate "fraternizing"; for those parents who feared otherwise, he wrote, "their fears do not speak . . . of their confidence in their own training."[34]

On August 4, the bodies of the three "Civil Rights Missionaries" were found in Neshoba County, buried to conceal their murders and, in the case of the Black youth, James Chaney, torture; the bodies of eight other Black boys and men had been found during the search, five of whom were never identified.[35] It was a confusing, distressing time, particularly for the young Black people who were fighting for their future, desegregating spaces, and increasingly engaging in integrated social relationships. They found that one white person might be willing to risk their life, while another was willing to murder. A Biloxi Freedom School student, Carolyn Weathersby, wrote poignantly about the subject in the school's newspaper, the *Biloxi Free Herald*, asking whether the two white victims, Andrew Goodman and Michael Schwerner, were killed because they had "love and cleanliness in their hearts.... I have [never] seen them in my life," she went on, "but I know them well enough to love them."[36] The culture was changing, but it could not change fast, dramatically, or thoroughly enough.

Judge Mize had little choice but to receive the message and rule in favor of integration.[37] He accepted the Biloxi, Jackson, and Leake County's desegregation plans and denied the NAACP and parents' request to enact something more dramatic and far-reaching than just "token integration."[38] In the fall of 1964, Biloxi became the first city in Mississippi to desegregate under the "freedom of choice" policy, beginning with first grade classes.[39] It was the judge's professed opinion that to start with anything more than one grade would cause "confusion and a slowing down" of the children's education. Dr. Kirby Walker, superintendent of the Jackson schools, had testified that, beyond the argument that younger children were "nearer together [in ability] than in any subsequent year," children at this age were also "more likely to adjust to change than older ones," adding that they were "more docile and amenable to teacher control," enabling teachers "to devote more time to instruction and less to . . . 'blending' student personalities." Furthermore, Walker suggested that, rather than "subterfuge or foot dragging," the plan would give teachers time to "redesign their program to fit 'such a mixture'" of students in later years.[40] Due to the one-grade-a-year arrangement, many of the children named as plaintiffs in the suit (including Gilbert Mason Jr.) were not eligible to take part in these historic first days of desegregation.

As registration drew nearer, a few private schools, such as the Bancroft Day School and Clarksdale School, opened in Jackson. Other private school corporations prepared to open more only, they said, if "trouble erupts."[41] Tuition grants had not been passed, as even adversaries of desegregation said that "token integration" was not likely to "create enough disturbance to warrant" lawmakers' agreeing to such controversial measures.[42] Under the Catholic bishop of Mississippi, Richard Gerow, all Catholic schools in the state also began to "admit pupils regardless of race" into the first grade, a position (shared by some other denominations) that led to dozens of churches being bombed and burned that year.[43] In Biloxi, journalist Kay Pittman reported "the feeling that everyone was sitting on a mental powder keg, ready to explode."[44] Over the years, however, the violence and racial murders had proved troubling to the consciousness of some and created what *Jet* magazine called a "strong economic jolt" that frightened others. The past month had seen a dramatic drop in tourism, following the murder of the three civil rights workers in Neshoba County, with "hotel and motel occupancy in the Gulfport-Biloxi" area at "only 8 per cent of capacity." The Sugar Bowl college football teams that usually trained in Biloxi had decided to relocate for fear of the safety of their Black players.[45] One reporter paid homage to the financial undercurrents, writing that the city wanted a transition in the schools "so quiet the tourists won't know anything unusual is afoot."[46]

Black parents hardly had time to celebrate the milestone.[47] The few families whose children would transfer had to prepare supplies and arrange carpools for transportation. Parents counseled their children on how to react to any trouble, fearing the bullying and exclusions they would encounter and teaching them how to report incidents.[48] The NAACP aided both parents and children during their meetings, but Gilbert Jr. said, "There was no role-playing or . . . defense training"; overall, the attitude was "the children will work it out."[49]

On Friday, August 14, 1964, Lopez Elementary on Howard Avenue in Biloxi became the first school below college level to open desegregated registration in the state.[50] While reporters expressed support of measures in place, forbidding journalists or cameras ("especially those from out of state"), they cautioned about the possibility of setting "a precedent which could jeopardize freedom of the press" as they waited to hear from the central office, notifying them of developments.[51] Police directed traffic while FBI agents watched from their cars. Husky athletic coaches and other male teachers were posted at the main entrances of most schools. Only parents or guardians could enter the school with the children. The first to arrive were what one report called two "neatly dressed" Black boys and a girl, "accompanied into the red brick building . . . by a half-dozen Negro adults." One Black mother with a daughter "in pigtails" told reporters, "We were treated very courteously. They couldn't have treated us better," but declined to be named (none of the children were named in the newspapers for their safety).[52] In the course of the day, four of the city's nine previously all-white schools admitted seventeen Black students: seven at Gorenflo, four at DuKate, three at Lopez, and two at Jeff Davis.[53] In Jackson, according to *Jet*, "only the occasional appearance of a Negro family and the presence of more white fathers with their children" and "Negro youngsters . . . accompanied by fathers, rather than mothers" was reported to "[make] the day seem different." This was one of the examples of the way gender played a part in these new, fluctuating racialized spaces. In both Biloxi and Jackson, reported the *Laurel Leader-Call*, the "well dressed" appearance of the Black families was reported, as well as their "becoming manner."[54] The numbers for both Black and white students in all three of the state's desegregating districts were down from the previous year, but it was expected that they would rise to the usual level after the opening of classes. It is unclear if it was usual for some families to register late or if some parents were suspected of waiting to see whether the schools opened without the violence seen in other states.[55]

"We don't anticipate one bit of trouble," Biloxi school superintendent Robert D. Brown said of the outlook for the rest of the year, as quoted in *Jet*. The reporter said Brown was "plainly pleased" to have pulled off the day "with a smoothness and peace that stunned the nation." Dr. Mason was said to have called off a scheduled news conference as "things were moving so smoothly he felt it best to stay out of it."[56]

However, it was not only the children who had to be prepared for troublesome encounters. On August 14, a week before the schools desegregated, Mason had finished an early morning delivery and retired to the hospital cafeteria for breakfast. A few months earlier, in March 1963, the New Biloxi Hospital was moved to a new building and renamed Howard Memorial. Although some staff members had tried to perpetuate the annex system, by which Black patients were separated from whites, they were not successful (though it is unclear if the rooms were in any other way segregated).[57] For better or worse (given the purported benefits of "rooming-in"), Black infants as well as white were received in the nursery from that time forward. That day, as Mason was eating in the recently integrated cafeteria, a seventeen-year-old white youth, William "Billy" Batia Jr., poured hot coffee down the doctor's back, scalding him.[58] Mason jumped up and asked "three times whether it was accidental or deliberate." When Batia replied, "It was no accident," Mason struck him on the nose, knocking Batia to the floor. Mason picked up a chair, anticipating the fight might continue, but others in the room quickly intervened. After he was examined by a coworker, Mason was arrested. His wife, Natalie, came to the station and bailed out her husband on a $300 bond, and the two combatants filed charges against each other.[59] Batia now contended that the event was accidental, and Mason was fined $300 and sentenced to ten days in jail for "assault and battery on a minor."[60] Mason appealed and, with the hospital staff behind him, it was found he had acted in self-defense and the charges were dropped.[61] It is, of course, not certain that the incident was connected to Biloxi's school desegregation or any of Mason's civil rights work; it may simply have been prompted by the fact that he was Black man sitting in a cafeteria with whites.

When classes opened in Biloxi on August 31, 1964, journalists from the *New York Times, Washington Post, Boston Globe*, and other major newspapers and TV networks were in Biloxi to cover the first day of desegregated school. Twelve girls and four boys broke the color barrier, attending school (as was normal for their grade) for a half-day during the first six weeks.[62] Very little was publicized about their identities, other than the daughter of Alexander Bellamy being mentioned by Mason in his autobiography.[63] US marshals guarded the entrances of the four schools, but there was no outbreak of violence as there had been at the University of Mississippi or in Little Rock. During Gilbert Jr's subsequent work to preserve Biloxi's civil rights history and the legacy of his father, he reflected in an interview that he found individuals who had taken part in that historic first-grade class "never felt they did anything really . . . special." He was pleased they would never know what it was like to grow up in a segregated school system. "You can imagine," he continued, "you had six- or seven-year-old Black children talking to white adults, [interacting with them] in ways their parents could not. But they got through it."[64]

In Leake County, only one student, Debora Lewis, desegregated the schools on September 2 (interestingly, a white boy had attempted to enroll at a historically Black elementary school, but his parents later withdrew the application); her father was fired from his job with a lumber company the next day. NAACP attorney Derrick Bell reported that "house to house visits by unnamed white persons" had dissuaded a greater desegregation effort.[65] Jackson opened on a desegregated basis on September 14, with forty-four Black students enrolled at previously all-white schools. At the end of the year, the students were presented with certificates from the NAACP, congratulating them on what they had done.[66]

Now wise to the loopholes that could be exploited in the words "all deliberate speed," and under the authority of the Civil Rights Act of 1964, the US Department of Education was telling school districts they must submit plans for the desegregation of every school by 1967 or lose all federal aid to the district.[67] The Harrison County School Board announced its plans to desegregate the first through fourth grades in 1965, fifth through eighth grades in 1966, and ninth through twelfth grades in 1967.[68] Biloxi arranged for a slight variation on that plan, opening the first through third and the twelfth grades to all students regardless of race in 1965, which added schools like Beauvoir and Fernwood to the forward movement.[69]

Why had the local school board opted to move ahead with desegregating an older class when that had been argued in court to be a more difficult undertaking? No explanation was given to the public, but Superintendent Brown spoke to the fears some had expressed that the quality of academics would be compromised by desegregation. "No concessions are being made to any students," he told the *Daily Herald*. "And the Biloxi system is continuously strengthening its program for the good of the community."[70]

Seven Black students registered at the previously all-white Biloxi High School: Jerry Black, John Esters, and Rosie Mumford (who had all been named in the desegregation suit), as well as Luther Buckley, Linda Cherry, Adrienne Martin, and a fourth boy.[71] According to Mason, lack of proximity to the previously all-white schools, the desire to graduate with their friends, and "apprehension" about attending school with white children was suspected of having influenced the low number of transferring students.[72] On September 2, 1965, the seven seniors arrived at Biloxi High in two automobiles, "which let them out in front and left."[73] With the rest of the senior class, they headed to the auditorium before their first day of classes began. Then they went to their homerooms to receive textbooks.[74] As the (all-white) faculty of the school never received class rosters ahead of time, they did not know whose classes the seven Black students would be in.[75] The year seemed to go well, with the most remarkable surprise arising during the end of the school dance, when the token Black students at the mostly white school did not pair up with each other but invited other Black peers as their dates, doubling the Black presence during the evening.[76]

A survey conducted by the Mississippi Council on Human Relations reported that the Gulf Coast and Hattiesburg had the most potential for an "acceptable experience" for desegregating students in the state.[77] A local white student during this time, Daniel Draughn, said he felt that bullying and ostracization of each race against the other were mostly subtle, seen in brief encounters in hallways and bathrooms.[78] Willie Jean McSwain remembered that bus drivers would neglect to pick up Black students, there were problems with "rapport with teachers," and some white teachers would humiliate Black students in the classroom with racialized comments and "jokes."[79] Initially, lunchrooms and other such spaces seemed "self-segregated," the *Clarion Ledger* reported, and a third to half of the students reported being excluded from extracurricular activities (sometimes for fear of their safety).[80] Gilbert Mason Jr. recalled attending high school with a talented trumpeter who was cut from the band over insurance concerns for bringing an integrated group on away games, rather than retaining the young man for home games, which were held in the stadium in Back-of-Town.[81]

Across the state, the *Clarion Ledger* reported that "nearly half" of Black families reported threats, crosses burned on their properties, and loss of jobs, housing, bank credit, or welfare payments.[82] Dr. Mason recalled that he had not heard of such consequences to the Black parents of Biloxi, harassments included the demeaning and unhygienic experience of having urine thrown on them, more than once, as they waited for their children.[83] Fortunately, this was not the story of every person in the *integrated* environment: as the fears of some parents proved true, desegregation did lead to social mixing across color lines. Gilbert Mason Jr., as intelligent, hard-working, civic-minded, and socially active as his parents, excelled in school and was able to form friendships across racial lines after he began to attend the desegregated Mary Michel Junior High in ninth grade.[84] Yet his experience was not without complications. He recalled that after gold medalist Tommie Smith and bronze medalist John Carlos raised fists on the 1968 Olympic podium, it became common to see Black spectators at football games do the same or refuse to stand when "Dixie" was played. Like the rest of the players, Mason continued to stand, without raising his fist, though he felt conscious of what he called the "dilemma" and "was never certain" about what was the correct choice. Occasionally, he encountered a teacher he suspected was prejudiced.[85] Most of all, it bothered him that, despite being voted "Most Intelligent" in Biloxi High's first Senior Hall of Fame, he was never invited to be a page in the state legislature or US Congress (as there were no Black legislators to appoint him) as some of his white peers were.[86] However, the concern that the curricula would be destroyed by desegregation of the schools was never realized, as, in Harrison County, students continued to win honors at every level of competition, across academics and extracurricular organizations.[87]

As these momentous changes were happening, the right to use the beaches was still on the mind of the Black community. Several Freedom School students wrote about the beaches in the school's first issue of its newspaper. Janice Thomas wrote about her frustration in driving twenty miles to Pass Christian to be allowed to swim. "Segregation on the beach should be done away with," she wrote.[88] Linda Davis's poem, titled "What's Wrong with My Skin," expressed feelings of belittlement and ostracism that she experienced on buses, in stores, and even walking down the road. "Each time I go on the beach," she wrote, "People look at me and make a long speech." But she was encouraged not to return hatred with hatred: "I won't fight back with violence / When I fight back, it will be in good sense / I'll fight with love and kindness / And I will win if I do my best."

After more than two hundred delays spanning four years, the federal beach case, *United States v. Harrison County*, finally came to trial in December 1964. Clemon Jimerson, who, despite the intensity of his late-night work in the local music scene, had maintained his grades well enough to earn a full music scholarship to Jackson State College, was among those from the 1960 wade-in subpoenaed to testify. After fifty-five witnesses were heard and 320 pieces of evidence exhibited, the trial ended in February 1965. (Unfortunately, many photographs used in the case were disposed of; historians have Leo Russell to thank for rescuing some from the garbage, many becoming the few images we have of the wade-ins today.[89]) Yet the beach did not open. Judge Sidney Mize delayed his ruling; a month later, he collapsed at the bench, was hospitalized, and died. Newspapers announcing his passing described him as the judge "whose reluctant decisions brought school desegregation to the state."[90] He had been spared the addition of beach integration to his epitaph.

The ruling fell to Judge William Harold Cox, who openly referred to Blacks with the n-word in court and berated civil rights attorneys for wasting his time with "lousy cases."[91] Unsurprisingly, Cox was in no hurry to issue a ruling in the beaches suit. Seven years into the fight, in summer 1966, Black people were still being arrested for trespassing on the beach, although the affidavits were later withdrawn. Even so, both Dr. Mason and Mayor Guice told reporters it had been "a pretty good summer" as far as beach use. Guice waved away all indication of racial ill-will in the continuing arrests, saying anyone could search the nation and "not find greater acceptance of the Negro than in Biloxi."[92] Unsurprisingly, in March 1967, Judge Cox ruled in favor of Harrison County, upholding the private title of the beaches. The government appealed the decision to the Fifth Circuit Court of Appeals. Ironically, after an unsuccessful run for reelection as governor of Mississippi, James Coleman, the originator of the SSC ten years prior, had been appointed to the Fifth Circuit and would now be handling the appeal.

Before the final conclusion was reached, yet another devastating blow to the heart of the civil rights movement rocked the foundation of all the community held dear: the evening of April 4, 1968, Martin Luther King Jr. was assassinated, shot on the balcony of his Memphis hotel in front of his friends and colleagues. The Mason family had returned from a meeting in the Baptist church basement to catch CBS news anchor Walter Cronkite reporting the evening news. Cronkite reported the death of King, whom Gilbert Mason Jr. called "the apostle of nonviolence." Gilbert Jr. recalled the "rough going" of the days ahead, the feeling of having the "wind knocked out," and the "community hand-holding" that followed. Deep down, he feared more than ever that his father "might meet the same fate." He remembered that his mother became more upset and worried about Dr. Mason's schedule, urging him to let her know his whereabouts consistently. But nothing could frighten him out of what Gilbert Jr. called his father's "fighter pilot mentality."[93]

Across the nation, memorials to Dr. King were soon arranged. "From all ends of the Coast," Dr. Mason was reported saying in the *Daily Herald*, "people of all races have called," devastated.[94] More than three thousand mourners of both races gathered at the Biloxi Stadium, where Mason served as master of ceremonies. Rev. John Aregood gave King's eulogy. Several other religious leaders, Dr. Felix Dunn, and Gulfport mayor Billy Meadows were also among the speakers.[95]

Finally, in mid-August 1968, Judge James Coleman issued the final decision in the beach desegregation case, ruling the beach property was indeed held in "perpetual public ownership" and that to find otherwise would violate the state constitution. He concluded that nothing of the littoral rights of the waterfront was lost to property owners and that, if anything, the beach had been given "free of charge" to them, as well as the entire public. (Despite Coleman's history and continuing support of states' rights, in his new position, he frequently voted "in favor of racial minorities" and desegregation. Perhaps he had changed with the times; perhaps as a judge, he felt a different level of autonomy or responsibility to the federal legislature. Perhaps he was simply one more complicated figure living among many—whose motivations and influences were a constantly shifting kaleidoscope.[96]) In any case, the US Supreme Court refused to hear further arguments. After almost a decade, because of Dr. Mason's unwavering perseverance, the bravery and integrity of so many Black Biloxians, and those whites also fighting to dismantle the bigotry of the hegemonic culture, the Biloxi beaches were open to all for the first time that season. It would take until 1970 to reverse the trespassing convictions of the 1963 wade-in.

No reaction from Dr. Mason or other demonstrators was recorded in the press it seems. When the ruling was issued, Mason and his family had been out of town at a Chicago convention of the Gulf Coast Medical Association.[97] When asked whether there was any community celebration of the verdict, wade-in survivor Clemon Jimerson replied, "That's what we're celebrating every year. Hey—we're still celebrating!"[98]

Chapter Eleven

SAND BETWEEN MY TOES

Continuing Work for Racial Equity

The Mississippi State Sovereignty Commission (SSC) watched Dr. Gilbert Mason until at least August 31, 1968, when he was on a list of delegates to the Democratic Convention in Chicago. By this time, his portrayal in the press was far more flattering. He was described as a "dapper general practitioner."[1] In 1968, his medical practice moved into a new building, a one-story brick structure that is now listed on the historical register.[2] Black doctors kept out of the all-white state (and, by extension, national) medical associations had formed the Mississippi Medical and Surgical Association and the Gulf Coast Medical, Dental, and Pharmaceutical Association.[3] Mason was a member of both and a secretary of the latter.[4] He went on to be named a diplomate of the American Board of Family Medicine, a fellow in the American Academy of Family Physicians, chair of its Health and Safety Committee, delegate to the Medical Committee for Civil Rights, and chief of the family practice section at Howard Memorial.[5] The Mississippi State Medical Association and the Coast Counties Medical Society, which for years had allowed him only as a "scientific" (not full) member, inducted him fully in 1966. Of particular importance to the Black community, Mason was a local leader in testing for and education about sickle cell anemia as it became better known in the 1970s.[6]

In 1969, Hurricane Camille hit the coast hard. Back-of-Town was flooded with over four feet of water, ruining homes and businesses, including those belonging to the Masons. While Dr. Mason was unable to see patients in his office for two weeks, he helped find food, water, housing, and other necessities for the displaced, including those in the low-income white neighborhood on the point, just as he would head other charity projects following natural disasters in the future.[7] He was one of the first three Black members appointed to the Governor's Emergency Council in the wake of the hurricane, and he was among those who spoke out about racial bias shown by

Red Cross aid workers after Camille. In 1969, Mason and Marvin Dickey resurrected the Biloxi Civic League, among other activities, to endorse the first Black candidates to run for office in Biloxi since the Civil War.[8] Mason was himself the first Black man elected to the Harrison County Democratic Executive Committee and served as a delegate to the state convention.

Dr. Mason, sensitive to representation across race, gender, and class, further advocated for women and more minorities to be included on the Coliseum Commission, to which he was appointed by four mayors of towns and cities in Harrison County—and where he demonstrated his continuing respect and familiarity with parliamentary procedure using Robert's Rules of Order, which had so impressed him as a young student in Jackson.[9] When the project was concluded, Mason protested the lack of Black officials initially invited to the opening ceremony and proposed (without success) that, rather than dedicate the building to Elvis Presley, who had so many monuments to his name, it be dedicated to the great Black soprano Leontyne Price, who was from Laurel, Mississippi.[10] Mason was very involved with city planning endeavors, instrumental in creation of a full-time emergency service for the hospital, and made recommendations for air and water emergency transportation and other improvements, which benefited all.[11] He was appointed to the Biloxi Planning Commission, worked on the Main Street Revitalization project, advocated against the closing of the L&N railway stop in Back-of-Town, and applied for and organized the use of community development grants for better housing and drainage in poor neighborhoods.[12] Under his guidance, the Civic Action Committee managed the "Turnkey Program" in Gulfport, a first of its kind home ownership program for low-income families (initiated by the National Council of Negro Women), which gave preoccupancy training in home maintenance and provided two hundred affordable homes, grouped around a community center for daycare and recreation.[13]

In 1970, seeing that, due to residential distribution (among other possible factors), schools in West Biloxi were still segregated, Mason brought another suit, *Gilbert R. Mason Jr. et al. v. Biloxi Municipal School District* with the intent of creating greater racial balance through bussing if necessary. Judge Walter L. Nixon Jr. had already attempted to rectify the "failure of white students to choose all black schools," due to the "unfounded" fear of "inferior education" by ordering desegregation of the staff and administration to an 80 percent white, 20 percent Black representation, without the desired shift in the student population. Nixon claimed that other impediments to a balanced freedom of choice—"fear of Blacks to attend white schools" and "artificial deterrents"—were "not present in the Biloxi school district."[14] Those who objected to plans to bus students did so, in part, citing the "hardships" and "safety hazard" it might cause families, the use of taxpayer dollars to do so, and the potential loss of Black administrators and teachers, as well as the closure of historically Black schools, to cause "instant integration."[15] Judge Nixon named a biracial committee to suggest solutions. In the end, he did rule to enact a bussing system to integrate the staff at each school "proportionate to the student enrollment" and to offer remedial education for those who had grown up in underfunded segregated schools "to overcome past inadequacies in their education."[16] White students from many parts of the city were bussed in to attend Nichols High and vice versa, regardless of their proximity to other schools.[17]

In addition to the work he had done with the public schools, Dr. Mason was appointed medical director of the county's integrated Head Start program, serving thousands of children who lived below poverty levels with medical and dental screenings and addressing vision, hearing, and speech problems as well as nutritional, educational, and psychological needs.[18] He advocated for adult education programs on the Board of Directors of the Community Education Extension at Mary Holmes College and as vice president and educator of the STAR vocational program, which served hundreds of graduates.[19] President Richard Nixon appointed Mason to the State Advisory Committee on Education. He also served on the State Advisory Committee to the United States Commission on Civil Rights, making recommendations for allocation of federal funds to aid desegregation and identifying areas of discrimination.[20] Locally, he continued to lead workshops on civil rights activism and contributed to Black history educational events, arranging films and displays on heritage, historical figures, arts, and culture.[21]

In his efforts to eliminate poverty, Mason was very involved in job creation as well. He worked on the State Manpower Council, the Harrison County Regional Economic Commission, and others.[22] The Civic Action Committee sponsored Youth Corps, giving teens summer work experience in national parks, and hired impoverished laborers to join national forest beautification projects.[23] He was treasurer and later president of the Biloxi USO, which provided entertainment for the Keesler airmen, organized drives to collect goods for military personnel overseas, arranged blood drives, and advocated for improvement in military housing and the conditions of military dependents at Howard Memorial Hospital.[24]

Befitting his role as a scout leader, Mason addressed the moral aspects of youth life in the community, asking that law enforcement prevent minors from playing pinball, gambling, entering pool halls, or obtaining access to pornographic material. He sought to have the Black youth baseball leagues added to the city's recreation program and to discontinue the dual recreation system altogether.²⁵ Further in the interest of justice, Mason continued to call for better investigation of murder cases and other questionable deaths in which racial bias was suspected to be a factor, such as the Gulfport shooting of Daniel Lee Lizana by a highway patrolman, who claimed self-defense despite evidence Lizana had been badly beaten before the shooting.²⁶

In addition to his lifelong dedication to the Baptist community, Mason was an invited speaker at the Gulf Coast Unitarian Fellowship, demonstrating again that his work on behalf of mutual understanding and cooperation bridged all spheres of his life.²⁷ Mason continued his connection to his alma mater, returning to speak at Howard on the topic of "The Brave Young Physicians" and to his fraternity, Alpha Phi Alpha.²⁸ He served as president of the local chapter and showed that he had retained the thespian skills of his high school years, taking first place in jabberwocks for his parts in the play *Lenox Avenue* and the skit *Black Night*.²⁹ In 1975, he and his wife celebrated their twenty-fifth wedding anniversary with vows they had written themselves, before departing on a second honeymoon.³⁰

Another aspect of civil rights work on the Gulf coast, which was not within the scope of this book or other historical research to cover adequately, is the elaborate multitude of intersections and networks among the figures involved. When one is studying events and individuals as separate entities, the intersection of their lives may not always be apparent. For example, in his role with the NAACP, Medgar Evers worked on Clyde Kennard's case; the two became friends and then sadly died less than a month apart. After the killing of Reverend George Lee, who had been Dr. Mason's pastor in Jackson, Lee's body was examined by Dr. Clinton Battle, who was later pushed out of Mississippi because of his civil rights activity.³¹ Many of the beach demonstrators were related through a network of extended family connections, as well as work affiliations and membership in churches and secular organizations. Mason's sister, Rozelia Mason Stamps, who lived in Jackson, was another member of his family involved in civil rights work deserving of further scholarship. Further research on and full recognition for the work of Natalie Lorraine Hamlar Mason, Dr. Mason's wife, in the civil rights movement in Harrison County, as well as her other civic contributions, are certainly deserved.³² In addition to the constant moral and legal support she gave her husband and community during the beach demonstrations, having raised her son to young adulthood in the mid-1960s, Natalie Mason began to pursue opportunities associated with her degree in social work. Alongside her dedication as a social worker at Gulfport Veterans Administration Hospital, she sat on the board of directors of Harrison County Mental Health Association and the State Department of

Youth Services (appointed by Governor Bill Waller) and served as treasurer of the National Association of Social Workers. She worked in programs for adult literacy, education, and community advocacy[33] and was the recipient of multiple awards for her work, including the Silver Star for Mental Health service and Social Worker of the Year by Gulf Coast Chapter of the National Association of Social Workers.[34]

Natalie Mason also had a profound impression on the young women she served as Girl Scout Troop Leader, Sunday School and Vacation Bible School teacher, and guiding other youth in the community. Gilbert Mason Jr. particularly remembered going with his mother to Ellzey's Hardware for a trashcan to collect water after a hurricane. When they arrived at the water department, situated on the same block, it appeared clear to her—though she was not quick to assume racial bias—that the workers were treating white people with priority, and she spoke up immediately to settle the issue. "I was very proud of her," her son recalled. "Greatly."[35]

Natalie Mason was politically active as well, particularly in the feminist movement and actions for women's rights. She served on the State Coordinating Committee of the International Women's Year (IWY), a national women's conference, which called for ratification of the Equal Rights Amendment (ERA), programs for battered women and children, low-cost childcare, equal employment opportunities, family planning services, and sex education. After the committee was criticized for only including white women among its delegates to the national convention, she was among the Black women, and the only one from the Gulf Coast, asked to "balance the state's representation."[36] Like Dr. Mason, Natalie Mason continued to experience the additional obstacle of racism in her civic work. At the IWY conferences, the anti-ERA group called Mississippians for God, Country, and Family passed out literature linking the civil rights movement with communism, while attorney Richard Barrett indicated the intersection between sexism and racism when he said the work to "bring women down to the level of men" would disrupt family life and the child's role as "the proper object to pass on Anglo-Saxon heritage and Western culture."[37]

Natalie Mason was also secretary and director of the integrated Mississippi Gulf Coast Young Democrats Club at its founding, which worked on such resolutions as changing the state code that prohibited women from serving on juries.[38] She worked with the Head Start program, as her church director of vacation Sunday School, and was the chairwoman of the Black Contributions to America programing, coordinating speakers to come to the Gulf Coast.[39] And like her husband, she maintained active ties to her sorority as a charter member of the Delta Sigma Theta Gulf Coast alumnae chapter.[40]

Gilbert Mason Jr. followed in his parents' footsteps as an honor student, peer leader, Eagle Scout and recipient of the Order of the Arrow award, lettered football player, performer in theater arts, and faithful member of his church congregation.[41] With other living participants of the Biloxi wade-ins, Mason, who became a doctor like his father, continues to devote himself to the preservation and awareness of the civil rights watersheds.[42] Likewise, his former wife, Givonna Joseph, and his daughter, Aria Mason, are among those whose stewardship of Black southern histories, including the Mason family and Biloxi wade-ins, continues to give illumination and dimension to the marginalized, yet founding, stories of our country's past.

Multiple memorials to Dr. Gilbert Mason Sr.'s legacy can be found on the Biloxi Gulf Coast. A section of the highway bears his name, as does an oceanic research vessel belonging to the National Science Foundation. July 30 has been proclaimed Gilbert Mason Day. Exhibits detailing the history of the wade-ins are on display in the local library and the Mississippi Civil Rights Museum. Local artist Demetrius Gayden included a representation of the 1963 wade-ins in his mural on the Inez Cafe, Main Street, with the organization and support of John Kemp and the NAACP and Steps Coalition.[43] For the fiftieth anniversary of the wade-ins, a historical marker was erected near the lighthouse; after its destruction in Hurricane Katrina, a new memorial marker was placed there in June 2022. Dr. Felix Dunn has also been commemorated for his role in the Gulfport wade-ins and other work on behalf of the community with the NAACP Dr. Felix Dunn Community Leader Award and a heritage marker near Jones Park in Gulfport. These testaments to bravery and perseverance sometimes bear the name of one man but are truly representations of many more, many whose names and actions are known only to the silent witnesses of the past. In the words of wade-in survivor Clemon Jimerson, "If not for Gilbert Mason, we wouldn't be talking today. But it was a total community effort. . . . In order to have a good leader, you got to have people that's willing to sacrifice."

Most beautiful of all are all the ways progress is celebrated and enjoyed by the generations that followed those who participated in opening the sand beaches for all. Clemon Jimerson Sr.'s son and namesake proposed to his wife-to-be on the beach, where he had grown up playing and surfing with friends of both races. And Myrtle Davis listened with joy each time her grandkids returned to her to say, "We went down to the beach and let the sand go between our toes."[44]

Epilogue

FLOTSAM, JETSAM

The Demise of the State Sovereignty Commission, Unforeseen Consequences, and Horizons Ahead

As with all change, there were unforeseen and far-reaching consequences to the movement for desegregation beyond the scars that some of the Biloxi beach demonstrators bore for the rest of their lives. Increasingly, state legislators came to view the Mississippi State Sovereignty Commission (SSC) as a waste of money and reported feeling that abolishing it would do more to improve the state's image than the commission itself.[1] Surviving SSC files certainly give the impression that hundreds of thousands of taxpayer dollars had been spent primarily on agents calling each other, driving around, and filing multiple copies of memos in which they largely reproduced, verbatim, newspaper articles they had meticulously cut out and filed. Funding to the SSC was cut, but it took years to officially disband the commission, which was likened to a spare tire by Representative John Johnson: "You don't use it, but it's there if you need it."[2]

In 1973, the SSC was finally disbanded. The director at that time, Erle Johnston, destroyed some of the records, but the suggestion to burn the rest was passed over. The American Civil Liberties Union (ACLU) brought a suit calling for the files to be turned over released to the public. Attorney General Albioun F. Summer accused the ACLU of trying to "impede" intelligence operations by revealing the methods of law enforcement, "which would expose society to more crime, violence and terrorism." Instead of opening the records to the public or destroying them, the court ordered them sealed for fifty years.[3] Once the records were opened in 1998, the over sixty thousand victims of the SSC's surveillance had ninety days to protest the release of files containing their names. The agents who had violated the constitutional rights of the victims had forfeited their own and could not ask for their files to be redacted.[4] The White Citizens' Council (WCC) also faded from prominence in the early 1970s. However, the "uptown Klan," as the Southern Poverty Law Center called the WCC, is alleged to have continued in the guise of the Council of Conservative Citizens and other white supremist groups.[5]

Public school desegregation was not a complete success. Early on, parents and teachers complained of overcrowding and both too little and too much integration (although it was capped at 40 percent nonwhite students). Dr. Mason and the Biloxi NAACP continued to object to the lesser quality of buses used to transport Black students, to illegal placement testing and discrimination in discipline, and to the selection of pep squad and honor students.[6] They advocated for appointment of Black representatives to the School Board and better qualified Black teachers, counselors, and administrators.[7] Meanwhile, the number of private schools in the state boomed, populated by white students fleeing the desegregated schools. Legislators succeeded in arranging tuition grants for students attending what they called any "nonsectarian private school," while cutting $12 million from the public school budget and diverting other resources such as textbooks into the private sector. The "white flight" into private schools continued, even increased, with support from elected leadership and judges, as bussing and other measures to create racial balance in schools began in the 1970s.[8] Even today, the redefinition of school districts has resulted in a sort of educational gerrymandering, creating charter schools that are disproportionately white.[9]

Neither did federal law result in true abolishment of voter disenfranchisement. After the 1965 Voting Rights Act nullified literacy tests and poll taxes, Mississippi redrew its voting districts, ensuring that historically Black districts became majority white. Less official obstacles to voters ranged from refusing to help illiterate voters to giving false instructions or mismarking voters' ballots for them.[10] Nevertheless, Mississippi's first Black legislator since Reconstruction, Robert Clark of Holmes County, was elected in 1967. Black votership grew from the tens of thousands to the hundreds of thousands.[11] Within a few decades, the number of Black elected officials (now including women) had grown to the highest of any state.[12]

The desegregation of public spaces and increasingly open residential practices resulted in the breakup, to various degrees, of historical Black neighborhoods and businesses, those areas of forced concentration where culture had developed and been sustained.[13] There is a history and continuing danger of demanding homogenization in exchange for equity and opportunity. There are balances to be struck among cultural fluidity, inclusivity, and preservation (particularly as diversity can contribute to compassion, innovation, and economic growth).[14] The work continuing to identify and preserve landmarks and commemorate cultural milestones in Biloxi is an important step in acknowledging the city's diverse history, in the hopes of creating an even more diverse—but united—future.

"There's not a total win here," Rev. John Aregood admitted about his civil rights work in Mississippi. "We're still struggling."[15]

Racism has not been eradicated from our global or national consciousness. It is still felt on the Mississippi Gulf Coast in new manifestations. During one wade-in remembrance, Constance Bailey reflected that criticism of the so-called "Black Spring Break" celebrations had made her feel that, although she had a right to be on the beach, she "did not feel welcome there."[16] Perhaps it takes more than one generation to undo the work of centuries—or perhaps it only takes more information, introspection, and effort. Either way, there is more to be done, more hands needed on the oars pulling us forward. And based on studies on innovation, we may go further, faster, taking the smoothest route possible if we ensure it is a diverse group of people navigating the way.

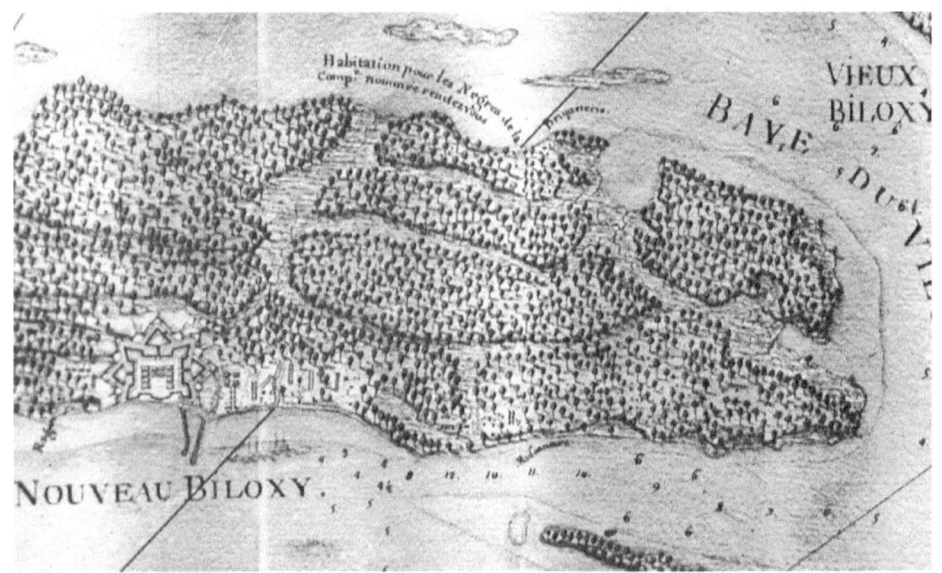

Pierre Le Blond de la Tour. Carte de partie de la coste du Nouveau Biloxy avec les isles des environs, ca. 1722. Courtesy of Research Laboratories of Archaeology.

Dr. Mason and son at Gulf Coast beach, possibly Gulfport, ca. 1956. Courtesy of Givonna Joseph.

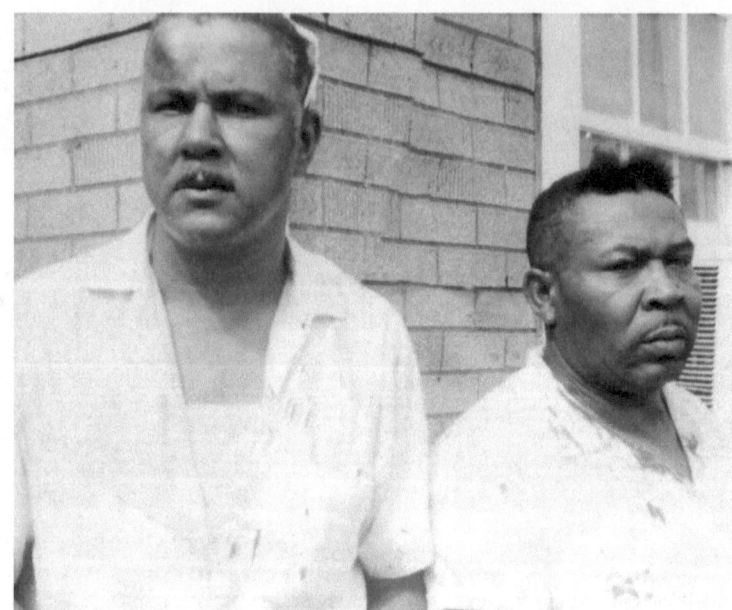
Ellis Brown (L) and Dorothy Galloway (R) waiting for treatment outside Dr. Mason's clinic after attack on the beach, April 24, 1960. Courtesy of Givonna Joseph.

Women and men on Division Street following the beach attack. Courtesy of Givonna Joseph.

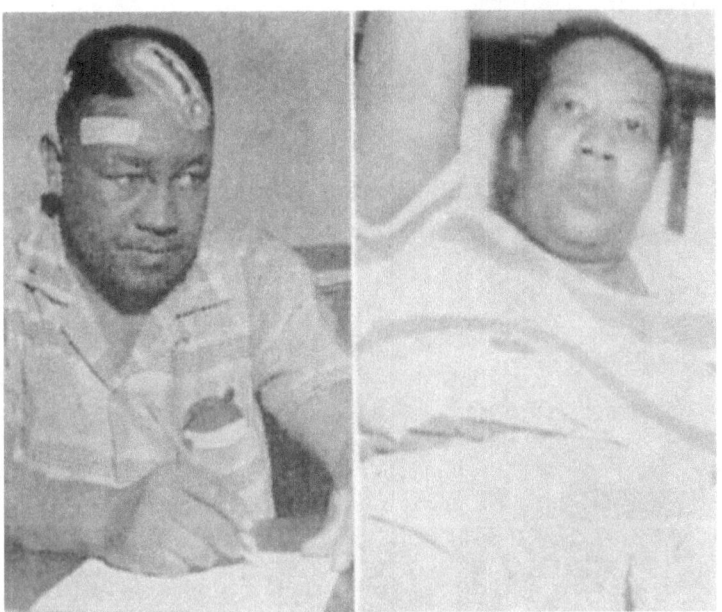

Wilmer McDaniels and Lavanie Rankin recovering from injuries sustained on the beach and Back-of-Town on April 24, 1960. From *Jet*, May 12, 1960.

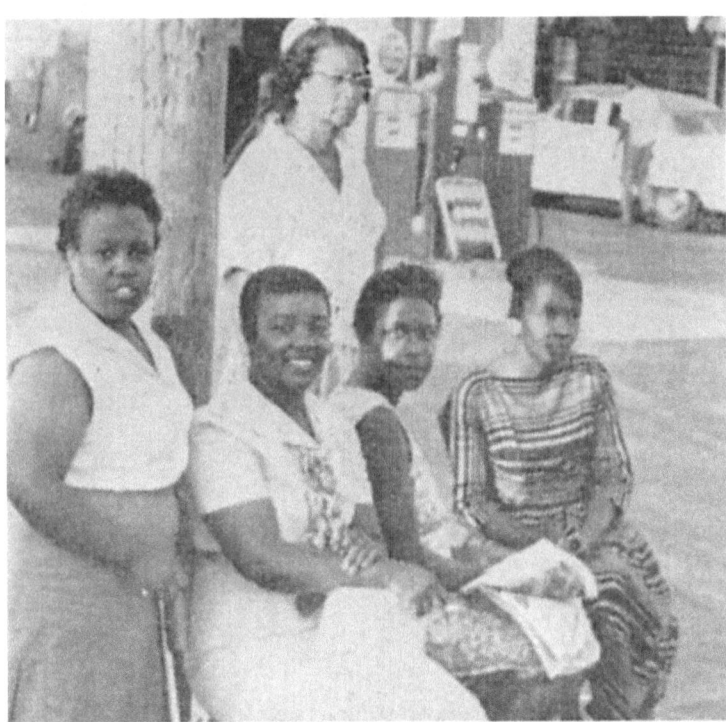

Vashti Tanner (rear) and other women promoting the boycott against businesses associated with the mob attack. From *Jet*, May 12, 1960.

Demonstrators led off the beach, 1963. Photograph thought to be by Jim Lund. Courtesy of Givonna Joseph.

White crowd turns over cars of demonstrators, 1963. Photograph thought to be by Jim Lund. Courtesy of Givonna Joseph.

Reverend Aregood and other demonstrators loaded into the back of a van by police, 1963. Photograph thought to be by Jim Lund. Courtesy of Givonna Joseph.

Police take demonstrators to jail, 1963. Photograph thought to be by Jim Lund. Courtesy of Givonna Joseph.

Hall Of Fame Honors Seniors

GILBERT MASON
Being elected Most Intelligent Boy was just one of the highlights of Gilbert's senior year. He was a semi-finalist in the National Achievement scholarship program for Outstanding Negro Students. President of JAS, he played football for two years.

Gilbert Mason Jr., Most Intelligent 1971, Biloxi High *Indian Echo*. Courtesy of Givonna Joseph.

ACKNOWLEDGMENTS

My gratitude, first and last, to the One that Is and Was and Will Be, for all good things.

Special thanks to Dr. Gilbert Mason Jr., Clemon P. Jimerson Sr., Givonna Joseph, Aria Mason, and Rev. Richard Ellerbrake for their generosity of time and energy, granting me interviews and sending historical records. My appreciation for their work extends to all the women and men named in this text, as well as those whose names were never publicized, whose work in pursuit of human dignity has and continues to create a culture more like the one I would wish my children to inherit.

My appreciation to all the journalists, historians, and preservationists whose sources are a beacon for anyone interested in Gulf Coast history, especially Ray Bellande and Dr. James Patterson Smith, whose monumental works helped me to orient my compass and navigate this history. Thank you to the librarians of Biloxi, especially Jane Shambra, for answering my archive questions long distance, as well as the librarians of Monmouth and Independence, Oregon, who helped me print numerous rough drafts and request obscure interlibrary loans.

I am indebted to editor Emily Bandy of University Press of Mississippi, for all the warmth and support—basically every writer's dream of working with their first editor. Thank you to everyone at University Press of Mississippi who worked on *Wading In* and to the peer readers, whose critiques helped make the text so much stronger and accessible. Special thanks to freelance editor Lynn Whittaker for her incredible attention to detail, giving my writing the clarity vital to and deserved by such an important and sensitive history.

My love and gratitude to my original illuminator of history and rough draft reader, my "mamushka." My love and missing-you to my first creative writing teacher, my father. To my copilot and my children, who give me the best and only reviews that really matter. To all my family, especially my little brother, for setting the bar on kindness, humor, wit, and dedication I expect from anyone new coming into my life. To my friends, there, through time and distance, silly times and serious—every time the world is having a crisis of compassion, I look back to you to remember there is hope. Thank you to my professors at Rogue Community College, Southern Oregon University, and Emory & Henry, especially those who pushed my creativity and work ethic, honing my ability to look at the milieu and minutiae of life and say, "*That's* the story."

To the readers! Without you, the efforts of every writer would be like striking a match in a vacuum. May you always honor the light and story of your own life.

NOTES

CHAPTER ONE. BLACK IN BILOXI: BACK-OF-TOWN

1. J. W. Powell, *Fifteenth Annual Report of the Bureau of Ethnology to the Secretary of the Smithsonian Institution, 1893–94* (Washington, DC: Government Printing Office, 1897), 164.

2. Daniel H. Usner, "Chitimacha Diplomacy and Commerce in Colonial Louisiana," *Louisiana History* 62, no. 2 (2021): 137–41, https://www.jstor.org/stable/27033052; and Alan Gallay, *The Indian Slave Trade: The Rise of the English Empire in the American South, 1670–1717* (New Haven, CT: Yale University Press, 2002), 308–14.

3. Gallay, *Indian Slave Trade*, 312.

4. Gwendolyn Midlo Hall, *Africans in Colonial Louisiana: The Development of Afro-Creole Culture in the Eighteen-Century* (Baton Rouge: Louisiana State University Press, 1992), 57.

5. Hall, *Africans in Colonial Louisiana*, 59–60, 63–64.

6. Dorothy Bauhoff, "Skilled Labor: An Overview," *Gale Library of Daily Life Encyclopedia*, https://www.encyclopedia.com/humanities/applied-and-social-sciences-magazines/skilled-labor-overview.

7. John N. Davidson, "Negro Slavery in Wisconsin," *Parkman Club Papers* 1 (1896): 106; and Hall, *Africans in Colonial Louisiana*, Appendix A, 382.

8. Hall, *Africans in Colonial Louisiana*, Appendix A, 384.

9. On September 27, 1781, it was determined that "Negroes should, on an average, be sold to the inhabitants for 660 livres . . . on three years' credit, payable by equal installments, either in tobacco or in rice." Charles Gayarreé, *History of Louisiana: The French Domination* (New York: William J. Widdleton, 1867), 272–73; and Hall, *Africans in Colonial Louisiana*, 65.

10. Hall, *Africans in Colonial Louisiana*, Appendix A, 385.

11. Pierre Le Blond de la Tour, Carte de partie de la coste du Nouveau Biloxy avec les isles des environs [map], ca. 1722, in "Research Laboratories of Archaeology. Early Maps of the American South—Local Haps: Harbors and Islands (Gulf Coast)," last updated November 26, 2021, https://rla.unc.edu/emas/local-gulf-harb.html#Bilo; and Warren L. Wise, "Fingerprints of Child Slaves Found in Charleston Old Bricks," *Post and Courier of Charleston*, May 18, 2019.

12. Laura Ewen Blokker and Heather A. Knight, "Louisiana Bousillage: The Migration and Evolution of a French Building Technique in North America," *Construction History* 28, no. 1 (2013): 29–33, http://www.jstor.org/stable/43856026; John Cuevas, *Cat Island: The History of a Mississippi Gulf Coast Barrier Island* (Jefferson, NC: McFarland), 55; and Adolph P. Felder,

"Old French Fort (de la Pointe—Krebs House), Pascagoula, Mississippi," National Park Service, Department of the Interior, Washington, DC, September 19, 1940.

13. Gayarreé, *History of Louisiana*, 254.

14. John F. H. Claiborne, *Mississippi, As a Province, Territory and State: With Biographical Notices of Eminent Citizens* (Jackson, MS: Power & Barksdale, 1880), 307.

15. Jennifer Trivedi, *Mississippi after Katrina: Disaster Recovery and Reconstruction on the Gulf Coast* (Lanham, MD: Rowman & Littlefield, 2020), 40; Ted Ownby, et al., *The Mississippi Encyclopedia* (Jackson: University Press of Mississippi, 2017), 1144; Edmond Boudreaux, *The Seafood Capital of the World: Biloxi's Maritime History* (Charleston: Arcadia Publishing, 2011), 38–39; Ronald W. Miller, National Register of Historic Places Inventory—Nomination Form, Magnolia Hotel, November 10, 1972, https://www.apps.mdah.ms.gov/nom/prop/9845.pdf; Elizabeth P. Reynolds, National Register of Historic Places Inventory—Nomination Form, Pradat House, Toledano House, Philbrick House, Red Brick House, Tullis House, United States Department of the Interior, National Park Service, August 26, 1976, https://www.apps.mdah.ms.gov/nom/prop/9880.pdf; and 1850 US Census, Harrison County, Mississippi, population schedule, unnamed township, 12 (handwritten).

16. In 1850 in Harrison County (including Pass Christian), most of the approximately fifty free men and women of color were the descendants of enslaved persons freed by Julia Asmard (née de la Brosse), to whom she bequeathed beachfront land and houses, and her son-in-law, Theodore Benoit, who purchased the freedom of the son he had by a neighbor's enslaved woman. Most of these free men and women identified as mulattos. Charles/Chalot and Madeline Asmar, a formerly enslaved couple, ran a dairy farm (as Julia Asmard's family had), and their children continued to work with cattle. Charles Asmar owned and freed at least one man. His daughter, Celeste, owned at least three enslaved people, two of whom she willed to her children. Bernard Benoit inherited and sold enslaved people from his father. I found no indication that Joseph St. Amand, a master cabinet maker from Louisiana, and his family or their neighbor Victor de Doudroy of Louisiana and his family were connected to Julia Asmard although she also owned property in New Orleans, as did master carpenter François Bertand and his family (two of Bertand's sons were working as masons by 1860). The census records do not list occupations for most of the freedmen. I did not track the ebb and flow of Freeman families over the next decades but include the occupations listed in the 1860 census: William Denton, cook; the Decoudreaux/Bradley family (likely related to Rosalie Benoit), dressmakers (and possibly boardinghouse keepers, given the white French workers residing in the house); J. Charlotte, tailor; V. Babine, carpenter; L. Saucier, wood chopper; and M. Bazile, washerwoman. Dan Ellis, "First People of the Pass Black Heritage: Free Persons of Color," July 2001, 11–12, http://pc.danellis.net/HTMLobj-21/BlackHeritage1.pdf; 1850 US Census, Harrison County, Mississippi, population schedule; and 1860 US Census, Harrison County, Mississippi, population schedule, unnamed township.

17. Ellis, "First People of the Pass," 14–15.

18. J. Michael Butler, "The Mississippi State Sovereignty Commission and Beach Integration, 1959–1963: A Cotton-Patch Gestapo?," *Journal of Southern History* 68, no. 1 (2002): 113, http://www.jstor.org/stable/3069692.

19. The 1850 census and slave schedule are divided into Pass Christian and an unnamed township, the latter of which included Deer Island, the brickworks on the Back Bay (now

D'Iberville), Ship Island, and the lightship that presumably preceded the lighthouse at that location (I could not find this station on any list of historical stations). In the unnamed township, of over five hundred white households, over three hundred held no enslaved persons. I have listed mainly those heads of house who held over ten enslaved persons; but some, holding fewer, I included to demonstrate the variety of professions these slave owners engaged in and, by extension, some indication of what tasks may have been expected of those enslaved. I have omitted others that seemed repetitious. If no number is listed, one enslaved person was held; if no profession is listed, it was given as "none." Please excuse any misspelling of surnames, caused by the unfixed nature of names in the era, the mistake of the census-taker, or myself in interpreting their handwriting. The list of Harrison County, Mississippi, slave owners (partial list) for August-September 1850 is as follows: J. Henderson, lawyer, 14; E. Fourniquet, lawyer, 10; W. Tegarden, doctor, 22; G. Tegarden, farmer, 7; S. Varderman, widow, 9; M. Standards, doctor, 26; J. Baxter, jailor, 2; R. Cowen, merchant, 8; L. Ent, planter, 11; S. Fowler, lumber merchant, 20; R. Lairds, blacksmith, 2; S. Taylor, baptist clergy; C. Goldstourgh, teacher, 3; J. Brown, farmer, 16; C. Taylor, seaman, 6; A. Nixon, hotel keeper, 10; P. Debreys, farmer, 10; P. Pradet, 16; J. Finel, carpenter, 4; B. Helley, boat pilot; B. Bonds, farmer, 10; E. Lavers, clerk; J. Bathes, tailor; A. Vache, grocer; I. Barat, baker, 2; J. Henley, sheriff, 4; B. Baloit, pastry cook; P. Green, blacksmith; J. Landy, farmer, 21; I. De Porte, mason, 2; M. Howards, lighthouse keeper, 5; J. Lambkin, 23; G. Reeves, 13; O. Smith, millwright, 3; William G. Kendall Brickyards, approx. 262; G. Tourma, sawmill, 10; N. Holley, ship carpenter, 4; W. Edwards, woodcutter, 9; W. Martin, gardener; R. Ranson, farmer, 30; G. Kibbe, farmer, 13; Hands, Iron Founder, 9; W. Coates, sawmill, 8; W. Holly, mariner, 13; J. Hester, farmer, 9; R. Saffolds, wood chopper, 16; J. Saucier, farmer, 18; J. Huddleston, sawmill, 18; R. Lizana, 18; C. Dedo, farmer, 7; W. Whitfield, farmer, 7; B. Whitfield, 30. D'Iberville Historical Society, "The Old Brickyard," 2017, Historical Marker, D'Iberville, Mississippi, accessed April 12, 2022, https://www.hmdb.org/m.asp?m=122401; 1850 US Census, Harrison County, Mississippi, population schedule; 1850 US Census, Harrison County, Mississippi, slave schedule, unnamed township, 1–15 (handwritten); Morgan MacKenzie, "American Lightships, 1820–1983: History, Construction, and Archaeology within the Maritime Cultural Landscape" (master's thesis (East Carolina University, 2011), https://media.defense.gov/2020/Sep/28/2002507185/-1/-1/0/LIGHTSHIP_AMERICAN_HISTORY%201820-1983.PDF; and Ray Bellande, "History of D'Iberville," Ocean Springs Archives, accessed April 2, 2022, https://oceanspringsarchives.net/history-diberville.

20. Edward W. Hearn and M. E. Carr, "Soil Survey of the Biloxi Area, Mississippi," US Department of Agriculture, 1904, 371–72, https://www.nrcs.usda.gov/Internet/FSE_MANUSCRIPTS/mississippi/biloxiMS1904/biloxiMS1904.pdf.

21. *Ocean Springs News*, March 20, 1909, 1, quoted in Ray L. Bellande, "An Early Black History of Ocean Springs," Ocean Springs Archives, accessed July 14, 2021, https://oceansprings archives.net/african-american-history.

22. John Muldowny, "Jefferson Davis: The Postwar Years," *Mississippi Quarterly* 23, no. 1 (1969): 22–23, http://www.jstor.org/stable/26473833.

23. Deanne Stephens Nuwer, "The Seafood Industry in Biloxi: Its Early History, 1848–1930," *Mississippi History Now*, June 2006, https://mshistorynow.mdah.ms.gov/issue/the-seafood-industry-in-biloxi-its-early-history-1848-1930; Kenneth P'Pool, "Historic Resources of Biloxi

(Partial Inventory: Historic and Architectural Sites)," April 10, 1984, https://www.apps.mdah.ms.gov/t_nom/Historic%20Resources%20of%20Biloxi.pdf; "Biloxi, Miss.," *Biloxi Herald*, August 11, 1888, 1; 1850 US Census, Harrison County, Mississippi, population schedule; 1880 US Census, Harrison County, Mississippi, population schedule, unnamed township; and 1900 US Census, Harrison County, Mississippi, population schedule, unnamed township.

24. Black sports teams, although segregated, also drew white attendees at their games. See Anthony J. Stanonis, *Faith in Bikinis: Politics and Leisure in the Coastal South Since the Civil War* (Athens: University of Georgia Press, 2014), 111–12; Andrew W. Kahrl, *The Land Was Ours: How Black Beaches Became White Wealth in the Coastal South* (Chapel Hill: University of North Carolina Press, 2016, 56–57; and "Black Tarpoons Play on Diamond Sunday," *Daily Herald*, July 20, 1928, 15.

25. Ellis, "First People of the Pass," 14; and Kahrl, *Land Was Ours*, 56–57.

26. Kate Derickson, "After Hurricane Katrina, Devastated Black Neighborhoods Created an Opportunity for Redevelopment That Focused on Gentrification," London School of Economics and Political Science, July 7, 2014, http://bit.ly/TYLSYL.

27. Black neighborhoods were known by derogatory terms like "Jig Town" or "N----r Town" by some white citizens. See "Meeks Takes Coliseum Seat; Mason, Gallotte Tangle Verbally," *South Mississippi Sun*, June 22, 1977, 12; and "Another Tragedy," *Biloxi Daily Herald*, September 19, 1900, 8.

28. "City within a City: African American Culture in Biloxi," Ohr-O'Keefe Museum of Art, https://georgeohr.org/exhibition/city-within-a-city/.

29. The first principal was Sylvanie Leon, who was paid $35 a month in contrast to the $60 per month paid to the white principal. In 1900, the salary gap had closed somewhat, as the one Black teacher, James Burns, was paid $40, only slightly less than the white teachers' $45; however, given that all the white teachers listed were women, his gender must be considered. In 1905, all schools were modernized with water closets. Julia C. Guice, Stephanie C. Richmond, and David Alfred Wheeler, *The Growth of the Biloxi Public School System* (Biloxi, 1979), 10, 16, 41–42, 84.

30. Laura Ewen Blokker, "East Biloxi African American and Civil Rights Historic Resources Survey 2017," Mississippi Department of Archives and History, July 31, 2017, 4, https://www.biloxi.ms.us/wp-content/uploads/2017/10/EastBiloxiInventory2017.pdf; "City News," *Biloxi Daily Herald*, January 12, 1901, 8; "City Paragraphs," *Biloxi Daily Herald*, April 7, 1906, 8; "The Miley Hotel," *Biloxi Daily Herald*, May 12, 1906, 3; "Crap Shooters in Police Court," *Biloxi Daily Herald*, February 11, 1907, 1; "Court Cases Brought Up for Trial: Another Blind Tiger," *Biloxi Daily Herald*, May 21, 1907, 1; "Local Courts Do Much Business," *Biloxi Daily Herald*, April 6, 1908, 1; "Court Cases," *Biloxi Daily Herald*, July 3, 1908, 1; "Mott Charged with Murder," *Biloxi Daily Herald*, July 18, 1907, 1; "Police Court," *Biloxi Daily Herald*, April 1, 1911, 5; and "Card Players at 'The Eagles Nest,'" *Biloxi Daily Herald*, March 18, 1912, 8.

31. Lidy is sometimes spelled "Leidy." Other locals who spoke out to prevent further violence included an unnamed journalist for *The Daily Herald* and Baptist pastor Edmond Young. Black citizens told the press the community was "heartily in accord" with the "very mild" punishment of Lidy. "Black Brute Hanged by Outraged Whites," *Biloxi Daily Herald*, November 10, 1908, 1; "Negro Seen to Follow Girl," *Biloxi Daily Herald*, November 11, 1908, 1; "No Meeting Held by Negros," *Biloxi Daily Herald*, November 12, 1908, 1; Edmond B.

Young, "The Right Sort of Talk," *Biloxi Daily Herald*, November 12, 1908, 4; James A. Burns, "Letters," *Biloxi Daily Herald*, November 14, 1908, 1; and Alan Lomax, *Mister Jelly Roll: The Fortunes of Jelly Roll Morton, New Orleans Creole and Inventor of Jazz* (Berkeley: University of California Press, 1973), 143.

32. In his inaugural address, Mississippi governor Andrew Longino bravely expressed clear condemnation of the "defective public sentiment" that led to lynchings. Despite the passage in March 1900 of Longino's antilynching bill, which allowed a victim's family to sue the county for damages where the murder took place and allowed the removal from their job of a sheriff or constable who did not prevent a victim from being taken from jail, "lynching bees" continued throughout the state without repercussions. The *Atlanta Constitution* objected that antilynching laws "give abroad a false impression of the people of Mississippi." The *Hattiesburg Progress* wrote that when a victim's "heirs come moping around claiming the $2000 reward, or whatever it may be termed, they will go the same way." The June 9, 1900, *Daily Herald* included the statement "If Biloxi had performed all the lynching acts with which she is accredited by the newspapers, she would have to . . . import a fresh supply of negros." That very night, Henry Askew and Ed Russell, two men innocent of the murder of Christinia Winterstein, were repeatedly "tortured" and hung behind the Mississippi City railroad station; Biloxians denied they had any part in it and were vocal in condemning the action. The murders were blamed on (nonlocal) newspapers for having enflamed tempers and on visitors from New Orleans and elsewhere who had come to view the scene of the crime. One paper alleged that Judge Gleason and District Attorney White had overseen the torture. However, when Governor Longino and the state attorney general visited the coast, no affidavits were signed. As to the viability of the antilynching law, when an unnamed Black man in Gulfport made "some unnecessary comments" about the lynching of Askew and Russell, "a party of white men started out after him and it was expected that he would be reported missing." Other victims of lynching included Warren Stewart in Ocean Springs, 1901; Sam Adams in Pass Christian, 1903; and Dave Poe, Tom Ranston, and "two Jenkins brothers" in Vancleave in 1908. It was recorded that "male citizens both white and colored" took part in the lynching of Sam Adams. "Gov. Longino on Lynching," *Daily Herald*, February 8, 1900, 4; "The Adams Bill," *Daily Herald*, February 6, 1900, 4; "Anti-Lynch Law," *Daily Herald*, March 18, 1900, 9; "A Dead Letter," *Daily Herald*, May 12, 1900, 4; *Daily Herald*, June 9, 1900, 3; "Jackson County Mob Hangs Four Negroes," *Hattiesburg Daily News*, March 11, 1908, 1; "No Developments," *Daily Herald*, June 5, 1900, 1; "The Latest," *Daily Herald*, June 6, 1900, 1; "Saturday's Horror," *Daily Herald*, June 7, 1900, 1; "Lynched," *Daily Herald*, June 10, 1900, 1; "At High Tension," *Daily Herald*, June 10, 1900, 1; "Lynching in Mississippi," *Poplarville Free Press*, June 14, 1900, 2; "The Responsibility," *Daily Herald*, June 15, 1900, 4; "Mississippi City Lynching," *Sea Coast Echo*, June 16, 1900, 1; "City News," *Daily Herald*, June 12, 1900, 8; "Saturday Night's Work," *Daily Herald*, June 12, 1900, 4; "Lively Gulfport," *Daily Herald*, June 13, 1900, 8; *Daily Herald*, June 19, 1900, 4; "Have They Remorse," *Daily Herald*, June 24, 1900, 4; "City News," *Daily Herald*, July 29, 1900, 8; "Hanged and Shot," *Daily Herald*, February 3, 1901, 8; "Rapist Lynched," *Daily Herald*, November 6, 1903, 1; and "Coroners Jury," *Daily Herald*, November 9, 1903, 5.

33. Lomax, *Mister Jelly Roll*; Danielle Dorsey, "Dorks of Black History: Jelly Roll Morton," DanielleDorky.com, 2019; and Jim O'Neal, "Biloxi Blues: Jelly Roll Morton and Main Street," Mississippi Blues Trail Blogspot, May 26, 2010.

34. Both the Miley Hotel and Eagles' Nest were repeatedly raided for gambling and sale of alcohol. "City within a City," 6; Daniella DiRienzo, "Biloxi, Mississippi Was Once a Resort Destination Known for Illegal Gambling, Bootleg Whiskey, and Great Music," Only in Your State, January 10, 2021, https://www.onlyinyourstate.com/mississippi/biloxi-was-once-a-resort-destination-ms/; Daniella DiRienzo, "Most People Have No Idea There's a Drowned Island Hiding in the Mississippi Gulf," Only in Your State, August 8, 2016, https://www.onlyinyourstate.com/mississippi/drowned-isle-of-caprice-in-ms/; "Local Happenings," *Biloxi Herald*, June 17, 1893, 8; Chas Harrison, "For Sale," *Daily Herald*, March 15, 1934, 2; and "General Secretary Back in Office," *Meridian Echo*, November 1, 1950, 1.

35. Kahrl, *Land Was Ours*, 11, 56–57.

36. "Col. Patterson Speaks to Club," *Daily Herald*, June 4, 1943, 2.

37. "Public Road to Beauvoir," *Biloxi Herald*, August 11, 1888, 8; and "Beach Driveway Oiled," *Daily Herald*, June 21, 1922, 3.

38. "Harrison County People Stirred by Storm Damage," *Daily Herald*, October 5, 1915, 1–8.

39. "Mississippi," United States Census Bureau, 26; and Ray L. Bellande, "Streets and Roads," Biloxi Historical Society, accessed July 10, 2021, https://biloxihistoricalsociety.org/streets-and-roads.

40. "Work Progressing on Beach Road," *Daily Herald*, May 1, 1923, 4; "Warrenite Surfacing Completed Halfway," *Daily Herald*, July 25, 1923, 4; "Bricks Arrive for Street Work," *Daily Herald*, July 31, 1923, 3; and "To Complete Beach Drive in Two Weeks," *Daily Herald*, May 26, 1948, 1.

41. T. M. Evans, "Epitaphs Written by the Legislature," *Daily Herald*, May 23, 1924, 7.

42. "Coast Sand Beach Is Step Nearer Reality," *Daily Herald*, December 22, 1947, 1, 16.

43. "Seeks Summary Judgment Sand Beach Complaint," *Daily Herald*, February 8, 1961, 1.

44. Zack J. Van Landingham, Beach Integration, Harrison County, October 20, 1959, SSC 2-56-1-17, p. 1.

45. Minnie Walter Myers, *Romance and Realism of the Southern Gulf Coast* (Cincinnati: Robert Clarke Company, 1898), 106; Lee Owens Jr., interview with Dora Feazant, Center for Oral History and Cultural History, University of Southern Mississippi, June 12, 2010; and "19 N. F. A. Boys Made Trip to Biloxi, Last Week," *Southern Advocate*, April 26, 1941, 1, 4.

46. Kahrl, *Land Was Ours*, 54; and Clara Griffin Watson, interviewed by Angela Sartin, Community Bridges Oral History Project, Center for Oral History and Cultural History, October 28, 1999, 18–19.

47. Earl Napoleon Moore, interviewed by Angela Sartin, Community Bridges Oral History Project, Center for Oral History and Cultural History, November 9, 1999, 20; "Don't Ask Integration, Coast Negros Say," *Daily News*, October 6, 1959, in SSC 5-4-0-4; and Gilbert R. Mason with James Patterson Smith, *Beaches, Blood, and Ballots: A Black Doctor's Civil Rights Struggle* (Jackson: University Press of Mississippi, 2007), 51.

48. Zack J. Van Landingham, Memo To: Director, State Sovereignty Commission, Subject: Beach Integration, Harrison County, Mississippi, October 20, 1959, SSC 2-56-1-17, p. 1.

49. First, third, fifth quotes: "Negroes Had Beach Area Three Years Ago But Lost It Due to Number of Reasons," *Biloxi Daily Herald*, May 2, 1960, 9. Second quote: "Beach Suit Filed by US," *Times Picayune*, May 18, 1960, in SSC 5-4-0-70. See also "Major Hiller Clarifies Story on Use of Beach," *Daily Times*, date unreadable, in SSC, May 12, 1960, 5-4-0-65.

50. Robert C. Thomas to Director, State Sovereignty Commission, Subject: Harrison County NAACP Activities, June 27, 1960, SSC 2-56-1-41, pp. 1–3.

51. "Rights Agency Calls for Probe in Mississippi," *Daily Herald*, September 9, 1961, 7; and Tom Cook, "Outlay for 28-Mile Man-Made Project Doubled in Four Years," *Daily Herald*, April 16, 1959, 1.

CHAPTER TWO. STILL WATERS RUN DEEP:
THE BEGINNING OF A HERO'S JOURNEY

1. Mason, *Beaches*, 11.
2. Mason, *Beaches*, 6, 9–12.
3. "The Tiger" was a weekly column produced by the Writers' Club of Jim Hill Junior High School, published in the *Mississippi Enterprise*, a Black-run newspaper since 1938. "The Tiger," *Mississippi Enterprise*, October 31, 1942, 3; November 14, 1942, 4; November 21, 1942, 3; November 28, 1942, 4; and February 6, 1943, 3. See also "Tattling Tess," *Mississippi Enterprise*, May 5, 1945, 5.
4. "Names of Negro Candidates on Ballots in State First Time Since Reconstruction," *Jackson Advocate*, June 2, 1962, 1–8.
5. Mason, *Beaches*, 15–16.
6. Mason, *Beaches*, 3, 15.
7. William D. Boyce, "The American Boy Scout Movement and Black History, a Story," *African American Registry*, https://aaregistry.org/story/the-african-american-boy-scout-movement-a-story/.
8. Gilbert Mason, interview with Bill Ellison, "Mississippi Moments: Dr. Gilbert Mason—Healthcare and Civil Rights," Center for Oral History and Cultural Heritage, University of Southern Mississippi, February 19, 2018, https://www.iheart.com/podcast/256-mississippi-moments-podcas-30950668/episode/msm-559-dr-gilbert-r-mason-39213499/.
9. Mason, *Beaches*, 13–14.
10. Dr. Gilbert R. Mason Sr., interviewed by Larry Crowe, November 11, 2002, The HistoryMakers Digital Archive, Session 1, tape 2, story 10; and Mason, *Beaches*, 17, 19.
11. Mason, *Beaches*, 21.
12. Mason, *Beaches*, 25.
13. Aria M. Mason, "The Woman Behind the Man: The Life and Work of Natalie H. Mason," https://gilbertrmason.com/the-life-of-natalie-h-mason.
14. Mason, *Beaches*, 24–26.
15. Mason, *Beaches*, 30.
16. Mason, *Beaches*, 37.
17. Dr. Mason's book describes it as the "old Shoreham." The original Shoreham Hotel, known subsequently as the Old Shoreham, was torn down in 1929. Mason may have worked at the Omni Shoreham, which was converted from long-term residences to hotel rooms in 1950. Mason, *Beaches*, 28–31; "The Old Shoreham Hotel at 15th and H Streets NW," Streets of Washington: Stories and Images of Historic Washington D.C., January 3, 2010, http://

www.streetsofwashington.com/2010/01/old-shoreham-hotel-at-15th-and-h.html; Allison DiLiegro, "The Omni Shoreham: Washington DC's Grande Dame Full of Political History and Beatlemania," Storied Hotels, January 12, 2019, https://storiedhotels.com/washington-dc-hotels/the-omni-shoreham-washington-dcs-grande-dame-full-of-political-history-and-beatlemania/; and Samuel P. Perry Jr., "Contends Equality of Man Must Become a World-Wide Principle," *Jackson Advocate*, September 12, 1942, 2.

18. This text is largely limited to gender-conforming and binary pronouns by historical record. Pauli Murray was a dynamic personality, a lawyer, poet, educator, and activist. Murray's struggles with gender labels and sexuality are an excellent, though tragic, example demonstrating that lived experience and identity may not be reflected in the records. "Pauli Murray Organizes Howard Student Sit-Ins," Student Nonviolent Coordinating Committee Digital, https://snccdigital.org/events/pauli-murray-organizes-howard-student-sit-ins/; Julie Cohen and Betsy West, *My Name Is Pauli Murray*, Amazon Studios, September 17, 2021, Min. 00:25–00:29; and Pauli Murray, "A Blueprint for First Class Citizenship," *The Crisis*, 1944, 358–59.

19. Neil Gale, "Thompsons Cafeteria Restaurants of Chicago, Illinois," *Digital Research Library of Illinois History Journal*, December 31, 2016; Mark Jones, "Eat Anywhere! Mary Church Terrell, the Lost Laws, and the End of Segregation in D. C. Restaurants," WETA, June 8, 2017; and "Eat Anywhere: High Court Opens D. C. Restaurants," *Washington Afro-American*, June 9, 1953, 1, 20.

20. Mason, *Beaches*, 31.

21. Mason, interview with Bill Ellison, "Healthcare and Civil Rights."

22. Mason, *Beaches*, 31–32; and Mason, "Woman Behind the Man."

23. Dr. Gilbert R. Mason Sr., interviewed by Larry Crowe, November 11, 2002, The HistoryMakers Digital Archive, Session 1, tape 3, story 3; and Mason, *Beaches*, 37.

24. Mason, *Beaches*, 36.

25. As one of the youngest among her eight siblings, Natalie Mason had been "kept . . . out of the kitchen" and didn't know how to cook well as a young homemaker. Her son, Dr. Gilbert Mason Jr., later said the women's social clubs on the coast "took her under their wing," teaching her the basics of making a casserole, "bacon and eggs and grilled pork chops or steak." Gilbert Mason Jr., interview with author, May 5, 2022; and Mason, *Beaches*, 36, 59.

26. "Mayor, Doctor Stand Opposed," *Commercial Appeal*, August 19, 1960, in SSC 5-4-0-127.

27. Another Black doctor, Dr. William P. Kyle, listed in Biloxi, age seventy-two in the 1950 census, was reportedly a veterinarian. Mason, *Beaches*, 37; "Remembering the Struggle and Looking Back with Dr. Gilbert Mason Jr.," Go to Places Monthly, https://gotoplaces.wordpress.com/2013/02/05/1345/; and Gilbert Mason Jr., interview with author.

28. Gilbert Mason Jr., interview with author.

29. Gilbert Mason Jr., interview with author.

30. Mason, *Beaches*, 38; and Dr. Gilbert R. Mason Sr., interviewed by Larry Crowe, November 11, 2002, The HistoryMakers Digital Archive, Session 1, tape 3, story 4.

31. Dr. Gilbert R. Mason Sr., interviewed by Larry Crowe, November 11, 2002.

32. Mason, *Beaches*, 40; and Mason, interview with Bill Ellison, "Healthcare and Civil Rights."

33. Mason, interview with Bill Ellison, "Healthcare and Civil Rights."

34. "History," National Medical Association, accessed August 30, 2021, https://www.nmanet.org/page/History.

35. Mason, *Beaches*, 37.

36. Mason, *Beaches*, 46; and Gilbert Mason Jr., interview with author.

37. Mason, interview with Bill Ellison, "Healthcare and Civil Rights."

38. "Table 11. Infant Mortality Rates by Race: United States, Select Years 1950–2015," CDC, www.cdc.gov/nchs/data/hus/2016/011.pdf; Ashley H. Hirai et al., "Contributors to Excess Infant Mortality in the US South," *American Journal of Preventive Medicine* 46, no. 3 (2014): 219–27, https://doi.org/10.1016/j.amepre.2013.12.006; Cristina Novoa and Jamila Taylor, "Exploring African Americans' High Maternal and Infant Death Rates," Center for American Progress, February 1, 2018; David J. Kelly et al., "Three-Month-Olds, but Not Newborns, Prefer Own-Face Faces," *Developmental Science* 8, no. 6 (2005): F31–F36, https://doi.org/10.1111/j.1467-7687.2005.0434a.x; Sandy Sangrigoli and Scania de Schonen, "Recognition of Own-Race and Other-Race Faces by Three-Month Old Infants," *Journal of Child Psychology and Psychiatry* 45 (2004):1–9; and Kelly M. Hoffman et al., "Racial Bias in Pain Assessment," *Proceedings of the National Academy of Sciences* 113, no. 16 (2016): 4296–4301, https://doi.org/10.1073/pnas.1516047113.

39. "Table 11. Infant Mortality Rates by Race."

40. Chester Higgins, "Talking About," *Jet*, October 15, 1964, 47; and David Pilgrim, "What Was Jim Crow," Ferris State University, September 2000.

41. Mason, *Beaches*, 6.

CHAPTER THREE. RIPTIDES:
HOW BLACK TAXPAYERS WERE FORCED TO FUND THEIR OPPRESSION

1. Earl M. Lewis, "The Negro Voter in Mississippi," *Journal of Negro Education* 26, no. 3 (1957): 329–50, https://doi.org/10.2307/2293416; and Susan Cianci Salvatore et al., "Civil Rights in America: Racial Voting Rights," National Park Service, 2009, 4–72, https://www.nps.gov/subjects/tellingallamericansstories/upload/CivilRights_VotingRights.pdf.

2. Salvatore et al., "Civil Rights in America," 8, 6–7, 13; and *Reconstruction: America's Unfinished Revolution, 1863–1877* (New York: Harper & Row, 1988), quoted in John Lewis and Archie E. Allen, "Black Voter Registration Efforts in the South," *Notre Dame Law Review* 48 (1972): 115, https://scholarship.law.nd.edu/cgi/viewcontent.cgi?article=2861&context=ndlr.

3. In 1870 and 1871, Congress passed the Enforcement Acts, making it a federal crime for groups of private individuals to band together and attempt to deprive others of their civil rights by violence or intimidation (such as patrolling the streets, visibly armed, on election day). Under these acts, thousands of Klansmen were prosecuted (and a few hundred were actually convicted). But shortly afterward, following the Colfax Massacre in Louisiana, the Supreme Court undermined the acts by ruling in the *United States v. Cruikshank* that only state officials, not private individuals, could be prosecuted thus. Salvatore et al., "Civil Rights in America," 10.

4. Salvatore et al., "Civil Rights in America," 27; Steven F. Lawson, *Black Ballots: Voting Rights in the South, 1944–1969* (Lanham, MD: Lexington Books, 1999), 56; and James W. Silver, *Mississippi: The Closed Society* (New York: Harcourt, Brace & World, 1964), 16.

5. Ronald G. Shafer, "The 'Mississippi Plan' to Keep Blacks from Voting in 1890: 'We Came Here to Exclude the Negro,'" *Washington Post*, May 1, 2021, https://www.washingtonpost.com/history/2021/05/01/mississippi-constitution-voting-rights-jim-crow/.

6. Shafer, "'Mississippi Plan.'"

7. Lewis and Allen, "Black Voter Registration," 107–8; Mary Frances Berry, *Racial and Ethnic Tensions in American Communities: Poverty, Inequality, and Discrimination*, vol. 7, The Mississippi Delta Report (Washington, DC: Commission on Civil Rights, 2001), 87; Salvatore et al., "Civil Rights in America," 12, 22; Marjorie Julian Spruill and Jesse Spruill Wheeler, "Mississippi Women and the Woman Suffrage Amendment," *Mississippi History Now*, December 2001, http://www.mshistorynow.mdah.ms.gov/articles/245/mississippi-women-and-the-woman-suffrage-amendment; Anna North, "The 19th Amendment Didn't Give Women the Right to Vote," *Vox*, August 18, 2020, https://www.vox.com/2020/8/18/21358913/19th-amendment-ratified-anniversary-women-suffrage-vote; and Meilan Solly, "What the First Women Voters Experienced When Registering for the 1920 Election," *Smithsonian Magazine*, July 30, 2020, https://www.smithsonianmag.com/history/what-first-women-voters-experienced-when-registering-1920-election-180975435/.

8. Lewis and Allen, "Black Voter Registration," 121; and Berry, *Racial and Ethnic Tensions*, 87.

9. Berry, *Racial and Ethnic Tensions*, 88.

10. Salvatore et al., "Civil Rights in America," 14.

11. Shafer, "'Mississippi Plan.'"

12. Salvatore et al., "Civil Rights in America," 53.

13. Abraham L. Davis and Barbara L. Graham, *The Supreme Court, Race, and Civil Rights* (Thousand Oaks, CA: Sage Publications, 1995), 51.

14. "Jim Crow Laws," National Park Service, April 17, 2018, https://www.nps.gov/malu/learn/education/jim_crow_laws.htm.

15. "Earl Brewer = Jeff D. Truly," *Daily Herald*, May 21, 1907, 1; "Judge Jeff Truly Is Not the Man for Governor," *Sea Coast Echo*, June 1, 1907, 1; and Jeff Truly, *Artificially Stimulated Immigration* (Jackson, MS: Tucker Printing House, 1907), in Mississippi Department of Archives and History, Broadside file/Politics/20th century/Folder 4/1907/2.

16. Stuart Grayson Noble, *Forty Years of the Public Schools in Mississippi*, Contributions to Education, no. 94 (New York: Columbia University, 1918), 14, 96.

17. Robert A. Brady and Vernon J. Ehlers, *Black Americans in Congress 1870–2007* (Washington, DC: Office of History and Preservation, US Government Printing Office, 2008), 181.

18. "Earl Brewer = Jeff D. Truly," 1.

19. M. V. O'Shea, *Public Education in Mississippi* (Jackson, MS: Jackson Printing Company, 1925), 40–41, 327–28, 334, https://babel.hathitrust.org/cgi/pt?id=uc1.$b66041&view=1up&seq=1.

20. O'Shea, *Public Education in Mississippi*, 9, 325–35.

21. A. A. Kincannon, "Manner of Apportioning Common School Fund," *Biennial Report of the State Superintendent of Public Education to the Legislature of Mississippi for Scholastic Years 1897-98 and 1898-99* (Jacksonville, FL: Vance Printing Co., 1900), insert 1.

22. Berry, *Racial and Ethnic Tensions*, 44.

23. Charles C. Bolton, "Mississippi's School Equalization Program, 1945–1954: 'A Last Gasp to Try to Maintain a Segregated Educational System,'" *Journal of Southern History* 66, no. 4 (2000): 789–90, https://doi.org/10.2307/2588011.

24. Bolton, "Mississippi's School Equalization Program," 786.

25. Okianer Christian Dark, "The Role of Howard University School of Law in *Brown v. Board of Education*," *Washington History* 16, no. 2 (2004): 83–85, http://www.jstor.org/stable/40073398.

26. Lewis and Allen, "Black Voter Registration," 120.

27. "Is Mississippi Hushing Up a Lynching? Mississippi Gunmen Take Life of Militant Negro Minister," *Jet*, May 26, 1955, 8–11; and A. H. McCoy to Herbert Bromwell, May 11, 1955, Jackson, Mississippi, SSC 2-5-2-36.

28. "Biography," Americans Who Tell the Truth, https://www.americanswhotellthetruth.org/portraits/clyde-kennard; Timothy J. Minchin and John A. Salmond, "'The Saddest Story of the Whole Movement': The Clyde Kennard Case and the Search for Racial Reconciliation in Mississippi, 1955–2007," *Journal of Mississippi History* 71 (Fall 2009): 191–234; and Steven A. Drizin et al., "Pardon Docket No. 06-0005 Before the Honorable Haley Barbour, Governor, State of Mississippi, in the Matter of Clyde Kennard," 2006, https://wwws.law.northwestern.edu/legalclinic/wrongfulconvictions/exonerations/documents/mskennardexhibits.pdf.

29. "Declaration of Constitutional Principles," March 12, 1956, 1–2, https://tigerprints.clemson.edu/cgi/viewcontent.cgi?article=2379&context=strom.

30. "Aims to Forestall New Coast Clash," *Jackson Daily News*, April 26, 1960, in SSC 5-4-0-37.

31. The SSC also investigated suspected cases of "passing" as white or Mexican. In one instance, it considered conspiring to get a young man drafted and sent to Vietnam to break up his suspected interracial relationship, at the request of the young woman's parents. Zack J. Van Landingham, letter to M. W. High, February 4, 1960, SSC 2-56-1-23; and Erle Johnston Jr. to Honorable Tom Scarbrough, Investigator, Subject: Raymond Carroll, January 15, 1965, SSC 2-56-2-74.

32. James Dickerson, *Dixie's Dirty Secret: The True Story of How the Government, the Media, and the Mob Conspired to Combat Integration and the Vietnam Antiwar Movement* (Armonk, NY: M. E. Sharpe, 1998), 27; and Zack Van Landingham to J. P. Coleman, Subject: B. L. Bell Informant-Administrative, January 12, 1959, SSC 2-10-0-6, pp. 1–3.

33. Zack J. Van Landingham to Director, State Sovereignty Commission, Subject: NAACP, Gulfport, Mississippi, June 2, 1959, SSC 2-56-1-12, p. 2; and Zack J. Van Landingham to Director, State Sovereignty Commission, Subject: NAACP, Gulfport, Mississippi, February 13, 1959, SSC 2-56-1-5, p. 2.

34. "Beach Suit Filed by MS," *Times Picayune*, May 18, 1960, in SSC 5-4-0-70.

35. P. D. East, "East Side," *Petal Paper*, October 20, 1960, 1.

36. For examples of WCC children's books, see James W. Silver, "Mississippi: The Closed Society," *Journal of Southern History* 30, no. 1 (1964): 3–34, https://doi.org/10.2307/2205371; and Zack J. Van Landingham, Memo to: File, Subject: NAACP, Biloxi, Mississippi, March 21, 1960, SSC 2-56-1-26.

37. "Claim South Hostile to KKK," *Hattiesburg American*, April 7, 1958, 6; "Report Coleman Did Good Job at Press Meet," *Daily Herald*, June 24, 1957, 1; "Integration Ban," *Daily Herald*, September 11, 1954; "Klan Meets," *Daily Herald*, June 11, 1960, 22; "Ku Klux Klan," History.

com, February 4, 2022, https://www.history.com/topics/reconstruction/ku-klux-klan; and "Attends KKK Meeting," *Daily Herald*, July 6, 1962, 8.

38. Martin Luther King Jr., "The Look to the Future," Speech, Monteagle, Tennessee, September 2, 1957, Duke University Repository, https://repository.duke.edu/dc/broadsides/bdsal40033.

39. Hal C. DeCell, Memo to: Ney M. Gore, Subject: Tupelo Investigation, October 16, 1957; and Robert C. Thomas to Director SSC, "Subject: Harrison County NAACP Activities," June 27, 1960, SSC 2-56-1-41, p. 2.

40. These appeals for mutual aid occurred even at a global level. For example, the Soviet Union used images and critiques of American race relations in its anti-American propaganda during the Cold War and succeeded in drawing Black American immigrants to the Soviet Union in search of liberation from racialized pressures. See Sanford Goldner, *The Jewish People and the Fight for Negro Rights* (Los Angeles: Committee for Negro-Jewish Relations, 1953); Gus Hall, *Marxism and Negro Liberation* (New York: New Century Publishers, 1951); Julia Ioffe, "The History of Russian Involvement in America's Race Wars," *The Atlantic*, October 17, 2017; Tom Scarbrough, "Harrison County," March 23, 1964, SSC 2-56-2-48, pp. 1–6; J. E. Stockstill, Letter to Rev. Richard Ellerbrake, July 11, 1960, SSC 7-0-1-156, pp. 1–3; Zack J. Van Landingham, Memo to Director State Sovereignty Commission, Subject: Camp Landon August 11, 1959, SSC 2-56-1-14; Zack J. Van Landingham to Director State Sovereignty Commission, Subject: NAACP, Gulfport, Mississippi, February 16, 1959, SSC 2-56-1-6; A. L. Hopkins, Title: B'Nai B'Rith Meeting at the Sun-N-Sand Motel, Biloxi, Mississippi, December 30, 1960, SSC 2-56-1-63; and Tom Scarbrough, Title: COFO Rental of Property at Point Cadet in Harrison County, Mississippi, October 19, 1964, SSC 2-56-2-62.

CHAPTER FOUR. WADING IN: PETITION, REJECTION, AND "OPERATION SURF"

1. Zack J. Van Landingham, Memorandum to Director, State Sovereignty Commission, Subject: NAACP, Gulfport, Mississippi, February 16, 1959, SSC 1-23-0-30, p. 1.

2. McDonnell is sometimes recorded as "McDonald." Zack J. Van Landingham, Memorandum to Director, State Sovereignty Commission, Subject: NAACP, Gulfport, Mississippi, February 16, 1959, SSC 1-23-0-30, pp. 1–2; and "Negro Doctor Breaks Color Line at Biloxi," *Clarion Ledger*, April 18, 1960, in SSC 5-4-0-14.

3. Zack J. Van Landingham, Memo to: Director State Sovereignty Commission, Subject: NAACP, Gulfport, Mississippi, June 2, 1959, SSC 2-56-1-12, pp. 1–2.

4. Hal DeCell, Note, December 3, 1958, SSC 2-5-1-55; Hal C. DeCell, Note, SSC 2-5-2-1; and Mason, *Beaches*, 45.

5. Hal C. DeCell, "Note," December 4, 1958, SSC 2-56-1-2.

6. Zack J. Van Landingham, Memo to Director, State Sovereignty Commission, Subject: NAACP, Gulfport, Mississippi, June 2, 1959, SSC 2-56-1-12, p. 2.

7. Mason, *Beaches*, 49–50.

8. Mason, *Beaches*, 26.

9. Camp Attawah took its name from the Choctaw language, which Boy Scout council members took to mean "break." The *New Choctaw Dictionary* does not show any word

with that spelling, but all words that appear to be in that phonetic family have meanings associated with being or residing for a while in one place. Dr. Joel O. Tate and Joseph N. Austin—figures associated with the desegregation of Biloxi beach—were among those who helped support and work with Camp Attawah and its council. See "Dam Completed at Negro Camp Site," *Daily Herald*, December 17, 1951, 19; J. H. C. Thomas, "Pine Burr Council Has Peppy, Powerful Program," *Hattiesburg American*, December 24, 1951, 28; "Troop Concludes Week's Camping," *Daily Herald*, August 5, 1950, 20; "Plans Completed for Central Lodge at Negro Scout Camp," *Hattiesburg American*, March 5, 1952, 3; "Negro Leaders in Gulfport Map Plans for Scout Camp Funds," *Daily Herald*, March 29, 1952, 5; "Colored Scout Camp Program Director Named," *Hattiesburg American*, June 7, 1952, 9; "Negro Boy Scout Camp Attaway to Open August 4," *Daily Herald*, August 1, 1957, 34; and Chahta Anumpa Tosholi Himona, *New Choctaw Dictionary* (Durant, OK: Choctaw Print Services, 2016), 31–32.

10. Gilbert Mason Jr., interview with author.

11. "Biloxi, MS, Weather History," Keesler AFB Station, May 4, 1959, https://www.wunderground.com/history/daily/us/ms/biloxi/KBIX/date/1959-5-4.

12. Gilbert Mason Jr., email message to author, June 2, 2021.

13. Saucier may also have been catcher for the historic Biloxi Black Cats. See "Black Cats Open Season with Mobile," *Biloxi Daily Herald*, April 16, 1960, 17.

14. Adell Lott, interview with Melissa Hall, April 24, 2010, Oral History Program of the University of Southern Mississippi, 2, https://usm.access.preservica.com/uncategorized/IO_ba7c2de5-c7e7--44d2-af56-5f04bde051e5/; and Krystal Allan, "Commemorating 'Bloody Wade-In' 50 Years Later," WLOX, April 25, 2010, https://www.wlox.com/story/12370959/commemorating-bloody-wade-in-50-years-later/.

15. Mason, *Beaches*, 52; Gilbert Mason Jr., email message to author; and Dr. Gilbert R. Mason Sr., interviewed by Larry Crowe, November 11, 2002, The HistoryMakers Digital Archive, Session 1, tape 3, story 7.

16. Mason, *Beaches*, 52; Butler, "Mississippi State Sovereignty Commission," 107–48; and Gilbert Mason Jr., interview with author.

17. Mason, *Beaches*, 52.

18. Adell Lott, interview with Melissa Hall.

19. Different sources give different accounts of this interaction; it is unclear if that is a product of imperfect memory or if different people recalled different moments in the interaction. For example, Dr. Mason records the police officer's language in a less vulgar way. See Mason, *Beaches*, 52; and Murray Saucier testimony, *United States v. Harrison County, Mississippi, et al.*, Civil Action No. 2262, U. S. District Court for the Southern District of Mississippi, 944–49, quoted in Butler, "Mississippi State Sovereignty Commission," 114.

20. Murray Saucier testimony, quoted in Butler, "Mississippi State Sovereignty Commission," 114.

21. In 1959, City Hall was still in its brick building on Main Street. In 1960, it moved to its present location, into the building that had formerly been the Biloxi post office. Ray L. Bellande, "Buildings, Architects, and Contractors: 1895," Biloxi Historical Society, https://biloxihistoricalsociety.org/buildings-architects-and-contractors; and "The Early Years," Biloxi, Mississippi, 2008, https://biloxi.ms.us/pdf/centennialdisplay.pdf.

22. Felix H. Dunn to Dewey Lawrence, May 22, 1959, Lawrence to Dunn, June 5, 1959, Box 158, Mississippi State Records Center, MDAH, quoted in Butler, "Mississippi State Sovereignty Commission," 115; and Zack J. Van Landingham, Beach Integration, Harrison County, October 20, 1959, SSC 2-56-1-17, p. 1.

23. Mason, *Beaches*, 53.

24. As an example of small differing accounts, Dr. Mason quotes Quave saying, "We're going to leave you down there," instead of the threat of arrest. Mason's book also says Natalie Mason came to the courthouse that day and heard the mayor threaten her husband. Natalie Mason, who did not drive, may have been attended by family friend Christopher Rosado. Mason, *Beaches*, 53–54; and Gilbert Mason testimony, *U. S. v. Harrison Co.*, No. 2262, 574–75, quoted in Butler, "Mississippi State Sovereignty Commission," 114.

25. Felix H. Dunn to Dewey Lawrence, May 22, 1959, Lawrence to Dunn, June 5, 1959, Box 158, Mississippi State Records Center, MDAH, quoted in Butler, "Mississippi State Sovereignty Commission," 115.

26. Zack J. Van Landingham, To: Director, SSC, Subject: NAACP, Gulfport, Mississippi, June 2, 1959, SSC 2-56-1-12.

27. Zack J. Van Landingham, To: Director, SSC, Subject: NAACP, Gulfport, Mississippi, June 2, 1959, SSC 2-56-1-12, p. 1.

28. "Looking Around," *Gulfport Pictorial Review*, July 3, 1959, in SSC 2-56-1-32.

29. Mason, *Beaches*, 56.

30. "Our History," NAACP, accessed May 6, 2022, https://naacp.org/about/our-history; "The Civil Rights Act of 1964: A Long Struggle for Freedom," Library of Congress, accessed May 6, 2022, https://www.loc.gov/exhibits/civil-rights-act/civil-rights-era.html; Mason, *Beaches*, 102–3; Butler, "Mississippi State Sovereignty Commission," 134, footnote 53; and Gilbert Mason Jr., interview with author.

31. Zack J. Van Landingham, Memo to: File 5-4, Subject: Beach Integration, Harrison County, Mississippi, May 4, 1960, SSC 2-56-1-33.

32. "Signers of Gulf Coast Beach Use Petition Lose Jobs," *Jackson Advocate*, October 17, 1959, 4; and Zack J. Van Landingham, Memo to File 5-4, Subject: Beach Integration, Harrison County, Mississippi, May 4, 1960, SSC 2-56-1-33, pp. 2–6.

33. Saul Dorsey, "Republic of New Afrika," Center for Study of Southern Culture, accessed September 23, 2021, http://mississippiencyclopedia.org/entries/republic-of-new-afrika/.

34. Isabelle Taft, "Black-Owned Businesses Once Thrived in Historic Coast Neighborhood," *Sun Herald*, February 26, 2021, https://www.sunherald.com/news/local/counties/harrison-county/article249516305.html.

35. "In Re: Lynching of Willlie Kirkland at Thomasville, Georgia," Howard Washington Raper Papers, Series 3, Box 15, Folder 749, SHC, quoted in Stanonis, *Faith in Bikinis*, 111.

36. Zack J. Van Landingham, To: File, Subject: NAACP, Hancock County, Mississippi, February 4, 1960, SSC 2-56-1-22, p. 2; and Zack J. Van Landingham, To: Director, SSC, Subject: NAACP, Gulfport, Mississippi, June 2, 1959, SSC 2-56-1-12.

37. Butler, "Mississippi State Sovereignty Commission," 121.

38. Joseph Austin testimony, *U. S. v. Harrison Co.*, No. 2262, 850–57, quoted in Butler, "Mississippi State Sovereignty Commission," 116; and "4 Miss. Negroes Petition for Use of Beach," *Jet*, October 22, 1959, 5.

39. Mason, *Beaches*, 56–57.

40. "Negroes Seek Use of Harrison Beach," *Daily Herald*, October 5, 1959, 1.

41. Zack J. Van Landingham, Beach Integration, Harrison County, SSC 2-56-1-17, p. 6.

42. Richard Ellerbrake, "From a Minister There . . . a Report on Biloxi," *Petal Paper*, May 19, 1960, 2.

43. "Local Happenings," *Biloxi Herald*, June 17, 1893, 8.

44. "Negroes Seek," October 5, 1959, 1.

45. Bob Thomas, Subject: Beach Disturbances, Biloxi, SSC 5-4-0-50, p. 3: and "Mayor, Doctor Stand Opposed," *Commercial Appeal*, August 19, 1960, SSC 5-4-0-127.

46. "Biloxi Seafood Workers Picket Meeting of NMU," *Daily Herald*, May 23, 1957, 1; "Hear Arguments in Biloxi Man's Assault Trial," *Daily Herald*, June 20, 1958, 1; and Zack J. Van Landingham, Memo to: Director, State Sovereignty Commission, Subject: Beach Integration, Harrison County, Mississippi, November 4, 1959, SSC 2-56-1-19.

47. Mason, *Beaches*, 60.

48. "Negroes Seek Use," 2.

49. Zack J. Van Landingham, To: Director SSC, Subject: NAACP, Harrison County, Mississippi, October 14, 1959, SSC 2-56-1-16, pp. 1–3.

50. Zack J. Van Landingham, To: Director SSC, Subject: NAACP, Harrison County, Mississippi, October 14, 1959, SSC 2-56-1-16, pp. 1–3.

51. "Negroes Seek Use," 1.

52. Mason, *Beaches*, 58; "Negro Told 'Mob' Out After Him," *Daily News*, October 7, 1959, in SSC 5-4-0-6; and "Dr. Gilbert Mason Son of Onetime Jackson Barber Arrested in Biloxi Beach Incident," *Jackson Advocate*, April 23, 1960, 1, 7.

53. Alice (nee Flowers) White, "Signers of Gulf Coast Beach Use Petition Lose Jobs," *Jackson Advocate*, October 17, 1959, 4.

54. "Signers of Gulf Coast Beach Use Petition Lose Jobs," *Jackson Advocate*, October 17, 1959, 1, 4.

55. "Don't Ask Integration Coast Negroes Say," *Daily News*, October 6, 1959, in SSC 5-4-0-3.

56. "Negro Physician Is Arrested by Biloxi Police," *Daily Herald*, April 18, 1960, 2; and "Coast Beaches Stay Deserted," *Times Picayune*, May 2, 1960, SSC 5-4-0-46.

57. "Never Requested Beach for Negro NAACP Declares," *Daily Herald*, May 19, 1960, 1; and "Signers," *Jackson Advocate*, October 17, 1959, 4.

58. "Signers," 4.

59. "Second Wooden Cross Is Burned in Coast Area," *Daily Herald*, October 10, 1959, 1; Austin testimony, quoted in Butler, "Mississippi State Sovereignty Commission," 118, footnote; "Tension Simmers in Biloxi," *State Times*, April 25, 1960, SSC 5-4-0-19; and Dickerson, *Dixie's Dirty Secret*, 27.

60. Mason, *Beaches*, 58.

61. Mr. Stanley "Rip" Daniels interviews Dr. Gilbert R. Mason, WJZD-FM, [title and date unknown]; and Mason, *Beaches*, 83.

62. Richard D. DeShazo, Robert Smith, and Leigh Baldwin Skipworth, "Black Physicians and the Struggle for Civil Rights: Lessons from the Mississippi Experience—Part 2: Their Lives and Experiences," *American Journal of Medicine* 127, no. 11 (November 2014), https://www.amjmed.com/article/S0002-9343(14)00492-6/pdf; and J. Todd Moye, *Let the People*

Decide: Black Freedom and White Resistance Movements in Sunflower County, Mississippi, 1945–1986 (Chapel Hill: University of North Carolina Press, 2004), 85–86.

63. Mason, *Beaches*, 60.

64. The self-appointed guardians included at least two women, Myrtle Bridges Davis and Blanche Elzy. In addition to the list of participants in Dr. Mason's autobiography, Lee Owens Jr. identified himself as a guard of Mason's residence. See Mason, *Beaches*, 59; Lee Owens Jr., interview with Dora Feazant, Center for Oral History and Cultural History, University of Southern Mississippi, June 12, 2010, 3:45–4:20; Laura Ewen Blokker, "East Biloxi African American and Civil Rights Historic Resources Survey 2017," 12; "Myrtle's Obituary," Marshall Funeral Home, October 2015, https://www.marshallfh.com/obituary/5056736; Gilbert Mason Jr., interview with author; and "Game Badly Protected," *Daily Herald*, December 21, 1900, 6.

65. The SSC appears to have stepped up its investigations in Biloxi at this time, escalating from recording license plate numbers in the parking lot to sending someone as a microphoned plant to sit in the front row of the Southern Christian Ministers' Conference of Mississippi as the attendees spoke on nonviolent resistance. The motto of the conference was "We Will Not Hate; We Will Not Retaliate; We Will Appreciate." Zack J. Van Landingham, Memo To: Governor Ross R. Barnett, Subject: Attempted Beach Integration, Mississippi Gulf Coast, February 4, 1960, SSC 2-56-1-21; and G. R. Haughton, *The Fall Session of the Southern Christian Ministers' Conference of Mississippi Presents: An Institute on Nonviolent Resistance to Segregation* (Jackson, MS: Pearl Street A. M. E. Church, 1959), 1–7, in SSC 2-126-1-29.

66. Zack J. Van Landingham, Memo To: File, Subject: NAACP, Harrison County, Mississippi, February 5, 1960, SSC 2-56-1-24.

67. Zack J. Van Landingham, Memo To: File, Subject: NAACP, Harrison County, Mississippi, February 5, 1960, SSC 2-56-1-24.

68. Zack J. Van Landingham, Memo To: Governor Ross R. Barnett, Subject: Attempted Beach Integration, Mississippi Gulf Coast, February 4, 1960, SSC 2-56-1-21, p. 6.

69. Zack J. Van Landingham, Beach Integration, Harrison County, SSC 2-56-1-17, p. 3; Bob Thomas to Governor Ross Barnett, Subject: Beach Disturbances, Gulfport, Harrison Co., Miss., SSC 5-4-0-51, pp. 1–3; and "Never Requested," *Daily Herald*, May 19, 1960, 1.

70. "Barnett Will Expose Forces Behind Mixing," *Daily Herald*, February 7, 1959, 13.

71. Mason, *Beaches*, 61.

72. Gilbert Mason Jr., interview with author.

73. Lott, interview with Melissa Hall, 3.

74. Gilbert Mason Jr., interview with author.

75. Gilbert Mason Jr., interview with author.

76. "Negro Physician Is Arrested by Biloxi Police," *Daily Herald*, April 18, 1960, 2.

77. Mason, *Beaches*, 63.

78. "Negro Jailed for White Beach Swim," *State Times*, April 18, 1960, in SSC 2-56-1-31.

79. Mason affidavit, May 3, 1960, NAACP Papers, quoted in Butler, "Mississippi State Sovereignty Commission," 124.

80. "Delay Decision in Mason Case in Biloxi Court," *Daily Herald*, April 19, 1960, 10.

81. Gilbert Mason Jr., interview with author.

82. Gilbert Mason Jr., interview with author; and Mason, *Beaches*, 62.

83. "Signers," *Jackson Advocate*, October 17, 1959, 4.

84. Zack J. Van Landingham, Memo to File 5-4, Subject: Beach Integration, Harrison County, Mississippi, May 4, 1960, SSC 2-56-1-33, p. 3.

85. Zack J. Van Landingham, Memo to File 5-4, Subject: Beach Integration, Harrison County, Mississippi, May 4, 1960, SSC 2-56-1-33; Wilson Evans II, interview with Dr. Orley B. Caudill, Center for Oral History and Cultural History, University of Southern Mississippi, June 11, 1981, 18; and "MS Honors Coast Civil Rights Activist," WLOX, July 2, 2011, https://www.wlox.com/story/15018161/ms-honors-coast-civil-rights-activist/.

86. "Negro Doctor Breaks Color Line at Biloxi," *Clarion Ledger*, April 18, 1960, in SSC 5-4-0-14.

87. "Traffic Charges Made Against Negro's Lawyer," *Daily Herald*, April 19, 1960, 10; and Bob Thomas, Subject: Beach Disturbances, Biloxi, SSC 5-4-0-50, p. 2.

88. Tom Scarbrough, Title: Harrison County, January 16, 1961, SSC 2-56-1-77; and "Trial of Beach Demonstrators Ends at Biloxi," *Daily Herald*, June 28, 1963, 1–2.

89. "Delay Decision," 10.

90. "Delay Decision," 10.

91. "Negro Physician Is Arrested," 2.

92. Bob Thomas, Subject: Beach Disturbances, Biloxi, SSC 5-4-0-50, p. 2.

93. Bob Thomas, Subject: Beach Disturbances, Biloxi, SSC 5-4-0-50, pp. 2–3.

94. The Pass Christian chief of police, Milton Ladiner, refuted a rumor that over a hundred Black people had gathered on the Pass Christian beach earlier in the week, "trying to get put in jail." Quoted in Bob Thomas, Subject: Beach Disturbances, Biloxi, SSC 5-4-0-50, p. 3.

95. Bob Thomas, Subject: Beach Disturbances, Biloxi, SSC 5-4-0-50, p. 1.

96. Several others, including Knox Walker and the president of the local chapter of the International Longshoremen Association, Wilson Evans, also owned shares of the Negro Juke Box and Cigarette Machine. Vending machine merchant Phillip Pelman of Gulfport said his machines were taken out of Harrison County, so Sheriff Dedeaux could give his spots to Dr. Dunn, allegedly as a bribe to stop beach desegregation efforts. Dunn, Evans, Walker, and others were alleged to also be partners in the Mississippi Valley Produce Company, which, through the "influence" of Evans, was supposedly given "first chance to purchase bananas of a certain grade . . . at the Port of Gulfport." Zack J. Van Landingham, Memo to File 5-4, Subject: Beach Integration, Harrison County, Mississippi, May 4, 1960, SSC 2-56-1-33, pp. 4–5; Bob Thomas, Subject: Beach Disturbances, Biloxi, SSC 5-4-0-50, p. 4; and "Alleged Facts in This Case That Cannot Be Confirmed," SSC 2-57-0-28, p. 1.

97. Bob Thomas, Subject: Beach Disturbances, Biloxi, SSC 5-4-0-50, p. 2.

98. Bob Thomas, Subject: Beach Disturbances, Biloxi, SSC 5-4-0-50, p. 3.

CHAPTER FIVE. BLOOD ON THE SAND, CAUSE OF INJURY: "INTEGRATIONAL"

1. "42 Seniors to Graduate from Nichols High," *Daily Herald*, May 31, 1961, 18.

2. In Ethel (Rainey) Clay's interview, she answers a question about the summer of 1960 with a reference to "the students who had the hoses put on them." My gratitude to the reader who pointed out Clay could only mean the violence in Birmingham in 1964, and she had either conflated her memories or, at least, the order of her wording could be mistakenly read

that way. Ethel R. Clay, interview with Louis Kyriakoudes, Mississippi Oral History Program, University of Southern Mississippi, April 24, 2010, 2–3, 11.

3. Mason, *Beaches*, 67.

4. Bob Thomas, Subject: Beach Disturbances, Biloxi, SSC 5-4-0-50, p. 5.

5. Mason affidavit, quoted in Butler, "Mississippi State Sovereignty Commission," 124; Bob Thomas, Subject: Beach Disturbances, Biloxi, SSC 5-4-0-50, p. 6; and Zack J. Van Landingham, Memo to: File 5-4, Subject: Beach Integration, Harrison County, Mississippi, May 4, 1960, SSC 2-56-1-33, p. 4.

6. Bob Thomas, Subject: Beach Disturbances, Biloxi, SSC 5-4-0-50, p. 3.

7. Gilbert Mason Jr., interview with author; and Richard Ellerbrake, "Report from Biloxi, Mississippi, Back Bay Mission No. 3," May 31, 1961, 2–5.

8. "Racial Violence Erupts at Biloxi," *Daily Herald*, April 25, 1960, 1.

9. Bob Thomas, Subject: Beach Disturbances, Biloxi, SSC 5-4-0-50, p. 3.

10. Clemon Jimerson Sr., interview with author, May 12, 2022.

11. Clemon P. Jimerson, interview with Curtis Austin, Mississippi Oral History Program, University of Southern Mississippi, April 24, 2010, 7.

12. Bobby C. Hope, interview with Elaine Fontas, Mississippi Oral History Program, University of Southern Mississippi, April 24, 2010, 2–5; and Clemon Jimerson Sr., interview with author.

13. Clemon Jimerson Sr. reports the first group as being closer to the Old Biloxi Cemetery, at about 1178 Beach Blvd. Mason, *Beaches*, 67; and "Racial Violence Erupts," 1.

14. Butler, "Mississippi State Sovereignty Commission," 126.

15. Bobby C. Hope, interview with Elaine Fontas, 3; and Mason, *Beaches*, 68.

16. Ethel R. Clay, interview by Louis Kyriakoudes, 8.

17. One unusual observer of the attacks was actor John Carroll. Carroll had been coming to Biloxi since October of the previous year and had been present at Sheriff Dedeaux's notorious election campaign speech. He had met Dedeaux in New Orleans and been convinced to move the planned location of a boat manufactory and a television show ("Duke of Orleans/Mississippi") to the area. It does not appear either plan was ever acted upon. During the day, Carroll bailed out a Black youth from New Orleans who had been arrested for an expired license and obstructing traffic on a motorcycle. It was noted that Carroll put his arm around the shoulders of the youth the whole time and that this type of interaction was something he often engaged in "for public relations," according to a friend. Carroll continued to observe the riot alongside Dedeaux. "John Carroll on Coast to Do Show, Build Plant," *Daily Herald*, October 16, 1959, 14; Bob Thomas, Subject: Beach Disturbances, Biloxi, SSC 5-4-0-50, p. 5; and Jim Lund, "African Americans Stage a Wade-In, Whites Watch from Seawall," *Daily Herald*, April 24, 1960, https://www.wlox.com/2019/05/15/community-comes-together-remember-biloxi-beach-wade-ins/.

18. Clemon Jimerson Sr., interview with author.

19. Zack J. Van Landingham, Memo to File 5-4, Subject: Beach Integration, Harrison County, Mississippi, May 4, 1960, 4.

20. "Racial Violence Erupts," 1.

21. Jim Lund, "A Group of Whites Chase Blacks," *Daily Herald*, April 24, 1960, https://www.sunherald.com/article145247704.html.

22. Alex Poinsett of *Jet* reported in the May 12, 1960, issue that Ellis Brown was the man Dr. Man saved from being beaten. He also listed Brown as being nineteen years old. According to the 1950 census, Ellis Brown would have been thirty-four in 1960. The *Daily Herald* reported that Joe Lonberger and Gilmore Fielder, like Dr. Mason, were arrested at the beach for "fighting nearby . . . after they had been attacked." They were ages eighteen and twenty-one. In subsequent interviews, Mason always listed the latter two as being the ones he intervened for. Dr. Gilbert R. Mason Sr. (The HistoryMakers A2002.202), interviewed by Larry Crowe, November 11, 2002, The HistoryMakers Digital Archive, Session 1, tape 3, story 9. See also Matthew Pitt, "Civil Rights Watershed in Biloxi, Mississippi," *Smithsonian Magazine*, April 19, 2010; "Five Negroes Fined in Two Justice of Peace Courts," *Daily Herald*, April 26, 1960, 15; Clemon Jimerson Sr., interview with author; Mason testimony, 960, quoted in Butler, "Mississippi State Sovereignty Commission," 129; and Alex Poinsett, "Biloxi Racial Flare-Up Causes $1 Million-Plus Business Loss," *Jet*, May 12, 1960, 16.

23. "Passenger Injured as Car Crashes into Oak Tree," *Daily Herald*, April 27, 1959, 14.

24. Mason, *Beaches*, 69; and "Racial Battle Enlivens Beach," *Commercial Appeal*, April 25, 1960, in SSC 5-4-0-18.

25. Sandy Daniels testimony, 1032–54, quoted in Butler, "Mississippi State Sovereignty Commission," 128.

26. Galloway affidavit, May 3, 1960, NAACP Papers, quoted in Butler, "Mississippi State Sovereignty Commission," 127.

27. Bob Thomas, Subject: Beach Disturbances, Biloxi, SSC 5-4-0-50, p. 4.

28. Myrtle Fleeton and her stepfather, William Fleeton, were part of this group. Myrtle Fleeton went on to own a beauty school in Biloxi for several years. Bernell Fletcher testimony, *U. S. v. Harrison Co.*, No. 2262, 912, quoted in Butler, "Mississippi State Sovereignty Commission," 126; and Clemon Jimerson Sr., interview with author.

29. W. Charles Ellis testimony, 1022–23, quoted in Butler, "Mississippi State Sovereignty Commission," 128.

30. Marzine Thames testimony, 1180, quoted in Butler, "Mississippi State Sovereignty Commission," 128.

31. Mason, *Beaches*, 68, 70; and "Racial Violence Erupts," 2.

32. Poinsett, "Biloxi Racial Flare-Up," 16.

33. Gordon Jackson, "'They Pulled the Brass Knuckles Out' at Historic Biloxi Civil Rights Protest," *Sunherald*, April 21, 2017, https://www.sunherald.com/news/local/counties/harrison-county/article146019724.html. This source incorrectly states that Bud Strong and Malcom Jackson were killed during the wade-ins.

34. Mason, *Beaches*, 69; and Clemon Jimerson Sr., interview with author.

35. Galloway affidavit, May 3, 1960, NAACP Papers, quoted in Butler, "Mississippi State Sovereignty Commission," 127.

36. Clemon Jimerson Sr., interview with author.

37. G. W. Carney, interview, Center for Oral History and Cultural History, University of Southern Mississippi, June 12, 2010, 1–3.

38. Clemon P. Jimerson, interview with Curtis Austin, 6; "Nolan McSwain," Marshall Funeral Home, https://www.marshallfh.com/obituary/5057694; Bellande, "History of D'Iberville"; and Clemon Jimerson Sr., interview with author.

39. Clemon Jimerson Sr., interview with author.

40. Clemon Jimerson Sr., interview with author.

41. Dr. Gilbert R. Mason Sr. (The HistoryMakers A2002.202), interviewed by Larry Crowe, November 11, 2002, The HistoryMakers Digital Archive, Session 1, tape 3, story 9; Matthew Pitt, "Civil Rights Watershed in Biloxi, Mississippi," *Smithsonian Magazine*, April 19, 2010; Clemon P. Jimerson, interview with Curtis Austin, 9; and "Our History," Infinity Funeral Homes, accessed August 9, 2012, https://www.infinityfuneralhomes.com/about-us/our-history.

42. "Racial Violence Erupts," 2.

43. Pitt, "Civil Rights Watershed."

44. Clemon Jimerson Sr., interview with author.

45. Lee Owens Jr., interview with Dora Feazant, minute 8:10; and "Lee's Obituary," Marshall Funeral Home, April 2001, https://www.marshallfh.com/obituary/lee-owens-jr.

46. Ethel R. Clay, interview by Louis Kyriakoudes, 7.

47. Bobby C. Hope, interview with Elaine Fontas, 2–5.

48. Eleanora Hayes, interview with Angela Sartin, Mississippi Oral History Program, University of Southern Mississippi, November 3, 1999, 19; Lee Owens Jr., interview with William Henderson, Mississippi Oral History Program, University of Southern Mississippi, April 26, 2000, 6; and Clemon Jimerson Sr., interview with author.

49. Clemon Jimerson, message to author, June 7, 2022.

50. Janice Kennedy, interview with Kendall Holder, Mississippi Oral History Program, University of Southern Mississippi, April 24, 2010, 2–3.

51. "Racial Battle Enlivens Beach," *Commercial Appeal*, April 25, 1960, in SSC 5-4-0-18.

52. Mason, *Beaches*, 69; "Keesler Airmen Restricted from Sand Beach Area," *Daily Herald*, April 26, 1960, 1, 9; and "Racial Violence Erupts," 2.

53. Clara Griffin Watson, interviewed by Angela Sartin, 12.

54. Richard Ellerbrake, email to author, August 31, 2021.

55. Ellerbrake, "Report from Biloxi," 2; Bob Thomas, Subject: Beach Disturbances, Biloxi, SSC 5-4-0-50, p. 4; and Thomas, "Beach Disturbances, Gulfport, Harrison Co., Miss.," SSC 5-4-0-51, pp. 5–6.

56. Galloway affidavit, May 3, 1960, NAACP Papers, quoted in Butler, "Mississippi State Sovereignty Commission," 127.

57. Bob Thomas, Subject: Beach Disturbances, Biloxi, SSC 5-4-0-50, p. 4.

58. Mason, *Beaches*, 69.

59. Pitt, "Civil Rights Watershed."

60. Clemon Jimerson Sr., interview with author.

61. Bruce William, letter to Bill Minor, July 25, 2000; Richard Ellerbrake, "Report on Biloxi," *Petal Paper*, May 19, 1960, 2; and Richard Ellerbrake, email to author, August 31, 2021.

62. Mason, *Beaches*, 70; and "Racial Violence Erupts," 1–2.

63. It was not clear if these men were injured at the beach or included victims of the fighting that lasted through the night. The eight listed were Algot L. Kropp, Mack L. Gilreath, Elliott L. Walker, Roger L. Cristianson, John C. Tilley, David Vermillion, Thomas C. Rinera Cesareo, and Paul D. Helper. "Tension Begins to Relax in Biloxi Section," *Daily Herald*, April 26, 1960, 1; and "Keesler Airmen Restricted from Sand Beach Area," *Daily Herald*, April 26, 1960, 1.

64. Mason, *Beaches*, 69; Bob Thomas, Subject: Beach Disturbances, Biloxi, SSC 5-4-0-50, p. 5; and Krystal Allan, "Commemorating 'Bloody Wade-In' 50 Years Later," WLOX, April 25, 2010.

65. Mason, *Beaches*, 70.

66. "Study Setting Aside of Beach Area for Negroes," *Daily Herald*, May 2, 1960, 1.

67. Dr. Gilbert R. Mason Sr. (The HistoryMakers A2002.202), interviewed by Larry Crowe, November 11, 2002, The HistoryMakers Digital Archive. Session 1, tape 3, story 9; and Mason, *Beaches*, 71.

68. "Four Are Hurt in Biloxi Riots," *Times Picayune*, April 25, 1960, in SSC 5-4-0-16.

69. Dr. Dunn also told the SSC he had "advised the entire meeting," especially the youth, against going to the beach in the first place and that the event was not organized by the NAACP. He said he wanted to step down as president of the NAACP branch, but the other members refused to allow it. He alleged, "he was for integration in every other field of endeavor such as school and so forth," but not the beaches, although it was clear the SSC agents were suspicious of these claims. The relationship between Dunn and the SSC had started to show strain although he hadn't participated in the wade-in. He had come to the SSC primarily to complain about two constables in Gulfport raiding the bars where his cigarette and gambling machines were held following the beach demonstration. Mason, *Beaches*, 102–5; and Zack J. Van Landingham, Memo to: File 5-4, Subject: Beach Integration, Harrison County, Mississippi, May 4, 1960, SSC 2-56-1-33.

70. "Never Requested Beach for Negro NAACP Declares," *Daily Herald*, May 19, 1960, 1; and Ellerbrake, "Report on Biloxi," 2.

71. Bob Thomas, Subject: Beach Disturbances, Biloxi, SSC 5-4-0-50, p. 4; Mason, *Beaches*, 75–76; "Bombs Cause Damage to Buildings," *Daily Herald*, October 2, 1962, 1; and Zack J. Van Landingham, Memo to File 5-4, Subject: Beach Integration, Harrison County, Mississippi, May 4, 1960, 4.

72. Ethel R. Clay, interview by Louis Kyriakoudes, 9.

73. "Racial Violence Erupts," 1–2; Bob Thomas, Subject: Beach Disturbances, Biloxi, SSC 5-4-0-50, p. 7; and "Registration of Firearms in Harrison Brisk," *Daily Herald*, April 26, 1960, 9.

74. Clemon Jimerson Sr., interview with author.

75. "All Biloxi Police Called to Duty in Race Crisis," *Clarion Ledger*, April 26, 1960, SSC 5-4-0-23; "Biloxi Patrolled by Armed Cops; Tension High," *New Orleans States*, April 25, 1960, SSC 5-4-0-22; and Mason, *Beaches*, 71, 73.

76. "Keesler Airmen Restricted from Sand Beach Area," *Daily Herald*, April 26, 1960, 1.

77. "Keesler Airmen Restricted," 1, 9; and "11 Wounded in Shootings After Race Riots Along Biloxi Beach," *Delta Democrat-Times*, April 25, 1960, 1–2.

78. Pitt, "Civil Rights Watershed"; Bob Thomas, Subject: Beach Disturbances, Biloxi, SSC 5-4-0-50, p. 6; and "Racial Violence Erupts," 1.

79. Walter Cook, interview with Clemon Jimerson, Mississippi Oral History Program, University of Southern Mississippi, June 10, 2010, 3.

80. "Five Negroes Fined in Two Justice of Peace Courts," *Daily Herald*, April 26, 1960, 15; and Mason, *Beaches*, 74.

81. Eleanora Hayes, interview with Angela Sartin, 20.

82. "Racial Violence Erupts," 2; and "Classifieds," *Daily Herald*, February 24, 1954, 15.

83. "Two Negroes Arrested in Petit Larceny," *Daily Herald*, October 10, 1946.

84. "Racial Violence Erupts," 2.
85. Myrtle Davis, interview by Louis Kyriakoudes, Mississippi Oral History Program, University of Southern Mississippi, June 12, 2010, 4–7.
86. "Biloxi Reported Quiet After Swimming Beach Riot Sunday," *Jackson Advocate*, April 30, 1960, SSC 5-4-0-42.
87. Tom Ethridge, "Mississippi Notebook," *Clarion Ledger*, April 28, 1960, SSC 5-4-0-35.
88. "Mayor, Doctor Stand Opposed," *Commercial Appeal*, August 19, 1960, in SSC 5-4-0-127; and Gilbert Mason Jr., interview with author.

CHAPTER SIX. FROM RIPPLES TO WAVES: SHIFTING BLAME, CALLS FOR PEACE, AND THE NATIONAL CAMPAIGN

1. "Coast Tense, Quiet; Negroes Fined for Packing Weapons," *Jackson Daily News*, April 26, 1960, in SSC 5-4-0-26.
2. "Biloxi Riots Enrage NAACP," *Hattiesburg American*, April 26, 1960, 1–2.
3. Wallace Dabbs, "Negroes Fail to Try Beach," *Clarion Ledger*, May 2, 1960, in SSC 5-4-0-48.
4. Ellerbrake, "Report on Biloxi," 2; "Five Negroes Fined," 15; "Ten Shot in Biloxi Riots," *Hattiesburg American*, April 25, 1960, 1; "Negro Swim Invasions Blamed: Gunfire Wounds 10 in Beachfront Rows," *Centralia Daily Chronicle*, April 25, 1960, 1; and Bob Thomas, Subject: Beach Disturbances, Biloxi, SSC 5-4-0-50, p. 8.
5. Ellerbrake, "Report on Biloxi," 5; and "Report Quiet Continuing in Biloxi Section," *Daily Herald*, April 27, 1960, 1.
6. "Federal Suit for Negroes' Right to Swim on Gulf Coast," *Jackson Advocate*, May 21, 1960, 1; "Coast Officials Prepare Legal Fight for Beach," *Daily Herald*, May 18, 1960, 1; and "Four Are Hurt in Biloxi Riots," *Times Picayune*, April 25, 1960, SSC 5-4-0-16.
7. "Racial Battle Enlivens Beach," *Commercial Appeal*, April 25, 1960, in SSC 5-4-0-18.
8. "Negroes Beat White Youth," *Clarion Ledger*, April 28, 1960, in SSC 5-4-0-34; and "Tension Simmers in Biloxi," *State Times*, April 25, 1960, SSC 5-4-0-19.
9. Chapman is sometimes reported as Chatman or Chattman. "Racial Violence Erupts," 2; and "Nichols School Has 28 Graduates," *Daily Herald*, June 1, 1960, 13.
10. Eleanora Hayes, interview with Angela Sartin, 20.
11. Bob Thomas, Subject: Beach Disturbances, Biloxi, SSC 5-4-0-50, p. 5.
12. Mason, *Beaches*, 76–77; "Five Negroes Fined," 15; and "Negroes Fined in Biloxi Rioting," *Commercial Appeal*, April 26, 1960, in SSC 5-4-0-25.
13. "Biloxi Riots Enrage NAACP," *Hattiesburg American*, April 26, 1960, 2.
14. Mason, *Beaches*, 80.
15. Mason, *Beaches*, 80; "Beach Measure Given Approval by Senate Body," *Daily Herald*, April 27, 1960, 1; "Beach Measure Is Explained by Law Official," *Biloxi Herald*, April 28, 1960, 1; and "Beach Measure Signed into Law by Gov. Barnett," *Daily Herald*, April 30, 1960, 1–2.
16. "Beach Measure Signed into Law," 1–2.
17. Dr. Gilbert Mason Jr. reported that after the attack on over six hundred civil rights demonstrators marching across the Edmund Pettus Bridge in Selma, Alabama, on March 7, 1965, a day known as "Bloody Sunday," the phrase may have been adopted to refer back

to the 1960 Biloxi riot. Bruce Biossot, "Nothing New in 'One Man, One Vote' Rule," *Raleigh Register*, March 18, 1965; and Gilbert Mason Jr., interview with author.

18. In 1957, a merger of two Black Congregational Christian churches and nine white Evangelical and Reformed churches, including the Back Bay Mission, formed one denomination as the United Church of Christ. Since its inception in the 1920s, the Back Bay Mission had offered sewing and cooking classes to the daughters of the poor "oyster and fisher folk" of Biloxi. In 1958–59, Reverend Ellerbrake's wife, Johann Havenner Ellerbrake, and Barbara Moffitt, secretary and receptionist of the mission, had agreed to extend those classes to include the Black daughters of the Main Street Baptist congregation. After finding the stove of the Main Street Baptist may have been leaking gas, the women moved this class as well to the mission—in the distinction often made at the time, these classes were said to be "desegregated" not "integrated." From there, both the Black and white young women were able to borrow books from the Mission library. Joy Hartman (who later married John Aregood and took his last name) also taught secretarial courses before 1963 at the request of Main Street Baptist's Rev. E. L. Jackson although it is not clear if they were desegregated. Richard Ellerbrake, "From a Minister There... A Report on Biloxi," *Petal Paper*, May 19, 1960, 5; "Apprehension in Biloxi about Race Situation," *Daily Herald*, April 29, 1960, 2; "Beach Study Group Named, Negro Mix Threat Voiced," *Jackson Daily News*, May 2, 1960, SSC 5-4-0-49; Richard Ellerbrake, email to author, April 26, 2022; Richard Ellerbrake, email to author, August 31, 2022; and Rev. John & Joy Aregood and Dr. Gilbert R. Mason Jr., interview with Louis Kyriakoudes, Mississippi Oral History Program, University of Southern Mississippi, May 3, 2001.

19. Richard Ellerbrake, letter to Bill Minor, July 14, 2000.

20. "Apprehension in Biloxi about Race Situation," *Daily Herald*, April 29, 1960, 2.

21. "Set Curfew for Military at 7 during Weekend," *Daily Herald*, April 28, 1960, 1–2.

22. "Time for Calmness: An Editorial," *Daily Herald*, April 28, 1960, 1.

23. "Negroes Fined in Biloxi Rioting," *Commercial Appeal*, April 26, 1960, in SSC 5-4-0-25.

24. "Keesler Airmen Restricted."

25. Mason, *Beaches*, 74.

26. "Little Rock Aftermath Proved High Cost of Bias," *Jet*, June 15, 1961, 18.

27. "Tension Simmers in Biloxi," *State Times*, April 25, 1960, SSC 5-4-0-19.

28. C. R. Darden, President of Mississippi State Conference NAACP, to Hon. John C. Stennis, February 18, 1960, Civil Rights Movement Archive, https://www.crmvet.org/docs/6002_naacp_lynch-let.pdf; and "Channels of Challenge: The Sword and the Spirit," *Daily Herald*, April 30, 1960, 6.

29. "Letters from the People: Deplores Violence (April 26, 1960)," *Daily Herald*, April 28, 1960, 4.

30. Joseph Reiff, *Born of Conviction* (New York: Oxford University Press, 2016), 44–45; and Garrett Kell, "Damn the Curse of Ham: How Genesis 9 Got Twisted into Racist Propaganda," Bible & Theology, The Gospel Coalition, January 9, 2021.

31. Reiff, *Born of Conviction*, 44–45.

32. "Ministers Call for 'Saneness and Goodwill,'" *Daily Herald*, April 29, 1960, 1–2.

33. "Mayor, Doctor Stand Opposed," *Commercial Appeal*, August 19, 1960, SSC 5-4-0-127; Bob Thomas, Subject: Beach Disturbances, Biloxi, SSC 5-4-0-50, p. 7; and "Set Curfew for Military at 7," 1–2.

34. "Little Rock Aftermath," 18; and "Report Quiet Continuing in Biloxi Section," *Daily Herald*, April 27, 1960, 1.

35. Mason, *Beaches*, 79; "Ten Shot in Biloxi Riots," *Hattiesburg American*, April 25, 1960, 13; and Ellerbrake, "Report on Biloxi," 2.

36. "Whites Club Negroes Invading Mississippi Beach," *Press Courier* (Oxnard, California), April 25, 1960, 1; and Bob Thomas, Subject: Beach Disturbances, Biloxi, SSC 5-4-0-50, p. 7.

37. "Biloxi Patrolled by Armed Cops; Tension High," *New Orleans States*, April 25, 1960, SSC 5-4-0-22.

38. "Negroes Had Beach Area Three Years Ago But Lost It Due Number of Reasons," *Biloxi Daily Herald*, May 2, 1960, 9; "Beach Suit Filed by US," *Times Picayune*, May 18, 1960, in SSC 5-4-0-70; and "Major Hiller Clarifies Story on Use of Beach," *Daily Times*, May 12, 1960, SSC 5-4-0-65.

39. Bob Thomas Memo to Governor Ross Barnett, Subject: Beach Disturbances, Gulfport, Harrison Co., Miss., SSC 5-4-0-51, pp. 1–3.

40. "Rand Speaks on State of Union," *Daily Herald*, June 10, 1960, 5.

41. "Biloxi Riots Enrage NAACP," *Hattiesburg American*, April 26, 1960, 2.

42. *Shreveport Times*, April 26, 1960, 6A, quoted in Butler, "Mississippi State Sovereignty Commission," 132.

43. "The Biloxi Incident," *Jackson Advocate*, April 30, 1960, 4.

44. "Tension Simmers in Biloxi," *State Times*, April 25, 1960, SSC 5-4-0-19.

45. "Tension Simmers in Biloxi."

46. Tom Scarbrough, Title: Harrison County, January 16, 1961, SSC 2-56-1-77, p. 2.

47. "Biloxi Incident," 4.

48. James M. Ward, "Dr. Mason and His Patients," *Jackson Daily News*, May 4, 1960, SSC 5-4-0-52.

49. Mason, *Beaches*, 82.

50. Dr. Gilbert R. Mason Sr. (The HistoryMakers A2002.202), interviewed by Larry Crowe, November 11, 2002, The HistoryMakers Digital Archive. Session 1, tape 3, story 10.

51. Mason, *Beaches*, 82.

52. Ward, "Dr. Mason and His Patients."

53. Mason, *Beaches*, 94.

54. "Car and Scooter Fires in Biloxi," *Daily Herald*, June 25, 1963, 6; and Mason, *Beaches*, 88–90.

55. Bob Thomas, Subject: Beach Disturbances, Biloxi, SSC 5-4-0-50, p. 7.

56. Gilbert Mason, interviewed by Bill Ellison, "Mississippi Moments: Dr. Gilbert Mason—In Memory of Medgar," Center for Oral History and Cultural Heritage, University of Southern Mississippi, June 25, 2013, https://mississippimoments.org/ms-mo-359-dr-gilbert-mason-sr-in-memory-of-medgar; and Gilbert Mason Jr., interview with author.

57. Mason, *Beaches*, 114, 124.

58. Mason, *Beaches*, 85–86.

59. Ethel R. Clay, interview by Louis Kyriakoudes, 2–3; and Clemon P. Jimerson, interview with Curtis Austin, 12.

60. In his autobiography, Mason gives the location of the meeting as the United Benevolence Association Hall; Mason, *Beaches*, 86. See also "Study Setting Aside of Beach

Area for Negroes," *Daily Herald*, May 2, 1960, 1; Laura Ewen Blokker, "Historic Resources Survey 2017"; and Bob Thomas, Beach Disturbances, Gulfport, Harrison Co., Miss., SSC 5-4-0-51, p. 4.

61. "Study Setting Aside of Beach Area," 1.

62. Wallace Dabbs, "Negroes Fail to Try Beach," *Clarion Ledger*, May 2, 1960, in SSC 5-4-0-48; and Poinsett, "Biloxi Racial Flare-Up," 15.

63. "Beach Study Group Named, Negro Mix Threat Voiced," *Jackson Daily News*, SSC 5-4-0-49; Mason, *Beaches*, 79, 83; Zack J. Van Landingham, Memo, Subject: NAACP, Biloxi, Mississippi, March 21, 1960, SSC 2-56-1-26; "KKK to Boycott Southern Cities for Integration," *Daily Herald*, September 15, 1961, 13; "Marvin M. Dickey," *Sun Herald*, August 6, 2003; Gilbert Mason Jr., interview with author; and Letter from Richard Woodruff to Erle Johnston Jr., February 3, 1965, SSC 99-89-0-116.

64. A. L. Hopkins, "Continued Investigation of the Boycott of White Merchants in Edwards, Mississippi, and Buy-Ins Sponsored by the APWR in this Town," October 27, 1966; and A. L. Hopkins, "Investigation in Fayette, Mississippi, on March 1, 1966, in Order to Ascertain If Persons of a Subversive Nature Were Involved in the Buy-Ins in Fayette Saturday, Feb. 26, 1966," March 4, 1966, SSC 2-51-0-44.

65. "Legal Status of Beach Is Given an Added Import in NAACP Plan for 'Wade-In' at U. S. Beaches," *Daily Herald*, May 9, 1960, 1; and "Chicago Needs No Help from Mississippi's KKK," *Jet*, August 3, 1961, 12.

66. Larry Still, "Chicago Police Plan to Prevent Race Violence: Chicago Beach Wade In Test," *Jet*, July 27, 1961, 16–19.

67. Ethel R. Clay, interview by Louis Kyriakoudes, 9.

68. Members of the 1959 Board of Supervisors, who would be the initial defendants in the case *United States v. Harrison County*, were Dewey Lawrence, Roy DeDeaux, Nick French, Gatha Ladner, and Dennis Broadus, along with Sheriff Curtis O. Dedeaux, Mayor Laz Quave, Biloxi chief of police Herbert McDonnell, and a private citizen, Mrs. Guice. "Dedeaux Elected to Harrison Sheriff Post: New Faces to Replace Incumbents," *Daily Herald*, August 26, 1959, 1–2.

69. "Police Accused of Aiding Mob," *Commercial Appeal*, August 9, 1960, SSC 5-4-0-119; and Amended Complaint: *US v. Harrison County, Mississippi et al.*, Civil Action No. 2262, July 20, 1961, Civil Rights Litigation Clearinghouse, https://clearinghouse.net/doc/78746/.

70. "Dr. Gilbert Mason Gives Credit to Providence for Swim Suit," *Jackson Advocate*, May 21, 1960, SSC 5-4-0-81.

CHAPTER SEVEN. WHITE SAND, WHITE SOLIDARITY:
THE CONTINUED POLICING OF HARRISON COUNTY BEACHES AND
UNITED STATES V. HARRISON COUNTY

1. "Beach Suit Filed by U.S.," *Times Picayune*, May 18, 1960, SSC 5-4-0-70.

2. "Federal Right to Bring Suit on Gulf Coast Is Challenged by Defense," *Jackson Advocate*, November 12, 1960, 6.

3. "Police Accused of Aiding Mob," *Commercial Appeal*, August 9, 1960, SSC 5-4-0-119.

4. "Serve Beach Suit Summons on Board," *Daily Herald*, May 20, 1960, 1.

5. Tom Cook, "Seawall Easement Claimed by County," *Daily Herald*, September 21, 1960, 1–2.

6. "Skrmetti Asks to Intervene in Sand Beach Suit," *Daily Herald*, June 23, 1960, 10; "Beach Owners Name Collins as President," *Daily Herald*, May 28, 1960, 1; and "Sand Beach Bid for Dredging of Areas Accepted," *Daily Herald*, July 12, 1962, 2.

7. "Private Ownership Sand Beach Claimed," *Daily Herald*, May 19, 1960, 1; and "Board Is Named in Another Beach Suit," *Daily Herald*, August 11, 1960, 1.

8. Jim Lund, "Grant Extension in Beach Hearing," *Daily Herald*, June 9, 1960, 1–2.

9. "Harrison County Sand Beach Suit Opens in Court," *Daily Herald*, September 20, 1960, 2.

10. "Private vs Public Ownership of Beach," *Daily Herald*, November 1, 1960, 1–2.

11. "Overrules Petition of Freedom Rider: Must Go in State Court First," *Daily Herald*, June 27, 1961, 1; "Judge Sets Hearing in Mix Cases," *Daily Herald*, February 20, 1964, 9; "Federal Grand Jury May Be Recessed Friday," *Daily Herald*, January 11, 1960, 1; and Zacharie Barber, "Justice, Southern Style: The Kidnapping and Murder of Mack Charles Parker," Northeast Texas Regional Phi Alpha Theta History Conference, 2014, 43, https://twu.edu/media/documents/history-government/Justice-Southern-Style-Ibid.-Volume-7-Spring-2014.pdf.

12. "Granted Two-Month Delay in U. S. Court," *Jackson Daily News*, June 9, 1960, 5-4-0-97-1-1-1; and "Reply Ordered in Beach Case," *Times Picayune*, September 13, 1960, 5-4-0-137-1-1-1.

13. "Lawsuit Delayed on Gulf," *State Times*, August 2, 1960, 5-4-0-116-1-1-1.

14. "U. S. Attorneys Charge Sheriff Knew of Gulf Mixing Attempt," *State Times*, August 10, 1960, 5-4-0-120-1-1-1.

15. "Refuses to Grant Beach Mixing Order," *Daily Herald*, December 7, 1961, 1.

16. Jim Lund, "Grant Extension in Beach Hearing," *Daily Herald*, June 9, 1960, 1–2.

17. "State Gives $20,000 to Citizens Council," *Hattiesburg American*, July 7, 2960, 1.

18. Richard Ellerbrake, letter to Albert Jones and Cosmin Eisendrath, July 8, 1960, SSC 7-0-1-152.

19. Albert Jones, Memo to File, NAACP Activities, Harrison County, Mississippi, July 11, 1960, SSC 2-56-1-49.

20. In contrast, J. E. Stockstill of Picayune, who served as attorney for the SSC, as well as serving a term in the state senate, wrote a letter to Ellerbrake, defending the necessity of the WCC's national propaganda campaign and "exposing the fallacy as well as the effect" of *Brown v. Board of Education* for "the protection of the pure White Anglo-Saxon" race. Stockstill told Ellerbrake, "It appears that your sentiment, your duties and your leanings [are] to nefarius [sic] Communistic Organizations that are sweeping this nation," and he demanded to know whether or not the pastor was, in fact, a Jew, as there was "plenty of authentic proof that the Jews have . . . embraced Communism, out of which has grown the NAACP," an organization he claimed was being "used for the main purpose of mixing the blood and destroying the White race," particularly in regards to the spread of syphilis. Such interracial relations, he wrote, would lead to the "final down-fall [sic]" of the Nation. Stockstill insisted that the "heads of all the various Church Organizations, [should] refrain from the present National wave of Church propaganda to mix the Black and White races," and that if they truly followed the edicts of the Apostle Paul, they could not "subscribe to the great movement [of] Communism . . . a God-less Revolution," that had been "fostered . . . by the Jewish nation." On the advice of other SSC members, this letter was likely never sent. J. E.

Stockstill, letter to Rev. Richard Ellerbrake, July 11, 1960, SSC 7-0-1-156. See also Herman B. DeCell to Albert Jones, Re: Rev. Richard Ellerbrake, Biloxi, July 15, 1960, SSC 2-56-1-56; "J. E. Stockstill," *Daily Herald*, September 22, 1971, 2; "Sovereignty Posts Filled," *Daily Herald*, March 11, 1960, 18; and "East Side," *Petal Paper*, October 20, 1960, 4.

21. Richard Ellerbrake, email to author, April 26, 2022.

22. "Adam to Preside Council Banquet on Coast," *Daily Herald*, June 18, 1960, 11; "Citizens Council Resets Banquet," *Daily Herald*, June 14, 1960, 7; "Fraud in Lincoln Exposed as Wells Releases Facts Tainting Adam's Victory," *Hattiesburg American*, September 1, 1927; Mason, *Beaches*, 90–91; SSC Robert C. Thomas, Subject: Harrison County NAACP Activities, June 27, 1960, SSC 2-56-1-41, p. 2; Mason, "In Memory of Medgar," June 25, 2013; Waltraut Stein, "The White Citizens' Councils," *Negro History Bulletin* 20, no. 1 (1956): 2–23, http://www.jstor.org/stable/44215197; "New York Beat," *Jet*, May 31, 1962, 63; and Gilbert Mason Sr., letter to member, June 19, 1960, SSC 2-56-1-36.

23. "Rights Agency Calls for Probe in Mississippi," *Daily Herald*, September 9, 1961, 7.

24. Robert C. Thomas, Assignment to Contact Nap Cassibry in Gulfport Relative to a Conversation He Had with Louis Hollis of the Citizen's Council Regarding Information He Has about Racial Conditions in Harrison County and DeSota National Park, July 25, 1960, SSC 2-56-1-59.

25. Robert C. Thomas, Memo to: Director SSC, Subject Harrison County NAACP Activities, June 27, 1960, SSC 2-56-1-41; and Albert Jones, letter to Billy Meadows, June 29, 1961, SCC 2-56-1-83.

26. Thomas, Assignment to Contact Nap Cassibry.

27. "Harrison Sheriff Uses New Law to Halt Mixing," *Daily Herald*, July 5, 1960, 1.

28. "Harrison Sheriff Uses New Law."

29. Albert Jones, Subject: Beach Integration and DeSoto National Forest Park Harrison County, Mississippi, July 5, 1960, SSC 5-4-0-115; Mason, *Beaches*, 110; Thomas, Assignment to Contact Nap Cassibry; "Negro History Week," *Daily Herald*, February 10, 1947, 5; and "Schools Seeking Federal Aid for Shop Building," *Daily Herald*, November 22, 1960, 2.

30. "Harrison Sheriff Uses New Law to Halt Mixing," 1.

31. Robert C. Thomas, Investigation of Disturbances at DeSoto National Forest Park, Harrison County Mississippi, on July 4, 1960, July 7, 1960, SSC 2-56-1-51, p. 2.

32. Robert C. Thomas, Investigation of Disturbances at DeSoto National Forest Park, Harrison County Mississippi, on July 4, 1960, July 11, 1960, SSC 2-56-1-54, 1–2.

33. Thomas, Investigation of Disturbances at DeSoto, July 7, 1960, 1–2; Thomas, Assignment to Contact Nap Cassibry; and "Inquiry Is Sought in Racial Incident," *Commercial Appeal*, July 9, 1960, SSC 2-56-1-42.

34. "Inquiry Is Sought."

35. Thomas, Investigation of Disturbances at DeSoto, July 7, 1960, p. 4.

36. Thomas, Investigation of Disturbances at DeSoto, July 11, 1960, p. 1.

37. Gilbert Mason Jr., interview with author.

38. "Sheriff Answers Rep. Diggs on Park Incident," *Daily Herald*, July 9, 1960, 1; and "DIGGS, Charles Coles, Jr.," History, Arts & Archives: House of Representatives, https://history.house.gov/People/Detail/12254.

39. "Behind Schedule in Taking of Depositions," *Daily Herald*, August 11, 1960, 2.

40. "Seeks Summary Judgment Sand Beach Complaint," *Daily Herald*, February 8, 1961, 2.

41. Tom Cook, "Seawall Easement Claimed by County," *Daily Herald*, September 21, 1960, 1–2.

42. *Harrison County, Mississippi, et al. v. Mrs. Lee Dicks Guice*, No. 42.276, May 7, 1962, SSC 2-56-2-39, pp. 2–9.

43. Cook, "Seawall Easement Claimed," 1–2.

44. "Private vs Public Ownership of Beach," *Daily Herald*, November 1, 1960, 1–2; "Issues Order against Getting Data of Council," *Daily Herald*, March 10, 1961, 2; and "Hearing Today on Sand Beach Legal Matter," *Daily Herald*, May 22, 1961, 8.

45. "Private Owners Hold Beach Strip Title," *Daily Herald*, May 7, 1962, 1.

46. Attorney General William Rogers "moved in on the . . . beach case" in early 1961. "Ticker," *Jet*, February 2, 1961, 16.

CHAPTER EIGHT. MANY OARS:
THE OTHER AVENUES OF CIVIL RIGHTS PROGRESS IN HARRISON COUNTY

1. Alex Poinsett, "Mississippi Segregation Faces First Real Test: Freedom Rides, Court Suits," *Jet*, July 20, 1961, 16–20.

2. Salvatore et al., "Civil Rights in America," 25–29, 44; Earl M. Lewis, "Negro Voter in Mississippi," 329; Answers to Interrogatories of State of Mississippi, Purpose of Laws 1890, 1954, 1960, 1962, Decrease in Negro Registration 1890–1954, *United States v. State of Mississippi* (U. S. District Court for the Southern District of Mississippi), Civil Action No. 3312, https://clearinghouse.net/doc/78672/; and Complaint, *United States v. State of Mississippi et al.*, Civil Action No. 3312, https://clearinghouse.net/doc/77058/; and Answers to Interrogatories of State of Mississippi, Statistics: Census—Registration—Voting 1890–1962, *United States v. State of Mississippi* (U. S. District Court for the Southern District of Mississippi), https://clearinghouse.net/doc/78670/.

3. C. R. Darden, to Hon. John C. Stennis.

4. Salvatore et al., "Civil Rights in America," 53.

5. Virgil Downing, "NAACP Activities in Harrison County," October 23, 1961, SSC 2-56-2-9; and Virgil Downing, "NAACP and COFO Activity in Jackson and Harrison Counties," December 23, 1964, SSC 2-56-2-70.

6. Clemon Jimerson Sr., interview with author.

7. Walter A. Bailey, letter to Ross Barnett, January 15, 1961, SSC 2-56-2-6; and Bob Thomas, Subject: Beach Disturbances, Biloxi, SSC 5-4-0-50, p. 2.

8. Mason, *Beaches*, 118–20.

9. "Numbers of Negroes Registered by County," SNCC report, Civil Rights Movement Archive, https://www.crmvet.org/docs/610000snccvr-stats.pdf.

10. "Raps Vote Method at Greenwood," *Daily Herald*, April 1, 1963, 1; "Seeking to Register at Jackson," *Daily Herald*, June 22, 1963, 8; "Barnett Defends Circuit Clerks in Federal Suit," *Daily Herald*, August 4, 1961, 1; "Gun Shots Hit Car Carrying Vote Workers," *Daily Herald*, March 7, 1963, 25; "Plans to Speak on Registration," *Daily Herald*, March 25, 1963, 6; "Lefore

County Scans Surge in Registration," *Daily Herald*, June 25, 1963, 9; and "Sheriff Denies Intimidation of Negro Prisoners," *Daily Herald*, July 1, 1963, 24.

11. "Barnett Says Marchers 'Dangerous as Bomb,'" *Delta Democrat-Times*, April 1, 1963, 1; and "Barnett Says Voter Efforts Are Dangerous," *Hattiesburg American*, April 1, 1963, 19.

12. Mason, *Beaches*, 78.

13. Mason, *Beaches*, 77–78; Stanonis, *Faith in Bikinis*, 132; Josh Foreman and Ryan Starrett, *Hidden History of the Mississippi Sound* (Charleston: The History Press, 2019), 119; and Jackson, "Brass Knuckles," *Sun Herald*, April 21, 2017.

14. "Harrison County Man Held in Connection with Beating," *South Mississippi Sun*, March 26, 1975, 9; "Two Inmates Hospitalized," *Biloxi Sun Herald*, May 31, 1975, 11; "Jailed Biloxi Man Slashes Wrists; Dies at Hospital," *Daily Herald*, June 4, 1975, 2; "Prisoner Dies After Slashing Wrists," *Hattiesburg American*, June 5, 1975, 20; Robert Ellzey, "Abernathy Reiterates Call for Pas-Point Area Boycott," *South Mississippi Sun*, June 18, 1975, 12; "Malcolm Hoyd Jackson," *Sun Herald*, June 8, 1975, A2; and "Malcolm Hoyd Jackson," Find A Grave, findagrave.com.

15. 1900 US Census, Biloxi, Harrison County, Mississippi, District 0030, p. 34; and 1910 US Census, Biloxi Ward 1, Harrison County, Mississippi, District 0033.

16. *Biloxi City Directory*, vol. 5 (Chillicothe, OH: Mullin-Kille, 1958), 752.

17. The Edgewater Gulf Hotel stood at what would be 2600 Beach Boulevard, Beauvoir at 2244.

18. "Authorities Check Cause of Negro's Death," *Daily Herald*, January 26, 1961, 2; "Elderly Negro Died When Hit by Automobile," *Daily Herald*, January 27, 1961, 2; "Cards of Thanks," *Daily Herald*, February 8, 1961, 2; "In Memoriam," *Daily Herald*, January 26, 1962, 2; "In Memoriam," *Daily Herald*, January 25, 1964, 2; and Bobby C. Hope, interview with Elaine Fontas, 1–2.

19. Berry Reece, "Coast Mayor, Negro Doctor Determined," *Jackson Daily News*, August 18, 1960.

20. Mason, *Beaches*, 121.

21. "Vote for Leadership by Electing Danny Guice," *Daily Herald*, May 8, 1961, 16; "Four Years of Progress for Biloxi," *Daily Herald*, April 11, 1961, 20; and Citizens' Councils, For Immediate Release, December 19, 1960, SSC 9-11-1-63.

22. In the midst of the mayoral campaigns, another event demonstrated the shift in white temperament and action regarding segregation. The biracial denomination that formed the United Church of Christ, including St. Paul Church of Christ and the Back Bay Mission, typically held its integrated ministerial meetings in the basements of one of the New Orleans churches. In 1961, it was proposed that the group meet in Biloxi, where the picture windows of the mission would leave the group clearly visible to the public. Put before the church's council, "by and large the idea was favorably received," with one woman becoming "rather disturbed because the matter of color had even been brought up." The two council members with "feelings quite the contrary" claimed their reservations were not from racial bias but respect of local law. Despite acknowledging that such a meeting would "alienate some members," causing the mission to "suffer financially," it was agreed upon, and three women of the congregation volunteered to prepare lunch. Reverend Ellerbrake wrote in his report of the meeting, "A year ago our women would never have been willing to serve Negroes," for reasons that were not made explicit; but the change nevertheless indicated a shift in white

sympathies. Ellerbrake was advised by the council to notify local law enforcement preceding the meeting, so it would be known "you're not planning a demonstration." However, the actions of the police force during the wade-ins made Ellerbrake feel that such a call might not secure their safety; perhaps the opposite. Therefore, the morning of the gathering, May 16, 1961, Ellerbrake called the FBI in New Orleans instead. It was an FBI agent who called the Biloxi chief of police to ensure the meeting was not disturbed, and this same agent watched over the small assembly (about twelve individuals) from a car parked behind the mission community center. In describing the day, Ellerbake wrote, "As usual I was wearing my clerical [collar], which we did in those days for self protection as much as anything." It transpired that some of the St. Paul congregation was upset by the event, causing a small drop in attendance. Richard Ellerbrake, "Report from Biloxi, Mississippi, Back Bay Mission No. 3," May 31, 1961, emailed to author May 16, 2022; and Richard Ellerbrake, email to author, April 26, 2022.

23. "Biloxi Joins Gulfport as Second Coastal City to Hire Negro Police," *Jackson Advocate*, November 4, 1961, 1, 8; and Zack J. Van Landingham, Memo to: Director State Sovereignty Commission, Subject: NAACP, Gulfport, Mississippi, June 2, 1959, SSC 2-56-1-12, pp. 1–2.

24. Schools that served the poorer white communities had also suffered from underfunding over the years. The children of the Back Bay and Point Cadet fishermen and seafood factory workers had not had their own schools until 1894. Biloxian Rachael Richardson recalled transferring in the 1970s from Michel Junior High, with its tennis courts and theater, to Central, where art class consisted of cheap mail-order kits more suitable for kindergarten-aged children and little to no instruction. Rachael Richardson, interview with author, June 10, 2020. See also "Colored People Hold Rally," *Daily Herald*, November 28, 1908, 10; "Negro School Bond Issue Before People of Biloxi on Tuesday," *Daily Herald*, August 4, 1947, 1, 4; and "Keesler Growth Strains School Plant at Biloxi," *Daily Herald*, February 15, 1951, 8.

25. Guice et al., *Growth of the Biloxi Public School System*.

26. Fannie L. Nichols, "Negro School Issue," *Daily Herald*, July 29, 1947, 11.

27. Irma D. Gorenflo, "Letters from the People," *Daily Herald*, October 2, 1945, 4; and Ray L. Bellande, "Dukate Family," Biloxi Historical Society, https://biloxihistoricalsociety.org/dukate-family.

28. "Public School Enroll 2831," *Daily Herald*, October 3, 1945, 5.

29. "Negro School Bond Issue Before People of Biloxi on Tuesday," *Daily Herald*, August 4, 1947; and "Public School Enroll 2831," 5.

30. "Negro School Bond Issue Before People," 4; and "Funds Are Received for School Planning," *Daily Herald*, October 9, 1945, 1.

31. "Miss Carter Is Essay Contest Winner," *Daily Herald*, May 13, 1948, 14; "Primary Library," *Daily Herald*, January 30, 1947, 6; "Aid Red Cross," *Daily Herald*, March 23, 1946, 5; "May Queen Chosen," *Daily Herald*, April 16, 1948, 5; and "Negro Health Week," *Daily Herald*, March 16, 1945, 9.

32. A. L. Hopkins, Contacting County and Municipal Superintendents of Education for the Purpose of Securing a List of the Names of Colored School Teachers in Jackson, Harrison, Stone, Forest, Covington and Simpson Counties and the Municipalities in These Counties, March 8, 1962, SSC 2-56-2-26.

33. "Name Negro School in Memory of Late Prof. MF Nichols," *Daily Herald*, March 26, 1948, 9; and "12 Graduates at Open Program Nichols School," *Daily Herald*, May 28, 1949, 3.

34. "$290,000 School," *Daily Herald*, May 27, 1952, 1, 9; and "Rights Agency Calls for Probe in Mississippi," *Daily Herald*, September 9, 1961, 7.

35. "Keesler Growth Strains School Plant at Biloxi," *Daily Herald*, February 15, 1951, 8.

36. "The General Condition of the Mississippi Negro," October 1963, SNCC, https://www.crmvet.org/docs/6310_sncc_ms-research.pdf.

37. "Complete First School in Construction Program of Biloxi Long-Range Project," *Daily Herald*, April 27, 1959, 16; Mimeographed Record, *United States v. Biloxi Municipal Separate School District et al.*, (US Court of Appeals for the Fifth Circuit), Docket Number: 63-02643, https://clearinghouse.net/doc/78366/; and Answers to Interrogatories of State of Mississippi, Comparison of Education for Negroes and White Persons 1890–1963, *United States v. State of Mississippi* (US District Court for the Southern District of Mississippi), Docket Number: 62-03312, https://clearinghouse.net/doc/78668/.

38. An event occurred that demonstrates both the presence of multiple "up-town" Klan-like groups and the resistance of white moderates in Harrison County early in the process of desegregation. On February 22, 1954, in anticipation of the outcome of *Brown v. Board of Education*, Robert L. Rice of Gulfport, Mississippi, formed the Heritage Crusade (which a local man, Jeremiah O'Keefe, later described as similar to a "Klan's group") to perpetuate "patriotic education 'based upon the interpretation of the Constitution,'" which focused on "states [sic] rights," especially "the right of continued segregation." The Heritage Crusade first proposed to hold a "semi-open meeting at the Harrison County courthouse" and advertised the "white's [sic] only" gathering in newspapers. However, the scheduled lead speaker, attorney Merle Palmer, seemed to get cold feet and announced he was "in no way connected with the organization." The meeting was canceled. The Heritage Crusade rescheduled its meeting for the Biloxi Community House since they were attempting to recruit from that city. O'Keefe had seen one of the group's "inflammatory" pamphlets and approached the Biloxi mayor, Laz Quave, who refused to cancel the meeting. O'Keefe gathered seven of his friends to "infiltrate" the meeting, being presided over by Robert Rice, George Houtz of Gulfport, and Vincent Carden of Biloxi. O'Keefe and his friends spread out in the audience. After the opening remarks, O'Keefe stood up and announced, "I fought the war, and many of my friends did, to prevent this kind of thing. And we don't want this in our town." After making a slighting remark about Rice's failed attempt to run for mayor of Gulfport, O'Keefe's friends stood up, and according to him, "the whole audience" walked out with them. This may have been what the press meant when it reported "several Biloxians questioned the advisability of the group meeting in Biloxi." The papers also reported that Lawrence Semski and John Sekul were among those who "questioned members," although O'Keefe later reported that Sekul was one of "the four organizers." "Rice Elected President of Heritage Crusade," *Daily Herald*, April 1954, 16; "Heritage Crusade to Hear Palmer," *Daily Herald*, April 5, 1954, 8; "Heritage Crusade Meeting Postponed," *Daily Herald*, April 7, 1954, 19; "Heritage Group Meets," *Daily Herald*, June 3, 1954, 7; Jeremiah J. O'Keefe, interview by Worth W. Long, Mississippi Oral History Program, University of Southern Mississippi, n.d.; Ira Harkey, *The Smell of Burning Crosses: An Autobiography of a Mississippi Newspaperman* (Jackson: University Press of Mississippi, 2019), chapter 10; and Memorandum for the United States in Opposition to Defendants' Motion to Dismiss (May 1, 1963) *US v. Biloxi Municipal Separate School District et al.*, Civil Action No. 2643 and *US v. Gulfport* (etc.) 2678, Civil Rights Litigation Clearing House.

39. Ethel R. Clay, interview by Louis Kyriakoudes, 10–11.

40. Jim Lund, "Portables Stay . . . Reach Decision on Gorenflo School," *Daily Herald*, August 22, 1967, 1–2.

41. Mason, *Beaches*, 144–45.

42. Jerry Mitchell, "Witness: Man Innocent in '60 Burglary," *Hattiesburg American*, January 1, 2006; "Pardon Docket No. 06-0005," 2006, 23; and Minchin and Salmond, "'Saddest Story of the Whole Movement,'" 196, 221.

43. "Will Try to Enter Daughter in Gulfport School Tuesday," *Laurel Leader-Call*, December 16, 1958, in SSC 1-28-0-50; "Negro Student Revolt Stuns Lily-Whites in Mississippi," *Pittsburgh Courier*, March 16, 1957, SSC 1-28-0-3; Richard F. Popper, "Clennon King Released from Whitfield; Sane," *Morning Star*, June 19, [year missing], SSC 1-28-0-45; Cliff Sessions, "Clennon King Is Missing; Wife Expresses Concern," *Mississippi State Times*, September 2, 1958, SSC 1-28-0-52; "Clennon King Now Publisher in California," *Daily Herald*, February 26, 1959, SSC 1-28-0-70; and "Prof. King: Rather Die Than Return to United States," *Jet*, December 30, 1965, SSC 1-28-0-91.

44. Mason, *Beaches*, 151; Ethel R. Clay, interview by Louis Kyriakoudes, 2; "Meredith Expected Ole Miss Campus," *Daily Herald*, September 20, 1962, 1; and "Hearing Aimed at Mixing Ole Miss Is Opened," *Daily Herald*, June 12, 1961, 1–2.

45. Mason, *Beaches*, 146.

46. "Rights Agency Calls for Probe in Mississippi," *Daily Herald*, September 9, 1961, 7.

47. Gilbert Mason Jr., interview with author; and Guice, Richmond, and Wheeler, *Growth of the Biloxi Public School System*, 20–22.

48. Taking his solitary art classes perhaps exacerbated the self-consciousness Gilbert Mason Jr. felt in being a successful student from a white-collar family, fearing that some of his peers may have believed he thought of himself as "better or higher-minded than the rest." Gilbert Mason Jr., interview with author.

49. "Negroes Would Like to Attend Kennedy Coffee," *Daily Herald*, October 4, 1960, 2.

50. Clemon Jimerson Sr., interview with author.

51. Gilbert Mason Jr., interview with author.

52. Medgar Evers addressed his letter to "Hon. Robert L. Carter, Mrs. Ruby Hurley, Mr. Roy Wilkins, and Mr. Gloster B. Current." Medgar W. Evers, letter to Mr. Robert L. Carter, October 11, 1960, in Mason, *Beaches*, insert 7; and Medgar W. Evers, letter to Dr. Gilbert Mason, October 18, 1960, in Mason, *Beaches*, insert 6.

53. From June 29 to July 15, 1962, Dr. Mason led a group of Boy Scouts from his Troop 416 (Otho Floyd, Phillip Johnson, Luther Buckley, Clemon Jimerson, and Stanley Woods) with some of the white scouts from Pascagoula Troops 407 and 430 on a road trip to Philmont Ranch in Cimarron, New Mexico, the "second largest scouting event in the world." Because the integrated group couldn't stay in hotels, Mason and the leader of the white troops arranged room and board at Marshall College in Wiley, Texas, and Texas Christian University in El Paso. In addition to their jamboree, "pow wow," hiking, camping, and other survival-training events, the group saw the bats in Carlsbad Caverns, the Grand Canyon, and other historical sites. "Scouts Return from Southwest," *Biloxi Herald*, July 16, 1962, 10; and Clemon Jimerson Sr., interview with author.

54. "Negro Parents Abandon School Integration Plans Here," *Jackson Advocate*, September 8, 1962, 7; and "Seeking to Mix Schools at Jackson," *Daily Herald*, August 16, 1962, 1.

55. "Mize Says Integrate; Big Dose for Citadel," *Laurel Leader-Call*, March 5, 1964, 1.

56. Larry Still, "How 'Ole Miss' Crisis Affects State's Negroes," *Jet*, October 18, 1962, 16–18.

57. "Bombs Cause Damage to Buildings," *Daily Herald*, October 2, 1962, 1; "Bailey Resigns Ku Klux Office," *Daily Herald*, October 1, 1962, 7; "Klan Sets Series of Rallies," *Daily Herald*, October 18, 1965, 18; "Klansman Criticizes Laurel Mayor's Attack," *Daily Herald*, November 9, 1965, 16; and "Biloxi, 1964, July-August," Sally Belfrage papers, 1962–1966, Historical Society Library Microforms Room, Micro 599, Reel 1, Segment 9, in COFO reports, Freedom Summer Digital Collection, Wisconsin Historical Society, https://content.wisconsinhistory.org/digital/collection/p15932coll2/id/36814.

58. "Report on Mississippi," Mississippi Advisory Committee to the United States Commission on Civil Rights, January 1963, SSC 4-0-1-82.

59. Memorandum for the United States in Opposition to Defendants' Motion.

60. "Reverse Dismissal of 3 School Cases," *Daily Herald*, February 14, 1964, 1.

61. "New York Beat," *Jet*, May 31, 1962, 63; and "Fire Bomb Home of Diggs Visit," *Daily Herald*, April 12, 1963, 1.

62. "Negroes Seek Answer from School Board in 10 Days," *Daily Herald*, May 21, 1963, 2.

63. "Suit Is Filed to Mix Biloxi Schools," *Daily Herald*, June 5, 1963, 1–2; "Adele Mingo Black," Obituary, Marshall Funeral Homes, December 14, 2015; "CPL Lewis Black (17 June 1921–2 January 1979)," Find a Grave, database citing Biloxi National Cemetery, Biloxi, Mississippi; "Harold Boglin," City Directory, Biloxi, Mississippi, 1958, 431; "Testimony Begins in Trespass Appeal Case," *Daily Herald*, November 21, 1963, 2; "Rehofus 'Rea' Staples Esters Sr. (18 May 1923–22 Sep 2014)," Find a Grave, database citing Biloxi National Cemetery, Biloxi, Mississippi; "Barbara Esters Obituary," *Sun Herald Legacy*, May 12, 2019; "Maude McKinley Obituary," *Sun Herald Legacy*, April 28, 2020; "PFC James William McKinley (9 Dec 1929–7 Aug 1990)," Find a Grave, database citing Biloxi National Cemetery, Biloxi, Mississippi; "Clifton Nunley Sr. Obituary," *Sun Herald Legacy*, February 9, 2005; "Christopher Rosado," City Directory, Biloxi, Mississippi, 1958, 676; and "Christopher Rosado (9 Nov 1913–15 Jun 1989)," Find a Grave, database citing Biloxi National Cemetery, Biloxi, Mississippi.

64. "File Briefs in Biloxi School Case," *Daily Herald*, June 20, 1963, 21.

65. "Order Federal Court to Hear Miss. School Cases," *Jet*, February 27, 1964, 6.

CHAPTER NINE. TIDES TURNING:
RESUMING THE FEDERAL TRIAL AND THE FINAL WADE-IN

1. Supervisor Dewey E. Lawrence also died in spring 1962. "Sand Beach Case May Be Nearing Date of Trial," *Daily Herald*, July 27, 1962, 1; and *United States v. Harrison County et al.*, Civil Action No. 2262, Amended Complaint, https://www.clearinghouse.net/chDocs/public/PA-MS-0003-0002.pdf.

2. Plaintiff's Memorandum in Opposition (October 22, 1962): *United States v. Harrison County, Mississippi et al.*, Civil Action No. 2262, Civil Rights Litigation, ClearingHouse.net;

"Refuses to Make Sand Beach Suit Class Action," *Daily Herald*, March 1, 1963, 1; and "Defense Files Two Motions in Beach Use Suit," *Daily Herald*, September 8, 1960, 1.

3. "Ask Waivers of Process Beach Suit," *Daily Herald*, November 20, 1963, 1.

4. Mason, *Beaches*, 132.

5. L. E. Cole Jr., Hattiesburg, Gulf Coast, Tylertown, and Poplarville, December 4, 1968, SSC 2-34-0-32, p. 1; Lee Cole, Memorandum to Director SSC, Subject: Activity-Southern District, January 29, 1969, SSC 2-64-2-28, pp. 1–2; Butler, "Mississippi State Sovereignty Commission," 141; and Citizens' Councils, "For Immediate Release," December 19, 1960, SSC 9-11-1-63.

6. John F. Kennedy, Civil Rights Address, Washington, DC, June 11, 1963, https://www.americanrhetoric.com/speeches/jfkcivilrights.htm.

7. "NAACP Leader Is Gunned Down in Driveway of Jackson Home," *Hattiesburg American*, June 12, 1963, 1, 16; and Michael Maxson, "Medgar Evers," Ferris State University, 2015, https://www.ferris.edu/HTMLS/news/jimcrow/witnesses/medgarevers.htm.

8. Harris G. Sims, "Fingerprints on a Rifle," *Lakeland Ledger*, June 24, 1963, 8, in FBI Records: The Vault, Medgar Evers Part 1 of 5; "White Citizens Legal Fund Is Started Today," *Greenwood Commonwealth*, June 1963, 19, in FBI Records: The Vault, Medgar Evers Part 1 of 5; "Beckwith Trial to Begin Today," 13, in FBI Records: The Vault, Medgar Evers Part 2 of 5; and "Beckwith, Assassin of Medgar Evers, Dies Serving Life Term," *Washington Post*, January 21, 2001.

9. Richard Ellerbrake, email to author, May 16, 2022.

10. Mason, *Beaches*, 133.

11. Gilbert Mason Jr., interview with author.

12. Sandra Trenholm, "Robert Kennedy on Civil Rights, 1963," The Gilder Lehrman Institute of American History, January 24, 1963, https://www.gilderlehrman.org/sites/default/files/inline-pdfs/05630_FPS_0.pdf; Simeon Booker, "Troops Sent to Miss.; Alabama Guard Federalized," *Jet*, June 20, 1968, 48; and Brian K. Landsberg, "JFK and the United States," in *John F. Kennedy History, Memory, Legacy: An Interdisciplinary Inquiry*, ed. John Delane Williams, Robert G. Waite, and Gregory S. Gordon (Grand Forks: University of North Dakota, 2010), 204–5.

13. "Biloxi School Suit Dismissed by Judge," *Daily Herald*, June 18, 1963, 1; and Memorandum for the United States in Opposition, 7–42.

14. Mason, *Beaches*, 134.

15. Around this time, a pamphlet credited to the NAACP was distributed in Jackson, urging Black citizens not to shop at white Capital Street businesses belonging to those "murderous segregationist[s] who plan and promote the murder" of men like Medgar Evers. (Ironically, the bulletin linked segregationists to Communism.) This group utilized deep shame tactics to promote Black compliance, calling those who did not join the boycott "Aunt Marys," "Uncle Toms," "Mule Team," and Master's "Good Nigras." "The Jackson Movement Information Bulletin: Murder Inc.," NAACP, circa December 1963, Civil Rights Movement Archive, https://www.crmvet.org/docs/6312jaxmurder.pdf; and Gilbert Mason Jr., interview with author.

16. "Nation's Only Negro Daily Newspaper Joins President Kennedy in Call to Stop All Public Demonstrations," *Jackson Advocate*, June 29, 1963, 1, 6; and Drew Pearson, "The Washington Merry-Go-Round," *The Chronicle*, June 10, 1963, 12.

17. Mason, *Beaches*, 134.

18. Butler, "Mississippi State Sovereignty Commission," 140.

19. It was around 1964–65 that Reverend Aregood also took a group of young people to the New York World's Fair. One young woman, Rena Flemming, remarked on her return, "I've been to New York before I've been to the [Biloxi] mall." Rev. John & Joy Aregood and Dr. Gilbert R. Mason Jr., interview with Louis Kyriakoudes; and Clemon Jimerson Sr., interview with author.

20. Myrtle Davis, interview by Louis Kyriakoudes, 6; James Lund, "71 Are Arrested in Biloxi Wade-In," *Daily Herald*, June 24, 1963, 2; and "When We Say Bloody, We Mean Bloody: Reflecting on the Biloxi Wade-Ins and Bloody Sunday," *Daily Herald*, February 23, 2021.

21. "Dr. Sekul New President of Medical Staff," *Daily Herald*, December 5, 1963, 10.

22. "Trial of Beach," *Daily Herald*, June 28, 1963, 1–2.

23. Lund, "71 Are Arrested in Biloxi Wade-In," 1.

24. Reverend Aregood thought Officer Gerald Ferrell may have been the policeman who tackled the man who ran onto the beach with the gun. Mason testimony, 968–69, quoted in Butler, "Mississippi State Sovereignty Commission," 140; Rev. John & Joy Aregood and Dr. Gilbert R. Mason Jr., interview with Louis Kyriakoudes; and "Dozen Arrested on Charges of Having Weapons," *Daily Herald*, June 24, 1963, in SSC 2-56-2-38.

25. Lund, "71 Are Arrested in Biloxi Wade-In," 1; Mason testimony, 968–69, quoted in Butler, "Mississippi State Sovereignty Commission," 140; Jim Bourdier, photographer, "Overturned Car," photograph, Associated Press, June 1963, History.com; and "Dozen Arrested on Charges of Having Weapons."

26. Clemon Jimerson Sr., interview with author.

27. Rev. John & Joy Aregood and Dr. Gilbert R. Mason Jr., interview with Louis Kyriakoudes.

28. Lund, "71 Are Arrested in Biloxi Wade-In," 2; and Myrtle Davis, interview by Louis Kyriakoudes, 6.

29. Dr. Gilbert R. Mason Sr. (The HistoryMakers A2002.202), interviewed by Larry Crowe, November 11, 2002, The HistoryMakers Digital Archive, Session 1, tape 4, story 4; and Rev. John & Joy Aregood and Dr. Gilbert R. Mason Jr., interview with Louis Kyriakoudes.

30. "Beach Trials Set Friday," *Daily Herald*, June 25, 1963, 14.

31. Richard Ellerbrake, letter to Bill Minor, July 14, 2000; and Myrtle Davis, interview by Louis Kyriakoudes, 6.

32. Rev. John & Joy Aregood and Dr. Gilbert R. Mason Jr., interview with Louis Kyriakoudes.

33. Mason, *Beaches*, 59, 137; and "Negro Dentist under Police Guard after Coast Incident," *Jackson Advocate*, June 29, 1963, 1, 5.

34. "Dozen Arrested on Charges of Having Weapons."

35. Mason, *Beaches*, 136; and "Car and Scooter Fires in Biloxi," *Daily Herald*, June 25, 1963, 6.

36. Rev. John & Joy Aregood and Dr. Gilbert R. Mason Jr., interview with Louis Kyriakoudes.

37. "Biracial Group at Gulfport Will Be Formed," *Daily Herald*, June 25, 1963, 1; and "Gulfport Biracial Committee Set Up," *Hattiesburg American*, June 28, 1963, 1–2.

38. "Explosion at Office of Dr. Dunn," *Daily Herald*, June 27, 1963, 1–2.

39. "Trial of Beach Demonstrators Ends at Biloxi," *Daily Herald*, June 28, 1963, 1–2.

40. Cornelius Kemp was later robbed and strangled to death in the parking lot of Howard Memorial Hospital during his shift as a taxi driver. Dr. Mason collected donations to help support Kemp's wife and fourteen children. "Biloxi Police Seek Suspect in Kemp Slaying," *Daily Herald*, February 18, 1972, 2; and "NAACP Sets Up Fund," *Daily Herald*, February 18, 1972, 10.

41. Gilbert Mason Jr., interview with author; and Clemon Jimerson Sr., interview with author.

42. "Eight Receive Maximum Penalty Beach Case," *Daily Herald*, June 29, 1963, 1–2.

43. "Jury Deliberates Hour, Returns Guilty Verdict," *Daily Herald*, November 23, 1963, 19.

44. Reiff, *Born of Conviction*, 289.

45. Reiff, *Born of Conviction*, 82–83.

46. "Protest Use of Mission for NAACP Meeting," *Daily Herald*, November 1, 1963, 24; Rev. John & Joy Aregood and Dr. Gilbert R. Mason Jr., interview with Louis Kyriakoudes; Drew Pearson, "Nazi-Like Organizations Spread Fear in McComb," *Laurel Leader-Call*, October 16, 1964, 4; Drew Pearson, "Moderate City Was Target of Recent Racial Bombing," *Laurel Leader-Call*, October 15, 1964, 4; and Drew Pearson, "Warren Made Sacrifice for Assassination Report," *Laurel Leader-Call*, September 28, 1964, 4.

47. "Window Broken Church Building," *Daily Herald*, November 20, 1963, 2; "Mission Robbed Monday Night," *Daily Herald*, November 26, 1963, 8; "Another Window at Mission Is Broken," *Daily Herald*, January 8, 1964, 16; "Back Bay Mission Windows Broken," *Daily Herald*, February 14, 1964, 22; "Windows Broken," *Daily Herald*, February 27, 1964, 14; and Rev. John & Joy Aregood and Dr. Gilbert R. Mason Jr., interview with Louis Kyriakoudes.

48. Attorney Richard Brown had previously worked on the defense of Mack Parker (before Parker was killed by a lynch mob) and Clyde Kennard's false theft charge. "Testimony Begins in Trespass Appeal Case," *Daily Herald*, November 21, 1963, 2; and Carter Dalton Lyon, "R. Jess Brown, Carsie A. Hall, and Jack H. Young, Sr.," *Mississippi Encyclopedia*, Center for Study of Southern Culture, July 10, 2017

49. "Restaurant at Greyhound Bus Station Closed," *Daily Herald*, November 21, 1963, 2.

50. Mason, *Beaches*, 139.

51. "Biloxi Beach Ruling," *Daily Herald*, December 12, 1966, 1.

52. Gilbert Mason Jr., interview with author.

CHAPTER TEN. HIGH TIDE, LOW TIDE: PROGRESS, PUSHBACK, AND DESEGREGATION

1. "Refuse Plea to Mix Biloxi Schools," *Daily Herald*, July 22, 1963, 1; and "Coast School Cases under Advisement," *Daily Herald*, December 5, 1963, 1.

2. "Mize Says Integrate; Big Dose for Citadel," *Laurel Leader-Call*, March 5, 1964, 1.

3. "Whites Seeking to Bar Mixing," *Daily Herald*, February 21, 1964, 1; "Negro Parents Seek Total Public School Desegregation," *Hattiesburg American*, May 18, 1964, 1, 6; and "Judge Orders State Schools to Take Negroes This Fall," *Delta Democrat-Times*, July 7, 1964, 1.

4. William Hodding Carter II, "Changes in Mississippi," *Delta Democrat-Times*, July 21, 1964, 4; and "Council Says to Stand Firm," *Laurel Leader-Call*, March 11, 1964, 25.

5. Erle Johnston Jr., to File, Subject: Extension Courses-Keesler Field, February 4, 1964, SSC 2-56-2-46, pp. 1–2.

6. "The University of Mississippi Announces Schedule of Courses for the Mississippi Gulf Coast, Spring 1964," *Daily Herald*, January 7, 1964, 2.

7. "Doors Closed . . . Pringle Reports on School Suits," *Daily Herald*, February 25, 1964, 1.

8. "Schools Must Mix," *Laurel Leader-Call*, March 4, 1964, 2.

9. "Won't Rehear Mixing Suit," *Laurel Leader-Call*, March 13, 1964, 14; "School Board Fights Suit," *Delta Democrat-Times*, April 2, 1964, 1; and "Biloxi Attorneys Ask for School Integration Dismissal," *Hattiesburg American*, March 31, 1964, 6.

10. "Biloxi Attorneys Ask for School Integration Dismissal," 6.

11. William Hodding Carter, "Desegregation Trial in Jackson," *Delta Democrat-Times*, May 22, 1964, 3; "Whites Seeking to Bar Mixing," *Daily Herald*, February 21, 1964, 1; Dudley Lehew, "Jackson Case Aims at Overruling '54 Decision," *Hattiesburg American*, May 20, 1964, 1, 12; Kenneth B. Clark and Mamie P. Clark, "Racial Identification and Preference in Negro Children," in *Readings in Social Psychology* (New York: Holt, 1958), 169–78, https://i2.cdn.turner.com/cnn/2010/images/05/13/doll.study.1947.pdf; Toni Sturdivant, "What I Learned When I Recreated the Famous 'Doll Test' That Looked at How Black Kids See Race," *The Conversation*, February 22, 2021; and Michael G. Proulx, "Professor Revisits Clark Doll Tests," *Harvard Crimson*, December 1, 2011.

12. "Whites Seeking to Bar Mixing," 1.

13. "At Jackson Hearing Educator Says Mixing Harmful," *Laurel Leader-Call*, May 19, 1964, 1–2; and "Jackson Lawyers Fight School Desegregation," *Hattiesburg American*, May 19, 1964, 1, 5.

14. "At Jackson Hearing Educator Says Mixing Harmful," 1–2.

15. Carter, "Desegregation Trial in Jackson," 3.

16. "Legislature Going Home Private School Hanging," *Delta Democrat-Times*, June 5, 1964, 1; "Private School Grants Passed by State Senate," *Delta Democrat-Times*, July 1, 1964, 1; and "Private School Plan Appearing Imminent," *Delta Democrat-Times*, July 15, 1964, 1.

17. "Dual School System Plan Nearly Ready for Report," *Delta Democrat-Times*, June 17, 1964, 1.

18. Timothy B. Tyson, *Blood Done Sign My Name: A True Story* (New York: Random House, 2005), 182; Gillian Brockwell, "Three Civil Rights Workers Were Missing. Sen. Eastland Said It Was Fake News," *Washington Post*, June 21, 2019, https://www.washingtonpost.com/history/2019/06/21/three-civil-rights-workers-were-missing-sen-eastland-said-it-was-fake-news/; James Saggus, "Governor Urges Serious Study of School Plans," *Hattiesburg American*, June 23, 1964, 1, 3; and Ed McCusker, "Mystery Surrounds Disappearance of Three Civil Rights Missionaries," *Hattiesburg American*, June 23, 1964, 1.

19. Virgil Downing, "Civil Rights Activity in Harrison County," July 20, 1964, in SSC 2-56-2-58; "Collegians to Invade for 'Freedom Summer,'" *Laurel Leader-Call*, March 18, 1964, 5; "Head Start . . . Program in Harrison," September 4, 1967, 9; Bolton, "Mississippi's School Equalization," 791–92; Berry, *Racial and Ethnic Tensions*, 62; Clemon Jimerson Sr., interview with author; and Donna McNair, "Civil Rights Workers Canvass for Voter Registration in Bayou Auguste Homes," *Biloxi Free Herald*, August 14, 1964, 3, https://www.crmvet.org/docs/640814_cofo_herald-c.pdf.

20. Clemon Jimerson was with Dr. Mason for the testing of compliance at the Sun 'n Sand. Mason, *Beaches*, 161; Gilbert Mason Jr., interview with author; and Clemon Jimerson Sr., interview with author.

21. Berry, *Racial and Ethnic Tensions*, 62; and Lester Smith, "Five Biloxi Students Test Public Accommodations Law," *Biloxi Free Herald*, August 14, 1964, 2, https://www.crmvet.org/docs/640814_cofo_herald-c.pdf.

22. "Biloxi, 1964, July-August," Sally Belfrage papers.

23. *Jackson Municipal Separate School District v. Darrell Kenyatta Evers, Biloxi Municipal Separate School District v. Gilbert R. Mason, Jr.*, and *Leake County School Board v. Dian Hudson et al.*, Nos. 21851–52, No. 21878, United States Court of Appeals Fifth Circuit, January 26, 1966, https://openjurist.org/357/f2d/653/jackson-municipal-separate-school-district-v-evers-biloxi-municipal-separate-school-district; and "Judge Orders State Schools to Take Negroes This Fall," *Delta Democrat-Times*, July 7, 1964, 1.

24. Jack Bell, "School Desegregation Order Made Permanent," *Hattiesburg American*, July 7, 1964, 1, 4.

25. *Jackson Municipal Separate School District v. Darrell Kenyatta Evers, Biloxi Municipal Separate School District v. Gilbert R. Mason, Jr.*, and *Leake County School Board v. Dian Hudson et al.*

26. "School Boards Submit Plans," *Laurel Leader-Call*, July 15, 1964, 1; "Jackson, Biloxi File Plans for Integration," *Delta Democrat-Times*, July 15, 1964, 1; and "School Board Attorneys Appeal Integration Orders," *Hattiesburg American*, August 4, 1964, 5.

27. "Negro Parents Seek Revision in Mix Plans," *Hattiesburg American*, July 16, 1964, 1, 6.

28. "Private School Plan Appearing Imminent," *Delta Democrat-Times*, July 15, 1964, 1; and "Segregation in Schools by Sex May Follow," *Hattiesburg American*, July 15, 1964, 4.

29. Carter, "Changes in Mississippi," 4.

30. "Citizens Council 'Fights' White Miss. Women," *Jet*, August 6, 1964, 56; and Tom Oxnard, "Women's Group Had Desegregation Role," *Delta Democrat-Times*, October 22, 1964, 4.

31. "Public School Backers Ask Statewide Support," *Delta Democrat-Times*, July 20, 1964, 1.

32. "Citizens Council Hits Public School Backers," *Delta Democrat-Times*, July 21, 1964, 1; and "League of Women Voters Opposes Scholarship Plan," *Hattiesburg American*, June 19, 1964, 3.

33. Carter, "Changes in Mississippi," 4.

34. "Columbus Writer Explains His 'Moderate' Civil Rights View," *Delta Democrat-Times*, August 25, 1964, 4.

35. Senator Eastland now implied the WCC, alongside the KKK, would be natural suspects in the case. "Arrests Imminent in CR Slayings," *Laurel Leader-Call*, August 6, 1964, 1; James Bonney, "18 Facing Trial in 'Rights' Case," *Laurel Leader-Call*, October 7, 1967, 1; and "Murder in Mississippi," Freedom Summer, *American Experience*, PBS.

36. Carolyn Weathersby, "The Three Civil Rights Workers," *Biloxi Free Herald*, August 14, 1964.

37. "Judge Sets Hearing in Mix Cases," *Daily Herald*, February 20, 1964, 9; and "School Hearing Wednesday," *Daily Herald*, February 24, 1964, 1.

38. "Council Says to Stand Firm," *Laurel Leader-Call*, March 11, 1964, 25.

39. "Gulfport Period Set Up," *Daily Herald*, February 11, 1967, 9; and Mason, *Beaches*, 159.

40. Elliott Chaze, "School Desegregation Plan Approved by Judge," *Hattiesburg American*, July 29, 1964, 2, 6.

41. "Private Schools to Open in Two Cities," *Hattiesburg American*, August 12, 1964, 1.

42. "Mississippi's Peaceful School," *Jet*, October 1, 1964, 48–49; and "Eight Charters for New Schools," *Laurel Leader-Call*, August 11, 1964, 1–2.

43. "Clarksdale Group Plans Private 1st-Grade This Fall," *Hattiesburg American*, August 11, 1964, 2; "Church Council Asks for Funds in Mississippi," *Delta Democrat-Times*, October 12, 1964, 2; "Continue Probe of Church Fire," *Hattiesburg American*, June 18, 1964, 10; and Tim Muldoon, "King Anniversary Recalls Bishop's Desegregation Efforts in Mississippi," *Catholic Telegraph*, April 6, 2018.

44. "Words of the Week," *Jet*, July 23, 1964, 30.

45. "Mississippi Has Money Woes," *Jet*, January 7, 1965, 24; "Miss. Sheriff Doesn't 'Know' Why Jury Called Him," *Jet*, October 8, 1964, 51; and "First Biloxi Crisis Meets No Violence," *Laurel Leader-Call*, August 15, 1964, 1–2.

46. Winfred Moncrief, "Covering the News," *Hattiesburg American*, August 10, 1964, 10.

47. "Doors Closed . . . Pringle Reports on School Suits," February 25, 1964, 1.

48. Mason, *Beaches*, 149–50.

49. Gilbert Mason Jr., interview with author.

50. This Lopez Elementary was closed in 1978, and the previously named West End Elementary became the current Lopez. "Negro First-Graders Register in Biloxi," *Hattiesburg American*, August 14, 1964, 1, 3; and Zan Skelton, "Biloxi Schools 1970–1979," in *The Biloxi Schools 1924-2001* (Biloxi: Publication Office, Biloxi Public School District, 2000), 14.

51. Moncrief, "Covering the News," 10; and "First Biloxi Crisis Meets No Violence," *Laurel Leader-Call*, August 15, 1964, 1–2.

52. "Jackson Schools Mix First Grade," *Laurel Leader-Call*, August 20, 1964, 1–2; "Jackson Is Calm," *Delta Democrat-Times*, August 21, 1964, 1; and "Negro First-Graders Register in Biloxi," 1, 3.

53. Zan Skelton, "Biloxi Schools 1960–1969," in *The Biloxi Schools 1924-2001* (Biloxi: Publication Office, Biloxi Public School District, 2000), 10; "Only 17 Negroes Sign Up at Biloxi," *Hattiesburg American*, August 15, 1964, 1; and "CR Heads Stunned at Low Enrollment," *Laurel Leader-Call*, August 21, 1964, 1–2.

54. "Mississippi's Peaceful School," 48–49; and "Jackson Schools Mix First Grade," 1–2.

55. "First Biloxi Crisis Meets No Violence," 1–2; and Moncrief, "Covering the News," 10.

56. "Mississippi's Peaceful School," 48–49.

57. Gilbert Mason, interview with Bill Ellison, "Healthcare and Civil Rights"; and Jeannette Crenshaw, "Care Practice #6: No Separation of Mother and Baby, with Unlimited Opportunities for Breastfeeding," *Journal of Perinatal Education* 16, no. 3 (2007): 39–43, https://doi.org/10.1624/105812407X217147.

58. Mason, *Beaches*, 155–56.

59. "Negro Dentist Arrested Following Hospital Scuffle," *Hattiesburg American*, August 15, 1964, 16.

60. "Negro Doctor to Appeal Conviction," *Hattiesburg American*, August 18, 1964, 4.

61. In his interview with Larry Crowe, Dr. Mason describes the cafeteria as segregated, with a small side room given to the Black staff. This may have been at New Biloxi Hospital or an early arrangement at Howard Memorial. Newspaper accounts of the fight with Batia describe the cafeteria as "recently integrated." It is unclear if Batia suffered any legal consequences. "Negro Doctor to Appeal Conviction," 4; and Dr. Gilbert R. Mason Sr. (The HistoryMakers A2002.202), interviewed by Larry Crowe, November 11, 2002, The HistoryMakers Digital Archive, Session 1, tape 5, story 1, https://www.iheart.com/podcast/256-mississippi-moments-podcas-30950668/episode/msm-559-dr-gilbert-r-mason-39213499/.

62. Skelton, "Biloxi Schools 1960–1969," 10.

63. Mason, *Beaches*, 157.

64. Gilbert Mason Jr., interview with author.

65. "NAACP Lawyer Asks Hearing on Leake," *Hattiesburg American*, September 12, 1964, 1; and "18 Negroes Seeking Transfer to Canton," *Hattiesburg American*, September 3, 1964, 4.

66. Gilbert Mason Jr., interview with author.

67. "Desegregation Rule Stymies Governors," *Delta Democrat-Times*, May 18, 1965, 1; Foster Davis, "Schools Must Comply with CR Act, Local School Officials Say," *Delta Democrat-Times*, January 14, 1965, 1; "U. S. Seeks Plans on School Funds," *Laurel Leader-Call*, February 5, 1965, 1–2; and Elsie W. Johnson, "Tubb States Compliance Local Option," *Laurel Leader-Call*, February 5, 1965, 1–2.

68. "Amended Plan of the Desegregation for the Harrison County School District," *Daily Herald*, October 9, 1965, 3.

69. "Harrison Has 5,470 Students," *Daily Herald*, September 2, 1965, 18; and "Record Enrollment at Biloxi Schools," *Daily Herald*, September 8, 1965, 1.

70. "Integrate Peacefully at Biloxi," *Daily Herald*, September 2, 1965, 1–2.

71. Biloxi High School, *Indian Echo*, vol. 28 (Dallas: Taylor Publishing Company, 1966), 147–60.

72. Before bussing, students who wanted to take advantage of their freedom of choice to attend predominantly white schools had to arrange carpooling or walked in groups. Gilbert Mason Jr., interview with author.

73. "Integrate Peacefully at Biloxi," *Daily Herald*, September 2, 1965, 1–2.

74. Skelton, "Biloxi Schools 1960–1969."

75. Gilbert Mason Jr., interview with author.

76. Gilbert Mason Jr., interview with author.

77. Bill Skelton, "Education Problem in Educators' Laps," *Clarion Ledger*, April 17, 1966, in SSC 4-0-3-37.

78. Daniel Draughn, interview with author, June 13, 2022.

79. Willie Jean McSwain, interview, Mississippi Oral History Program, University of Southern Mississippi, April 24, 2010, 3.

80. Skelton, "Education Problem in Educators' Laps."

81. Gilbert Mason Jr., interview with author.

82. Skelton, "Education Problem in Educators' Laps."

83. Mason, *Beaches*, 157–58.

84. Gilbert Mason Jr., interview with author; and Rev. John & Joy Aregood and Dr. Gilbert R. Mason Jr., interview with Louis Kyriakoudes.

85. When John and Joy Aregood's first son was set to enter Lopez Elementary in 1972, Joy's memory of the teacher, Mrs. David, who had taught her own fourth grade class, as a "screaming racist" with a family "involved in all the parades" was a factor in the family's decision to relocate to Illinois. Rev. John & Joy Aregood and Dr. Gilbert R. Mason Jr., interview with Louis Kyriakoudes.

86. Gilbert Mason Jr., interview with author.

87. Skelton, "Biloxi Schools 1960–1969," 12.

88. Janice Thomas, "Freedom School Trip to Pass Christian," *Biloxi Free Herald*, August 14, 1964, 3; and Linda Davis, "What's Wrong with My Skin," *Biloxi Free Herald*, August 14, 1964, 2, https://www.crmvet.org/docs/640814_cofo_herald-c.pdf.

89. Clemon Jimerson Sr., interview with author.

90. "State Pays Last Respects to Mize," *Hattiesburg American*, April 27, 1965, 1; and "Judge Dismisses Sand Beach Suit," *Daily Herald*, March 9, 1967, 1.

91. Jack Nelson, "Papers Show RFK Sought Action against Judge Cox," *Daily Herald*, August 9, 1971, 15.

92. "At Biloxi . . . Want Negroes Named as School Trustees," *Daily Herald*, August 2, 1966, 1, 9.

93. Gilbert Mason Jr., interview with author.

94. "Memorial Service for King," *Daily Herald*, April 6, 1968, 21.

95. "Over 3000 at Memorial for King at Biloxi," *Daily Herald*, April 8, 1968, 29; "Court Says Miss. Can't Deny Negroes Use of Beaches," *Jet*, January 12, 1967, 4; and Clemon Jimerson Sr., interview with author.

96. "Appeals Court Decrees Beach Public," *Daily Herald*, August 16, 1968, 1–8; and "Coleman, J(ames) P(lemon)," *Scribner Encyclopedia of American Lives*, June 10, 2022, https://www.encyclopedia.com/humanities/encyclopedias-almanacs-transcripts-and-maps/coleman-james-plemon.

97. Untitled Document, Chicago, Illinois, August 25–31, 1968, SSC 9-31-8-61; "Masons Attend Chicago Meeting," *Daily Herald*, August 19, 1968, 42; Dr. Gilbert R. Mason Sr. (The HistoryMakers A2002.202), interviewed by Larry Crowe, November 11, 2002, The HistoryMakers Digital Archive, Session 1, tape 4, story 2; and Mason, *Beaches*, 139–40.

98. Clemon Jimerson Sr., interview with author.

CHAPTER ELEVEN. SAND BETWEEN MY TOES: CONTINUING WORK FOR RACIAL EQUITY

1. Tom Cook, "Biloxi Negro Named to County Demo Committee," *Daily Herald*, May 22, 1968, 1.

2. "Dr. Mason Is Building New Medical Clinic," *Daily Herald*, August 20, 1968, 47.

3. Mason, *Beaches*, 39; and "About Us" and "Message from MMSA President," http://mmsa-online.com/.

4. Gilbert Mason, interview with Bill Ellison, "Healthcare and Civil Rights."

5. "Elect Dr. Gilbert R. Mason," *Daily Herald*, May 1, 1973, 10; Gilbert Mason, interview with Bill Ellison, "Healthcare and Civil Rights"; "Dr. Mason Joins Family Practice," *Daily Herald*, June 14, 1971, 5; "Dr Mason Named Fellow in Academy," *Daily Herald*, November 21, 1972, 5; "Finch Passes Up Medical Group's Choice to Name Mason," *Daily Herald*, February 9, 1977, 12; and "Dr. Mason Is Candidate for Post," *Daily Herald*, April 4, 1973, 14.

6. Jo Ann Klein, "Black Community Finds Itself in Uncomfortable Spotlight," *Daily Herald*, January 30, 1973, 15.

7. Tim Kriehn, "Officials Said Satisfied with Disaster Act," *Daily Herald*, March 25, 1973, 2; "Tuesday Donation Deadline," *Daily Herald*, March 4, 1971, 36; Mason, *Beaches*, 176; and

"Hypocrisy, Racism of Red Cross Hurts Black Hurricane Victims," *Muhammad Speaks* 9, no. 19 (January 23, 1970), https://jstor.org/stable/community.28592051.

8. "Civic League Plans Series of Meetings," *Daily Herald*, June 26, 1969, 22; and "Biloxi Civic League Endorses Duckworth," *Daily Herald*, October 6, 1971, 33.

9. James H. Downey, "Governor Named Five to Council," *Daily Herald*, January 1, 1970, 1; Tim Kriehn, "Planners Endorse Coliseum Site," *Daily Herald*, September 8, 1972, 13; Bob Bishop, "Mayors Name Mason to Coliseum Commission," *Biloxi Sun Herald*, January 17, 1976, 1; and Bob Bishop, "Meeks Takes Coliseum Seat; Mason, Gallotte Tangle Verbally," *South Mississippi Sun*, June 22, 1977, 12.

10. Bob Bishop, "Mason Complains Blacks Not on List for Coliseum Opening," *South Mississippi Sun*, October 12, 1977, 88.

11. "Commission Votes to Recommend Updating of Comprehensive Plan," *South Mississippi Sun*, February 8, 1974, 2; and Marie Langlois, "Capital Improvements Report Accepted by Biloxi Planners," *Daily Herald*, February 8, 1974, 2.

12. "Physician, Ice Executive Named Biloxi Planners," *Daily Herald*, July 15, 1969, 13; "Main Street Project Groundbreaking Held," *Daily Herald*, June 8, 1976, 11; "Biloxi Commission Okays Trash Zoning," *South Mississippi Sun*, June 7, 1974, 12; and Marie Langlois, "Group of Biloxi Citizens Contend Black Area Neglected," *Daily Herald*, October 3, 1974, 2.

13. "Home-Ownership Plan, First in U.S., at Gulfport," *Daily Herald*, September 16, 1967, 1.

14. Billy Ray Quave, "Biloxi Ordered to Close Nichols Senior High School," *Daily Herald*, July 12, 1970, 1–11.

15. One of the most significant objections to forced bussing is that it was an about-face on the idea that no child would be forced to attend any particular school on the basis of their race. Although Gene G. Arnn of D'Iberville wrote to the *Daily Herald* on the bussing issue to say there was no longer an objection to desegregation in itself, he included in his argument against bussing the statement that "we have already lost our right to freely choose our customers or sell our private property," indicating racial mixing, as much as safety concerns, was still an issue in the argument. Whereas little to no concern had been evident for the effect on the few Black children who were enrolled in predominantly white schools under the initial stages of desegregation, with new redistricting and bussing plans in place statewide elsewhere in Mississippi, efforts were made for "concentrating whites" in areas where they would be the minority in predominantly Black schools to "create enough of a haven" that the former would not transfer to private institutions. "Whites Getting Concessions in Desegregation," *Daily Herald*, July 20, 1970, 15; Gene G. Arnn, "Bussing to Schools," *Daily Herald*, January 22, 1970, 4; Billy Ray Quave, "Dr. Mason Calls for School Action," *Daily Herald*, May 22, 1970, 1–2; Jim Sellers, "Biloxi School District Gets Okay to File New Mix Plan," *Biloxi Daily Herald*, June 20, 1970, 1, 5; Billy Ray Quave, "Judge Nixon Promises Biloxi School Plan Soon," *Daily Herald*, June 29, 1970, 10; and Quave, "Biloxi Ordered to Close Nichols Senior High School," 1.

16. Billy Ray Quave, "Judge Nixon to Organize School Mix Study Group," *Daily Herald*, June 2, 1970, 2.

17. Rachael Richardson, interview with author, June 10, 2022.

18. "Dr. Mason Is Candidate for Post," 14; and Tom Cook, "Head Start . . . Program in Harrison," *Daily Herald*, September 4, 1967, 9.

19. "More Education and Training Goal of Star," *Daily Herald*, February 23, 1966, 5; James Lund, "Biloxi Center . . . STAR in Second Cycle," *Daily Herald*, August 16, 1966, 14; and "Star's Third Cycle Class Has 96 Grads," *Daily Herald*, December 24, 1966, 19.

20. During the time Dr. Mason worked with the State Advisory Committee to the Civil Rights Commission, it reported such problem areas as ongoing segregation in the 4-H Clubs and homemaker activities overseen by the Mississippi Cooperative Extension Service. When the committee was hearing complaints against bias in the welfare system, welfare department official Thomas Pruitt said the state legislature would not grant more money for Aid to Dependent Children (one of the several problems recipients named with the system) "because of the high illegitimacy rate among Negro recipients." Mason replied that "the abortion rate among whites is three times the rate among Negroes." "Dr. Mason Is Candidate for Post," 14; David Lawrence, "Mississippi Committee Named," *Daily Herald*, July 3, 1970, 4; "Discrimination Reported in Extension Unit," *Daily Herald*, August 8, 1969, 28; and Laura Engle, "Miss. Welfare Applicants Tell of Refusals, Insults," *Southern Courier*, February 2, 1967, in SSC 4-0-4-36.

21. "Coast Council Meets at Long Beach Motel," *Daily Herald*, September 14, 1965, 17; and "Negro History Week Keeping Set Wednesday," *Daily Herald*, February 11, 1969, 14.

22. Ironically, for a short period of time, the Board of Supervisors, under its president, Laz Quave Sr., took over the Civic Action Committee despite protests from Dr. Mason. The board soon "divested itself of . . . responsibility" for the committee, but at the same time, Mason resigned. Quave told the press, "It is my opinion he has done an outstanding job." "Elect Dr. Gilbert R. Mason," *Daily Herald*, May 1, 1973, 10.

23. "County Civic Action Group Names Director," *Daily Herald*, January 12, 1967, 19; Tom Cook, "Supervisors . . . Pondering Civic Action Program," *Daily Herald*, March 21, 1968, 1–2; and Tom Cook, "CAP Board Action," *Daily Herald*, June 6, 1969, 1–8.

24. "Heads Biloxi USO Council," *Daily Herald*, November 9, 1965, 23; "Dr. Mason Will Head Coast USO," *Daily Herald*, October 10, 1969, 15; and "Beautification . . . Include[s] USO Grounds in Biloxi Program," *Daily Herald*, May 3, 1969, 26.

25. "Want Negroes Named," *Daily Herald*, August 2, 1966, 1.

26. "Let Reason Rule," *Daily Herald*, April 13, 1972, 4.

27. "Unitarian Fellowship," *Daily Herald*, October 22, 1966, 6.

28. "Biloxian Speaks at Howard University," *Daily Herald*, May 22, 1974, 58.

29. "Fraternity Chapter Wins," *Daily Herald*, May 22, 1974, 26; and "Jabberwock Held," *Daily Herald*, April 30, 1968, 18.

30. "Masons Celebrate 25th Anniversary," *Daily Herald*, July 31, 1975, 26.

31. Gilbert Mason, interview with Bill Ellison, "Mississippi Moments: Dr. Gilbert Mason—In Memory of Medgar," Center for Oral History and Cultural Heritage, University of Southern Mississippi, June 25, 2013.

32. Mason, "Woman Behind the Man."

33. Gilbert Mason Jr., interview with author.

34. Linda Williams, "Coast's IWY Delegate Hopes Houston Won't Be Another Jackson," *South Mississippi Sun*, November 14, 1977, 12; "Waller Appoints Biloxian," *South Mississippi Sun*, November 8, 1974, 7; "Tea Scheduled to Launch Drive," *Daily Herald*, February 28, 1974, 31; and "Social Workers Honor Members at Banquet," *Daily Herald*, April 1, 1976, 20.

35. Gilbert Mason Jr., interview with author.

36. Williams, "Coast's IWY Delegate," 12; and Linda Williams, "Feminists, Anti-Feminists See IWY Meeting as Grassroots Test," *South Mississippi Sun*, November 14, 1977, 1.

37. Linda Williams, "ERA Debate Turns into Loud Struggle at Meeting," *Biloxi Sun Herald*, July 9, 1977, 1, 12.

38. Carter Speaks, "Young Demos on Coast United," *Daily Herald*, December 31, 1965, 2.

39. "Head Start Seminar Slated for June 16–18," *Daily Herald*, June 15, 1971, 2; "Bible School Ends," *Daily Herald*, June 24, 1967, 10; and "Biloxi News," *Daily Herald*, February 26, 1971, 24.

40. "Sorority Forms Alumnae Unit for Coast Area," *Daily Herald*, March 21, 1966, 20.

41. "35 Initiated BHS Honors Society," *Daily Herald*, March 23, 1970, 19; "BHS Sophomore Competition in Class Election," *Daily Herald*, September 26, 1968, 19; "Gilbert Mason Jr. Gets Award of Eagle Scout," *Daily Herald*, July 25, 1971, 3; "Michel Football Players Awarded Letters Friday," *Daily Herald*, January 13, 1968, 16; and "Thespians Perform," *Daily Herald*, December 5, 1969, 22.

42. "Gilbert Mason Jr. Gets Award of Eagle Scout," 3; "Mason Gets Scholarship for $1,000," *Daily Herald*, March 4, 1971, 29; and "Top Athletes, Citizens Cited at Biloxi," *Daily Herald*, March 26, 1971, 22.

43. Josh Jackson, "Mural Commemorating Civil Rights Achievements Unveiled at Iconic Inez Cafe," WLOX, January 31, 2022.

44. Myrtle Davis, interview by Louis Kyriakoudes, 9.

EPILOGUE. FLOTSAM, JETSAM: THE DEMISE OF THE STATE SOVEREIGNTY COMMISSION, UNFORESEEN CONSEQUENCES, AND HORIZONS AHEAD

1. "Hayden Campbell Resigns Sovereignty Commission," *Laurel Leader-Call*, January 4, 1966, 22; James Saggus, "Sovereignty Commission Gets Vote of Confidence," *Hattiesburg American*, March 13, 1973, 2; and "Sovereignty Commission Gets Funds," *Daily Herald*, May 25, 1966, 1.

2. "Not Easy to Kill," *South Mississippi Sun*, April 9, 1976, 6.

3. Andrew Reese, "Summer Criticizes ACLU Suit," *Delta Democrat-Times*, June 7, 1977, 14.

4. "Judge Hears in Arguments in Sovereignty Case," *Laurel Leader-Call*, September 21, 1993, 3A.

5. "Resolution Introduced Condemning Conservative Group," *Laurel Leader-Call*, February 5, 1999, 3; and "League of the South Considers Black Spring Break in Biloxi a Call to Arms," Southern Poverty Law Center, September 15, 2000, https://www.splcenter.org/fighting-hate/intelligence-report/2000/league-south-considers-%E2%80%98black-spring-break%E2%80%99-biloxi-call-arms.

6. "NAACP Spokesman Charges Discrimination in Biloxi Schools," *Daily Herald*, March 12, 1975, 15.

7. "Want Negroes Named," *Daily Herald*, August 2, 1966, 1.

8. "State's Unified Schools Continue Peaceful," *Delta Democrat-Times*, September 3, 1970, 1, 17; Hugh Morgan, "Jackson Busing Continues Despite Order from Williams," *Hattiesburg American*, September 13, 1971, 1; LaTanya L. Dixon, "From Statehood to School Desegregation:

Racial Disparities in the Public Education of Mississippi, 1817–1969," *AERA Open*, October 2020, https://doi.org/10.1177/2332858420975396; Jules Loh, "Jackson State Fence like 'Berlin Wall,'" *Daily Herald*, September 27, 1970, 1, 7; "White Voter Drive Said 'Success,'" *Daily Herald*, June 26, 1971, 7; Ed Williams, "Judge's Candidacy Brings Questions of Propriety," *Daily Herald*, October 9, 1971, 34; "Citizens Council Planning College," *Daily Herald*, May 29, 2974, 63; and Hank Klibanoff, "Some Private Schools to Refuse Multiracial Student Recruit Teams," *Sun Herald*, October 8, 1974, 19.

9. Jeff Bryant, "Why Are Federal Funds Flowing to 'White Flight' Privatized Charter Schools?," *Dissident Voice*, July 3, 2021, https://dissidentvoice.org/2021/07/why-are-federal-funds-flowing-to-white-flight-privatized-charter-schools/; and Peter Greene, "White Flight, without the Actual Flight," *Forbes*, November 12, 2019, https://www.forbes.com/sites/petergreene/2019/11/12/white-flight-without-the-actual-flight/?sh=55a4bbf853c6.

10. Lewis and Allen, "Black Voter Registration," 125.

11. Berry, *Racial and Ethnic Tensions*, 89.

12. Berry, *Racial and Ethnic Tensions*, 91.

13. Blokker, "East Biloxi African American and Civil Rights," 7; and Clemon P. Jimerson, interview with Curtis Austin, 11.

14. Graham Jones, Bernardita Chirino Chace, and Justin Wright, "Cultural Diversity Drives Innovation: Empowering Teams for Success," *International Journal of Innovation Science* 12, no. 3 (August 10, 2020), https://www.emerald.com/insight/content/doi/10.1108/IJIS-04-2020-0042/full/pdf?title=cultural-diversity-drives-innovation-empowering-teams-for-success; Remus Serban, "Here's How Workplace Diversity Boosts Profitability," Hub Gets, July 19, 2017, https://www.hubgets.com/blog/workplace-diversity-boosts-profitability/; and Desmund Adams, "Harnessing the Power of Diversity for Profitability," *Forbes*, March 3, 2022, https://www.forbes.com/sites/forbesbusinesscouncil/2022/03/03/harnessing-the-power-of-diversity-for-profitability/?sh=205e520b459a.

15. Rev. John & Joy Aregood and Dr. Gilbert R. Mason Jr., interview with Louis Kyriakoudes.

16. Constance Bailey, "Keeping the Civil Rights Movement Alive: Black Spring Break," *Mississippi FolkLife*, October 19, 2021, http://www.mississippifolklife.org/exhibits/keeping-the-civil-rights-movement-alive-black-spring-break; Casey Malone Maugh Funderburk and Wendy Atkins-Sayre, "Forgetting the 1960 Biloxi, Mississippi, Wade-Ins: Collective Memory, Forgetting, and the Politics of Remembering Protest," in *Like Wildfire: The Rhetoric of the Civil Rights Sit-Ins*, ed. Sean Patrick O'Rourke and Lesli K. Pace (Columbia: University of South Carolina Press, 2020), 261–27, https://www.usm.edu/association-office-professionals/uploads/forgettingthewadeinsarticle.pdf; Bobby C. Hope, interview with Elaine Fontas, 7; and Gordon Jackson, "'They Pulled the Brass Knuckles Out' at Historic Biloxi Civil Rights Protest," *Sun Herald*, April 21, 2017.

SELECTED BIBLIOGRAPHY

BOOKS

Boudreaux, Edmond. *The Seafood Capital of the World: Biloxi's Maritime History*. Charleston: Arcadia Publishing, 2011.

Claiborne, John F. H. *Mississippi, As a Province, Territory, and State: With Biographical Notices of Eminent Citizens*. Jackson, MS: Power & Barksdale, 1880.

Clark, Kenneth B., and Mamie P. Clark. "Racial Identification and Preference in Negro Children." In *Readings in Social Psychology*, 169–78. New York: Holt, Rinehart & Winston, 1958.

Cuevas, John. *Cat Island: The History of a Mississippi Gulf Coast Barrier Island*. Jefferson, NC: McFarland & Co., 2011.

Dickerson, James. *Dixie's Dirty Secret: The True Story of How the Government, the Media, and the Mob Conspired to Combat Integration and the Vietnam Antiwar Movement*. Armonk, NY: M. E. Sharpe, 1998.

Foreman, Josh, and Ryan Starrett. *Hidden History of the Mississippi Sound*. Charleston: History Press, 2019.

Funderburk, Casey Malone Maugh, and Wendy Atkins-Sayre. "Forgetting the 1960 Biloxi, Mississippi, Wade-Ins: Collective Memory, Forgetting and the Politics of Remembering Protest." In *Like Wildfire: The Rhetoric of the Civil Rights Sit-Ins*, edited by Sean Patrick O'Rourke and Lesli K. Pace, 261–27. Columbia: University of South Carolina Press, 2020.

Gallagher, Charles A., and Cameron D. Lippard. *Race and Racism in the United States: An Encyclopedia of the American Mosaic*. Santa Barbara, CA: ABC-CLIO, 2014.

Gallay, Alan. *The Indian Slave Trade: The Rise of the English Empire in the American South, 1670–1717*. New Haven, CT: Yale University Press, 2002.

Gayarreé, Charles. *History of Louisiana: The French Domination*. New York: William J. Widdleton, 1867.

Goldner, Sanford. *The Jewish People and the Fight for Negro Rights*. Los Angeles: Committee for Negro-Jewish Relations, 1953.

Guice, Julia C., Stephanie C. Richmond, and David Alfred Wheeler. *The Growth of the Biloxi Public School System*. Biloxi, 1979.

Hall, Gus. *Marxism and Negro Liberation*. New York: New Century Publishers, 1951.

Hall, Gwendolyn Midlo. *Africans in Colonial Louisiana: The Development of Afro-Creole Culture in the Eighteenth-Century*. Baton Rouge: Louisiana State University Press, 1992.

Harkey, Ira. *The Smell of Burning Crosses: An Autobiography of a Mississippi Newspaperman*. Jackson: University Press of Mississippi, 2019.

Himona, Chahta Anumpa Tosholi. *New Choctaw Dictionary*. Durant, OK: Choctaw Print Services, 2016.

Kahrl, Andrew W. *The Land Was Ours: How Black Beaches Became White Wealth in the Coastal South*. Chapel Hill: University of North Carolina Press, 2012.

Landsberg, Brian K. "JFK and the United States." In *John F. Kennedy History, Memory, Legacy: An Interdisciplinary Inquiry*, edited by John Delane Williams, Robert G. Waite, and Gregory S. Gordon. Grand Forks: University of North Dakota Press, 2010.

Lawson, Steven F. *Black Ballots: Voting Rights in the South, 1944–1969*. Lanham, MD: Lexington Books, 1999.

Lomax, Alan. *Mister Jelly Roll: The Fortunes of Jelly Roll Morton, New Orleans Creole, and Inventor of Jazz*. Berkeley: University of California Press, 1973.

Mason, Gilbert R., with James Patterson Smith. *Beaches, Blood, and Ballots: A Black Doctor's Civil Rights Struggle*. Jackson: University Press of Mississippi, 2007.

Moye, J. Todd. *Let the People Decide: Black Freedom and White Resistance Movements in Sunflower County, Mississippi, 1945–1986*. Chapel Hill: University of North Carolina Press, 2004.

Myers, Minnie Walter. *Romance and Realism of the Southern Gulf Coast*. Cincinnati: Robert Clarke Company, 1898.

O'Shea, M. V. *Public Education in Mississippi*. Jackson, MS: Jackson Printing Company, 1925. https://babel.hathitrust.org/cgi/pt?id=uc1.$b66041&view=1up&seq=1.

Ownby, Ted, et al., *The Mississippi Encyclopedia*. Jackson: University Press of Mississippi, 2017.

Powell, J. W. *Fifteenth Annual Report of the Bureau of Ethnology to the Secretary of the Smithsonian Institution, 1893–94*. Washington, DC: Government Printing Office, 1897.

Reiff, Joseph. *Born of Conviction*. New York: Oxford University Press, 2016.

Silver, James W. *Mississippi: The Closed Society*. New York: Harcourt, Brace, & World, 1964.

Skelton, Zan. *The Biloxi Schools 1924–2001*. Biloxi, MS: Publication Office, Biloxi Public School District, 2000.

Stanonis, Anthony J. *Faith in Bikinis: Politics and Leisure in the Coastal South Since the Civil War*. Athens: University of Georgia Press, 2014.

Trivedi, Jennifer. *Mississippi after Katrina: Disaster Recovery and Reconstruction on the Gulf Coast*. Lanham, MD: Rowman & Littlefield, 2020.

Tyson, Timothy B. *Blood Done Sign My Name: A True Story*. New York: Random House, 2005.

ARTICLES

"4 Miss. Negroes Petition for Use of Beach." *Jet*, October 22, 1959.

Adams, Desmund. "Harnessing the Power of Diversity for Profitability." *Forbes*, March 3, 2022. https://www.forbes.com/sites/forbesbusinesscouncil/2022/03/03/harnessing-the-power-of-diversity-for-profitability/?sh=205e520b459a.

Bailey, Constance. "Keeping the Civil Rights Movement Alive: Black Spring Break." *Mississippi FolkLife*, October 19, 2021. http://www.mississippifolklife.org/exhibits/keeping-the-civil-rights-movement-alive-black-spring-break.

Barber, Zacharie. "Justice, Southern Style: The Kidnapping and Murder of Mack Charles Parker." Northeast Texas Regional Phi Alpha Theta History Conference, 2014. https://twu.edu/media/documents/history-government/Justice-Southern-Style-Ibid.-Volume-7-Spring-2014.pdf.

"Biloxi Racial Flare-Up Causes $1 Million-Plus Business Loss." *Jet*, May 12, 1960.

Blokker, Laura Ewen, and Heather A. Knight. "Louisiana Bousillage: The Migration and Evolution of a French Building Technique in North America." *Construction History* 28, no. 1 (2013): 27–48. http://www.jstor.org/stable/43856026.

Bolton, Charles C. "Mississippi's School Equalization Program, 1945–1954: 'A Last Gasp to Try to Maintain a Segregated Educational System.'" *Journal of Southern History* 66, no. 4 (2000): 781–814. https://doi.org/10.2307/2588011.

Booker, Simeon. "Troops Sent to Miss.; Alabama Guard Federalized." *Jet*, June 20, 1968.

Bryant, Jeff. "Why Are Federal Funds Flowing to 'White Flight' Privatized Charter Schools?" *Dissident Voice*, July 3, 2021. https://dissidentvoice.org/2021/07/why-are-federal-funds-flowing-to-white-flight-privatized-charter-schools/.

Butler, J. Michael. "The Mississippi State Sovereignty Commission and Beach Integration, 1959–1963: A Cotton-Patch Gestapo?" *Journal of Southern History* 68, no. 1 (2002). https://doi.org/10.2307/3069692.

"Chicago Needs No Help from Mississippi's KKK." *Jet*, August 3, 1961.

"Citizens Council 'Fights' White Miss. Women." *Jet*, August 6, 1964.

"Coleman, J(ames) P(lemon)." *Scribner Encyclopedia of American Lives*, June 10, 2022. https://www.encyclopedia.com/humanities/encyclopedias-almanacs-transcripts-and-maps/coleman-james-plemon.

"Court Says Miss. Can't Deny Negroes Use of Beaches." *Jet*, January 12, 1967.

Crenshaw, Jeannette. "Care Practice #6: No Separation of Mother and Baby, with Unlimited Opportunities for Breastfeeding." *Journal of Perinatal Education* 16, no. 3 (2007): 39–43. https://doi.org/10.1624/105812407X217147.

Dark, Okianer Christian. "The Role of Howard University School of Law in *Brown v. Board of Education*." *Washington History* 16, no. 2 (2004). http://www.jstor.org/stable/40073398.

Davidson, John N. "Negro Slavery in Wisconsin." *Parkman Club Papers* 1 (1896): 103–32.

Derickson, Kate. "After Hurricane Katrina, Devastated Black Neighborhoods Created an 'Opportunity' for Redevelopment That Focused on Gentrification." London School of Economics and Political Science, July 7, 2014. http://bit.ly/TYLSYL.

DeShazo, Richard D., Robert Smith, and Leigh Baldwin Skipworth. "Black Physicians and the Struggle for Civil Rights: Lessons from the Mississippi Experience. Part 2: Their Lives and Experiences." *American Journal of Medicine* 127, no. 11 (2014). https://www.amjmed.com/article/S0002-9343(14)00492-6/pdf.

DiLiegro, Allison. "The Omni Shoreham: Washington DC's Grande Dame Full of Political History and Beatlemania." Storied Hotels. January 12, 2019. https://storiedhotels.com/washington-dc-hotels/the-omni-shoreham-washington-dcs-grande-dame-full-of-political-history-and-beatlemania/.

DiRienzo, Daniella. "Biloxi, Mississippi Was Once a Resort Destination Known for Illegal Gambling, Bootleg Whiskey, and Great Music." Only in Your State. January 10, 2021. https://www.onlyinyourstate.com/mississippi/biloxi-was-once-a-resort-destination-ms/.

DiRienzo, Daniella. "Most People Have No Idea There's a Drowned Island Hiding in the Mississippi Gulf." Only in Your State. August 8, 2016. https://www.onlyinyourstate.com/mississippi/drowned-isle-of-caprice-in-ms/.

Dixon, LaTanya L. "From Statehood to School Desegregation: Racial Disparities in the Public Education of Mississippi, 1817–1969." *AERA Open*, 2020. https://doi.org/10.1177/2332858420975396.

Dorsey, Danielle. "Dorks of Black History: Jelly Roll Morton." Danielle Dorky. 2019. http://danielledorky.com/2014/02/18/dorks-black-history-jelly-roll-morton/.

Ellis, Dan. "First People of the Pass Black Heritage: Free Persons of Color." July 2001. http://pc.danellis.net/HTMLobj-21/BlackHeritage1.pdf.

Foster, L. H. "Race Relations in the South, 1960." *Journal of Negro Education* 30, no. 2 (1961): 138–49. https://doi.org/10.2307/2294337.

Greene, Peter. "White Flight, without the Actual Flight." *Forbes*, November 12, 2019. https://www.forbes.com/sites/petergreene/2019/11/12/white-flight-without-the-actual-flight/?sh=55a4bbf853c6.

Hearn, Edward W., and M. E. Carr. "Soil Survey of the Biloxi Area, Mississippi." US Department of Agriculture, 1904. https://www.nrcs.usda.gov/Internet/FSE_MANUSCRIPTS/mississippi/biloxiMS1904/biloxiMS1904.pdf.

Higgins, Chester. "Talking About." *Jet*, October 15, 1964, 47.

Hirai, Ashley H., William M. Sappenfield, Michael D. Kogan, Wanda D. Barfield, David A. Goodman, Reem M. Ghandour, and Michael C. Lu. "Contributors to Excess Infant Mortality in the US South." *American Journal of Preventive Medicine* 46, no. 3 (2014): 219–27. https://doi.org/10.1016/j.amepre.2013.12.006.

Hoffman, Kelly M., Sophie Trawalter, Jordan R. Axt, and M. Norman Oliver. "Racial Bias in Pain Assessment." *Proceedings of the National Academy of Sciences* 113, no. 16 (2016): 4296–301. https://doi.org/10.1073/pnas.1516047113.

"Hypocrisy, Racism of Red Cross Hurt Black Hurricane Victims." *Muhammad Speaks* 9, no. 19 (January 23, 1970). https://jstor.org/stable/community.28592051.

"Is Mississippi Hushing Up a Lynching? Mississippi Gunmen Take Life of Militant Negro Minister." *Jet* 8, no. 3, (1955): 8–11.

Jackson, Josh. "Mural Commemorating Civil Rights Achievements Unveiled at Iconic Inez Cafe." WLOX, January 31, 2022. https://www.wlox.com/2022/02/01/mural-commemorating-civil-rights-achievements-unveiled-iconic-inez-caf/.

Jones, Graham, Bernardita Chirino Chace, and Justin Wright. "Cultural Diversity Drives Innovation: Empowering Teams for Success." *International Journal of Innovation Science* 12, no. 3 (August 10, 2020). https://www.emerald.com/insight/content/doi/10.1108/IJIS-04-2020-0042/full/pdf?title=cultural-diversity-drives-innovation-empowering-teams-for-success.

Kell, Garrett. "Damn the Curse of Ham: How Genesis 9 Got Twisted into Racist Propaganda." Bible & Theology, The Gospel Coalition. January 9, 2021. https://www.thegospelcoalition.org/article/damn-curse-ham/.

Kelly, David J., Paul C. Quinn, Alan M. Slater, Kang Lee, Alan Gibson, Michael Smith, Liezhong Ge, and Olivier Pascalis. "Three-Month-Olds, But Not Newborns, Prefer Own-Race Faces." *Developmental Science* 8, no. 6 (2005): 31–36. https://doi.org/10.1111/j.1467-7687.2005.0434a.x.

"Ku Klux Klan." History. Last modified February 4, 2022. https://www.history.com/topics/reconstruction/ku-klux-klan.

"League of the South Considers Black Spring Break in Biloxi a Call to Arms." Southern Poverty Law Center, September 15, 2000. https://www.splcenter.org/fighting-hate/intelligence-report/2000/league-south-considers-%E2%80%98black-spring-break%E2%80%99-biloxi-call-arms.

Lewis, John, and Archie E. Allen. "Black Voter Registration Efforts in the South." *Notre Dame Law Review* 48 (1972): 105–32. https://scholarship.law.nd.edu/cgi/viewcontent.cgi?article=2861&context=ndlr.

"Little Rock Aftermath Proved High Cost of Bias." *Jet*, June 15, 1961.

Lyon, Carter Dalton. "R. Jess Brown, Carsie A. Hall, and Jack H. Young Sr." *Mississippi Encyclopedia*, Center for Study of Southern Culture, 2017. https://mississippiencyclopedia.org/entries/r-jess-brown-carsie-a-hall-and-jack-h-young-sr/.

Minchin, Timothy J., and John A. Salmond. "'The Saddest Story of the Whole Movement': The Clyde Kennard Case and the Search for Racial Reconciliation in Mississippi, 1955–2007." *Journal of Mississippi History* 71 (Fall 2009): 191–234.

"Miss. Sheriff Doesn't 'Know' Why Jury Called Him," *Jet*, October 8, 1964.

"Mississippi Has Money Woes." *Jet*, January 7, 1965.

"Mississippi's Peaceful School." *Jet*, October 1, 1961.

Muldoon, Tim. "King Anniversary Recalls Bishop's Desegregation Efforts in Mississippi." *Catholic Telegraph*, April 6, 2018. https://www.thecatholictelegraph.com/king-anniversary-recalls-bishops-desegregation-efforts-in-mississippi/50487.

Muldowny, John. "Jefferson Davis: The Postwar Years." *Mississippi Quarterly* 23, no. 1 (1969): 22–23. http://www.jstor.org/stable/26473833.

"Murder in Mississippi." Freedom Summer, *American Experience*, PBS. Accessed June 12, 2022. https://www.pbs.org/wgbh/americanexperience/features/freedomsummer-murder/.

Murray, Pauli. "A Blueprint for First Class Citizenship." *The Crisis*, 1944.

Noble, Stuart Grayson. *Forty Years of the Public Schools in Mississippi*. Contributions to Education, No. 94. New York: Columbia University, 1918, 14.

O'Neal, Jim. "Biloxi Blues: Jelly Roll Morton and Main Street." Mississippi Blues Trail Blogspot, May 26, 2010. https://mississippibluestrail.blogspot.com/2010/05/biloxi-blues-jelly-roll-morton-and-main.html.

Poon, Linda. "Remembering Beaches as Battlegrounds for Civil Rights." Bloomberg, June 21, 2017. https://www.bloomberg.com/news/articles/2017-06-21/the-bloody-wade-ins-that-brought-equal-rights-to-beaches.

"Prof. King: Rather Die Than Return to United States." *Jet*, December 30, 1965, SSC 1-28-0-91.

Proulx, Michael G. "Professor Revisits Clark Doll Tests." *Harvard Crimson*, December 1, 2011. https://www.thecrimson.com/article/2011/12/1/clark-dolls-research-media/.

Sangrigoli, Sandy, and Scania de Schonen. "Recognition of Own-Face and Other-Race Faces by Three-Month Old Infants." *Journal of Child Psychology and Psychiatry* 45, no. 7 (2004): 1219–27. https://doi.org/10.1111/j.1469-7610.2004.00319.x.

Serban, Remus. "Here's How Workplace Diversity Boosts Profitability." Hub Gets, July 19, 2017. https://www.hubgets.com/blog/workplace-diversity-boosts-profitability/.
Silver, James W. "Mississippi: The Closed Society." *Journal of Southern History* 30, no. 1 (1964): 3–34. https://doi.org/10.2307/2205371.
Stein, Waltraut. "The White Citizens' Councils." *Negro History Bulletin* 20, no. 1 (1956): 2–23. http://www.jstor.org/stable/44215197.
Still, Larry. "Chicago Police Plan to Prevent Race Violence: Chicago Beach Wade in Test." *Jet*, July 27, 1961.
Still, Larry. "How 'Ole Miss' Crisis Affects State's Negroes." *Jet*, October 18, 1962, 16–18.
Sturdivant, Toni. "What I Learned When I Recreated the Famous 'Doll Test' That Looked at How Black Kids See Race." *The Conversation*, February 22, 2021. https://theconversation.com/what-i-learned-when-i-recreated-the-famous-doll-test-that-looked-at-how-black-kids-see-race-153780.
Usner, Daniel H. "Chitimacha Diplomacy and Commerce in Colonial Louisiana." *Louisiana History* 62, no. 2 (2021). https://www.jstor.org/stable/27033052.
Wise, Warren L. "Fingerprints of Child Slaves Found in Charleston Old Bricks." *Post and Courier of Charleston*, May 18, 2019. https://apnews.com/article/1648af4d6b2c4626abf3914f2f4078f0.
"Words of the Week." *Jet*, July 23, 1964.

MISSISSIPPI STATE SOVEREIGNTY COMMISSION (SSC) RECORDS

Bailey, Walter A. Letter to Ross Barnett. January 15, 1961. SSC 2-56-2-6.
Citizens' Councils. For Immediate Release. December 19, 1960. SSC 9-11-1-63.
Cole, L. E., Jr. Hattiesburg, Gulf Coast, Tylertown, and Poplarville. December 4, 1968. SSC 2-34-0-32.
Cole, Lee. Memorandum to Director SSC, Subject: Activity-Southern District. January 29, 1969. SSC 2-64-2-28.
DeCell, Hal C. Note. December 4, 1958. SSC 2-56-1-2.
Downing, Virgil. Civil Rights Activity in Harrison County. July 20, 1964. SSC 2-56-2-58.
Downing, Virgil. NAACP Activities in Harrison County. October 23, 1961. SSC 2-56-2-9.
Downing, Virgil. NAACP and COFO Activity in Jackson and Harrison Counties. December 23, 1964. SSC 2-56-2-70.
Ellerbrake, Richard. Letter to Albert Jones and Cosmin Eisendrath. July 8, 1960. SSC 7-0-1-152.
Hopkins, A. L. Contacting County and Municipal Superintendents of Education for the Purpose of Securing a List of the Names of Colored School Teachers in Jackson, Harrison, Stone, Forest, Covington, and Simpson Counties and the Municipalities in These Counties. March 8, 1962. SSC 2-56-2-26.
Hopkins, A. L. Continued Investigation of the Boycott of White Merchants in Edwards, Mississippi, and Buy-Ins Sponsored by the APWR in This Town. October 27, 1966. SSC 2-51-0-44.
Hopkins, A. L. Investigation in Fayette, Mississippi, on March 1, 1966, in Order to Ascertain If Persons of a Subversive Nature Were Involved in the Buy-Ins in Fayette Saturday, Feb. 26, 1966. March 4, 1966. SSC 2-51-0-44.

Johnston, Erle Jr. Letter to File, Subject: Extension Courses-Keesler Field. February 4, 1964. SSC 2-56-2-46.

Johnston, Erle Jr. Letter to Honorable Tom Scarbrough, Investigator, Subject: Raymond Carroll. January 15, 1965. SSC 2-56-2-74.

Jones, Albert. Letter to Billy Meadows. June 29, 1961. SSC 2-56-1-83.

Jones, Albert. Memo to File: NAACP Activities, Harrison County Mississippi. July 11, 1960. SSC 2-56-1-49.

Jones, Albert. Subject: Beach Integration and DeSoto National Forest Park Harrison County, Mississippi. July 5, 1960. SSC 5-4-0-115.

Mason, Gilbert, Sr. Letter to Member. June 19, 1960. SSC 2-56-1-36.

McCoy, A. H. Letter to Herbert Bromwell. May 11, 1955. Jackson, Mississippi. SSC 2-5-2-36.

Mississippi Advisory Committee to the United States Commission on Civil Rights. Report on Mississippi. January 1963. SSC 4-0-1-82.

Scarbrough, Tom. Harrison County. January 16, 1961. SSC 2-56-1-77.

Scarbrough, Tom. Harrison County. March 23, 1964. SSC 2-56-2-48.

Scarbrough, Tom. Title: COFO Rental of Property at Point Cadet in Harrison County, Mississippi. October 19, 1964. SSC 2-56-2-62.

Stockstill, J. E. Letter to Rev. Richard Ellerbrake. July 11, 1960. SSC 7-0-1-156.

Thomas, Bob. Memo to Governor Ross Barnett, Subject: Beach Disturbances, Biloxi, Harrison Co., Mississippi. May 2, 1960. SSC 5-4-0-50.

Thomas, Bob. Memo to Governor Ross Barnett, Subject: Beach Disturbances, Gulfport, Harrison Co., Mississippi. SSC 5-4-0-51.

Thomas, Robert C. Assignment to Contact Nap Cassibry in Gulfport Relative to a Conversation He Had with Louis Hollis of the Citizen's Council Regarding Information He Has about Racial Conditions in Harrison County and DeSota National Park. July 25, 1960. SSC 2-56-1-59.

Thomas, Robert C. Investigation of Disturbances at DeSoto National Forest Park, Harrison County Mississippi, on July 4, 1960. July 7, 1960. SSC 2-56-1-51.

Thomas, Robert C. Investigation of Disturbances at DeSoto National Forest Park, Harrison County Mississippi, on July 4, 1960. July 11, 1960. SSC 2-56-1-54.

Thomas, Robert C. Memo to: Director SSC, Subject Harrison County NAACP Activities. June 27, 1960. SSC 2-56-1-41.

Untitled Document, Chicago, Illinois. August 25–31, 1968. SSC 9-31-8-61.

Van Landingham, Zack J. Letter to M. W. High. February 4, 1960. SSC 2-56-1-23.

Van Landingham, Zack J. Memo to Director, State Sovereignty Commission, Subject: Beach Integration, Harrison County, Mississippi. October 20, 1959. SSC 2-56-1-17.

Van Landingham, Zack J. Memo to Director, State Sovereignty Commission, Subject: NAACP, Gulfport, Mississippi. February 13, 1959. SSC 2-56-1-5.

Van Landingham, Zack J. Memo to Director, State Sovereignty Commission, Subject: NAACP, Gulfport, Mississippi. February 16, 1959. SSC 1-23-0-30.

Van Landingham, Zack J. Memo to Director, State Sovereignty Commission, Subject: NAACP, Gulfport, Mississippi. June 2, 1959. SSC 2-56-1-12.

Van Landingham, Zack J. Memo to File 5-4, Subject: Beach Integration, Harrison County, Mississippi. May 4, 1960. SSC 2-56-1-33.

Van Landingham, Zack J. Memo to File, Subject: NAACP, Biloxi, Mississippi. March 21, 1960. SSC 2-56-1-26.

Van Landingham, Zack J. Memo to: File, Subject: NAACP, Harrison County, Mississippi. February 5, 1960. SSC 2-56-1-24.

Van Landingham, Zack J. Memo to: Governor Ross R. Barnett, Subject: Attempted Beach Integration, Mississippi Gulf Coast. February 4, 1960. SSC 2-56-1-21.

Van Landingham, Zack J. Memo to J. P. Coleman, Subject: B. L. Bell Informant-Administrative. January 12, 1959. SSC 2-10-0-6.

Van Landingham, Zack J. To: Director SSC, Subject: NAACP, Harrison County, Mississippi. October 14, 1959. SSC 2-56-1-16.

Van Landingham, Zack J. To: File, Subject: NAACP, Hancock County, Mississippi. February 4, 1960. SSC 2-56-1-22.

INTERVIEWS

Aregood, Rev. John & Joy, and Dr. Gilbert R. Mason Jr. Interview with Louis Kyriakoudes. Mississippi Oral History Program, University of Southern Mississippi, May 3, 2001. Recorded digitally in two files.

Carney, G. W. Interview. Center for Oral History and Cultural History, University of Southern Mississippi, June 12, 2010.

Clay, Ethel R. Interview by Louis Kyriakoudes. Mississippi Oral History Program, University of Southern Mississippi, April 24, 2010.

Davis, Myrtle. Interview by Louis Kyriakoudes. Mississippi Oral History Program, University of Southern Mississippi, June 12, 2010.

Dr. Gilbert R. Mason Sr. (The HistoryMakers A2002.202), interviewed by Larry Crowe, November 11, 2002. The HistoryMakers Digital Archive. Session 1, tape 2, story 10. Dr. Mason talks about transferring to Lanier High School and skipping eleventh grade.

Dr. Gilbert R. Mason Sr. (The HistoryMakers A2002.202), interviewed by Larry Crowe, November 11, 2002. The HistoryMakers Digital Archive. Session 1, tape 2, story 15. Dr. Mason describes why he enrolled at Tennessee State University in Nashville.

Dr. Gilbert R. Mason Sr. (The HistoryMakers A2002.202), interviewed by Larry Crowe, November 11, 2002. The HistoryMakers Digital Archive. Session 1, tape 3, story 2. Dr. Mason describes his experiences attending Howard University College of Medicine.

Dr. Gilbert R. Mason Sr. (The HistoryMakers A2002.202), interviewed by Larry Crowe, November 11, 2002. The HistoryMakers Digital Archive. Session 1, tape 3, story 3. Dr. Mason describes his experiences with racism as an intern at Homer G. Phillips Hospital in St. Louis, Missouri.

Dr. Gilbert R. Mason Sr. (The HistoryMakers A2002.202), interviewed by Larry Crowe, November 11, 2002. The HistoryMakers Digital Archive. Session 1, tape 3, story 4. Dr. Mason describes the racism he faced working as a doctor.

Dr. Gilbert R. Mason Sr. (The HistoryMakers A2002.202), interviewed by Larry Crowe, November 11, 2002. The HistoryMakers Digital Archive. Session 1, tape 3, story 5. Dr. Mason describes why he continued to practice medicine in Biloxi, Mississippi, rather than move to Ohio.

Dr. Gilbert R. Mason Sr. (The HistoryMakers A2002.202), interviewed by Larry Crowe, November 11, 2002. The HistoryMakers Digital Archive. Session 1, tape 3, story 9. Dr. Mason talks about organizing and participating in the "Bloody Sunday" wade-in on the Gulf Coast beach.

Dr. Gilbert R. Mason Sr. (The HistoryMakers A2002.202), interviewed by Larry Crowe, November 11, 2002. The HistoryMakers Digital Archive. Session 1, tape 3, story 10. Dr. Mason talks about being reprimanded by the Gulf Coast Medical Society for his civil rights activities.

Dr. Gilbert R. Mason Sr. (The HistoryMakers A2002.202), interviewed by Larry Crowe, November 11, 2002. The HistoryMakers Digital Archive. Session 1, tape 4, story 2. Dr. Mason talks about the ruling that effectively desegregated the Gulf Coast beach in 1969.

Dr. Gilbert R. Mason Sr. (The HistoryMakers A2002.202), interviewed by Larry Crowe, November 11, 2002. The HistoryMakers Digital Archive. Session 1, tape 4, story 4. Dr. Mason describes what happened to the money intended for his bail after the Gulf Coast beach wade-ins of 1963.

Dr. Gilbert R. Mason Sr. (The HistoryMakers A2002.202), interviewed by Larry Crowe, November 11, 2002. The HistoryMakers Digital Archive. Session 1, tape 5, story 1. Dr. Mason describes a racist incident at Howard Memorial Hospital in Biloxi, Mississippi.

Dr. Gilbert R. Mason Sr. (The HistoryMakers A2002.202), interviewed by Larry Crowe, November 11, 2002. The HistoryMakers Digital Archive. Session 1, tape 5, story 5. Dr. Mason talks about his family.

Dr. Gilbert R. Mason Sr. (The HistoryMakers A2002.202), interviewed by Larry Crowe, November 11, 2002. The HistoryMakers Digital Archive. Session 1, tape 5, story 9. Dr. Mason narrates his photographs.

Draughn, Daniel. Interview with author, June 13, 2020.

Evans, Wilson, II. Interview with Dr. Orley B. Caudill. Center for Oral History and Cultural History, University of Southern Mississippi, June 11, 1918.

Hayes, Eleanora. Interview with Angela Sartin. Mississippi Oral History Program, University of Southern Mississippi, November 3, 1999.

Hope, Bobby C. Interview with Elaine Fontas. Mississippi Oral History Program, University of Southern Mississippi, April 24, 2010.

Jimerson, Clemon, Sr. Interview with author, May 12, 2022.

Jimerson, Clemon P. Interview with Curtis Austin. Mississippi Oral History Program, University of Southern Mississippi, August 24, 2010.

Kennedy, Janice. Interview with Kendall Holder. Mississippi Oral History Program, University of Southern Mississippi, April 24, 2010.

Kennedy, John F. Civil Rights Address. Washington, DC, June 11, 1963. https://www.american rhetoric.com/speeches/jfkcivilrights.htm.

Lott, Adell. Interview with Melissa Hall, "An Oral History with Adell Lott." Oral History Program of the University of Southern Mississippi, April 24, 2010.

Mason, Gilbert. Interview with Bill Ellison, "Mississippi Moments: Dr. Gilbert Mason—Healthcare and Civil Rights." Center for Oral History and Cultural Heritage, University of Southern Mississippi, February 19, 2018. https://www.iheart.com/podcast/256 -mississippi-moments-podcas-30950668/episode/msm-559-dr-gilbert-r-mason -39213499/.

Mason, Gilbert. Interview with Bill Ellison, "Mississippi Moments: Dr. Gilbert Mason—In Memory of Medgar." Center for Oral History and Cultural Heritage, University of Southern Mississippi, June 25, 2013.
Mason, Gilbert, Jr. Interview with author, May 5, 2022.
McSwain, Willie Jean. Interview. Mississippi Oral History Program, University of Southern Mississippi, April 24, 2010.
Moore, Earl Napoleon. Interview with Angela Sartin. Community Bridges Oral History Project, COHCH, November 9, 1999.
O'Keefe, Jeremiah J. Interview by Worth W. Long. Mississippi Oral History Program, University of Southern Mississippi, n.d.
Owens, Lee, Jr. Interview with Dora Feazant. Center for Oral History and Cultural History, University of Southern Mississippi, June 12, 2010.
Owens, Lee, Jr. Interview with William Henderson. Mississippi Oral History Program, University of Southern Mississippi, April 26, 2000.
Richardson, Rachael. Interview with author, June 10, 2020.
Watson, Clara Griffin. Interviewed by Angela Sartin. Community Bridges Oral History Project, Center for Oral History and Cultural History, October 28, 1999.
Watson, Minnie. Interview for American History TV. "Medgar Evers House," CSPAN3, April 28, 2014. https://www.c-span.org/video/?319880-1/medgar-evers-house.

OTHER SOURCES

1850 US Census, Harrison County, Mississippi, population schedule, unnamed township, 1–69 (handwritten). Dwelling number/family number? [publication/roll number].
1850 US Census, Harrison County, Mississippi, slave schedule, unnamed township, 1–15 (handwritten). Dwelling number/family number? [publication/roll number].
1860 US Census, Harrison County, Mississippi, population schedule, unnamed township, 12 (handwritten). Dwelling number/family number? [publication/roll number].
1900 US Census, Harrison County, Mississippi, population schedule, unnamed township, 12 (handwritten). Dwelling number/family number? [publication/roll number].
"Adele Mingo Black." Obituary, Marshall Funeral Homes, December 14, 2015.
Amended Complaint: *US v. Harrison County, Mississippi, et al.*, Civil Action No. 2262. July 20, 1961. Civil Rights Litigation Clearinghouse. https://clearinghouse.net/doc/78746/.
Answers to Interrogatories of State of Mississippi, Comparison of Education for Negroes and White Persons 1890–1963, *United States v. State of Mississippi* (US District Court for the Southern District of Mississippi), Docket Number: 62-03312. https://clearinghouse.net/doc/78668/.
Answers to Interrogatories of State of Mississippi, Purpose of Laws 1890, 1954, 1960, 1962; Decrease in Negro Registration 1890–1954, *United States v. State of Mississippi* (US District Court for the Southern District of Mississippi), Civil Action No. 3312. https://clearinghouse.net/doc/78672/.
Answers to Interrogatories of State of Mississippi, Statistics: Census—Registration—Voting 1890–1962, *United States v. State of Mississippi* (US District Court for the Southern District of Mississippi). https://clearinghouse.net/doc/78670/.

SELECTED BIBLIOGRAPHY

Bauhoff, Dorothy. "Skilled Labor: An Overview." *Gail Library of Daily Life Encyclopedia.* Accessed June 10, 2021. https://www.encyclopedia.com/humanities/applied-and-social-sciences-magazines/skilled-labor-overview.

Bellande, Ray L. "African-American History." Ocean Springs Archives. Accessed June 10, 2021. https://oceanspringsarchives.net/african-american-history.

Bellande, Ray L. "Buildings, Architects, and Contractors: 1895." Biloxi Historical Society. Accessed June 10, 2021. https://biloxihistoricalsociety.org/buildings-architects-and-contractors.

Bellande, Ray L. "Dukate Family." Biloxi Historical Society. https://biloxihistoricalsociety.org/dukate-family.

Bellande, Ray L. "An Early Black History of Ocean Springs." Ocean Springs Archives. Accessed June 10, 2021. https://oceanspringsarchives.net/african-american-history.

Bellande, Ray L. "History of D'Iberville." Ocean Springs Archives. Accessed April 2, 2022. https://oceanspringsarchives.net/history-diberville.

Bellande, Ray L. "Streets and Roads." Biloxi Historical Society. Accessed June 10, 2021. https://biloxihistoricalsociety.org/streets-and-roads.

Berry, Mary Frances. *Racial and Ethnic Tensions in American Communities: Poverty, Inequality, and Discrimination.* Volume 7: The Mississippi Delta Report. Washington, DC: Commission on Civil Rights, 2001.

"Biloxi, 1964, July-August." Sally Belfrage papers, 1962–1966, Historical Society Library Microforms Room, Micro 599, Reel 1, Segment 9. Accessed via COFO reports, Freedom Summer Digital Collection, Wisconsin Historical Society. https://content.wisconsinhistory.org/digital/collection/p15932coll2/id/36814.

Biloxi City Directory, Vol. 5. Chillicothe, OH: Mullin-Kille, 1958.

"Biloxi, MS, Weather History." Keesler AFB Station. May 4, 1959. https://www.wunderground.com/history/daily/us/ms/biloxi/KBIX/date/1959-5-4.

"Biography: Clyde Kennard." Americans Who Tell the Truth. https://www.americanswhotellthetruth.org/portraits/clyde-kennard.

Blokker, Laura Ewen. "East Biloxi African American and Civil Rights Historic Resources Survey 2017." Mississippi Department of Archives and History. July 31, 2017. https://www.biloxi.ms.us/wp-content/uploads/2017/10/EastBiloxiInventory2017.pdf.

Bourdier, Jim. "Overturned Car." Associated Press. June 1963. History.com. https://www.history.com/news/how-civil-rights-wade-ins-desegregated-southern-beaches.

Boyce, William D. "The American Boy Scout Movement and Black History, a Story." *African American Registry.* https://aaregistry.org/story/the-african-american-boy-scout-movement-a-story/.

Brady, Robert A., and Vernon J. Ehlers. *Black Americans in Congress 1870–2007.* Office of History and Preservation. Washington, DC: US Government Printing Office, 2008.

Bruce, William. Letter to Bill Minor. July 25, 2000.

"Christopher Rosado (9 Nov 1913–15 Jun 1989)." Find a Grave, database citing Biloxi National Cemetery, Biloxi, Mississippi.

"Christopher Rosado." City Directory, Biloxi, Mississippi, 1958, 676.

"City within a City: African American Culture in Biloxi." Ohr-O'Keefe Museum of Art. https://georgeohr.org/exhibition/city-within-a-city/.

"The Civil Rights Act of 1964: A Long Struggle for Freedom." Library of Congress. Accessed May 6, 2022. https://www.loc.gov/exhibits/civil-rights-act/civil-rights-era.html.

Cohen, Julie, and Betsy West. *My Name Is Pauli Murray*. Amazon Studios. September 17, 2021. Min. 00:25–00:29.

Complaint, *United States v. State of Mississippi et al.*, Civil Action No. 3312. https://clearinghouse.net/doc/77058/.

"CPL Lewis Black (17 June 1921–2 January 1979)." Find a Grave, database citing Biloxi National Cemetery, Biloxi, Mississippi.

Darden, C. R. President of Mississippi State Conference NAACP to Hon. John C. Stennis, February 18, 1960. Civil Rights Movement Archive. https://www.crmvet.org/docs/6002_naacp_lynch-let.pdf.

Davis, Abraham L., and Barbara L. Graham. *The Supreme Court, Race, and Civil Rights*. Thousand Oaks, CA: Sage Publications, 1995.

"Declaration of Constitutional Principles." March 12, 1956. https://tigerprints.clemson.edu/cgi/viewcontent.cgi?article=2379&context=strom.

D'Iberville Historical Society. "The Old Brickyard." 2017. Historical Marker. D'Iberville, Mississippi. https://www.hmdb.org/m.asp?m=122401.

Dorsey, Saul. "Republic of New Afrika." Center for Study of Southern Culture. Accessed September 23, 2021. http://mississippiencyclopedia.org/entries/republic-of-new-afrika/.

"Dr. Gilbert R. Mason, Sr., Medical Office." National Register of Historic Places Registration Form. https://www.apps.mdah.ms.gov/nom/prop/101916.pdf.

Drizin, Steven A., Bobby Owens, Barry Bradford, Agnieszka Mazur, Mona Ghadiri, and Callie McCune. "Pardon Docket No. 06-0005 Before the Honorable Haley Barbour, Governor, State of Mississippi, in the Matter of Clyde Kennard." 2006. https://wwws.law.northwestern.edu/legalclinic/wrongfulconvictions/exonerations/documents/mskennardexhibits.pdf.

"The Early Years." 2008. https://biloxi.ms.us/pdf/centennialdisplay.pdf.

Ellerbrake, Richard. Letter to Bill Minor. July 14, 2000.

Ellerbrake, Richard. Re: Biloxi Wade-Ins, email to author. April 26, 2022.

Ellerbrake, Richard. Re: Biloxi Wade-Ins, email to author. August 31, 2022.

Ellerbrake, Richard. Re: Biloxi Wade-Ins, email to author. August 31, 2021.

Ellerbrake, Richard. Re: Biloxi Wade-Ins, email to author. May 16, 2022.

Ellerbrake, Richard. "Report from Biloxi, Mississippi, Back Bay Mission No. 3." May 31, 1961.

Evers, Medgar W. Letter to Dr. Gilbert Mason. October 18, 1960. In Mason, *Beaches, Blood, and Ballots: A Black Doctor's Civil Rights Struggle*, 6.

Evers, Medgar W. Letter to Mr. Robert L. Carter. October 11, 1960. In Mason, *Beaches, Blood, and Ballots: A Black Doctor's Civil Rights Struggle*, 7.

Felder, Adolph P. "Old French Fort (de la Pointe—Krebs House), Pascagoula, Mississippi." National Park Service, Department of the Interior, Washington, DC, September 19, 1940.

Foley, Brendan. "Slaves in the American Maritime Economy, 1638–1865: Economic and Cultural Roles." www.mit.edu/people/bpfoley/slavery2.html.

Gale, Neil. "Thompsons Cafeteria Restaurants of Chicago, Illinois." *Digital Research Library of Illinois History Journal*, December 31, 2016. https://drloihjournal.blogspot.com/2016/12/thompsons-cafeteria-restaurants-of.html.

"The General Condition of the Mississippi Negro." SNCC. October 1963. https://www.crmvet.org/docs/6310_sncc_ms-research.pdf.

"Harold Boglin." City Directory, Biloxi, Mississippi, 1958, 431.

Harrison County, Mississippi, et al. v. Mrs. Lee Dicks Guice, No. 42.276, May 7, 1962. In SSC 2-56-2-39.

Haughton, G. R. "The Fall Session of the Southern Christian Ministers' Conference of Mississippi Presents: An Institute on Nonviolent Resistance to Segregation." Jackson, MS: Pearl Street A. M. E. Church, 1959. In SSC 2-126-1-29.

"History." National Medical Association. Accessed August 30, 2021. https://www.nmanet.org/page/History.

"In Re: Lynching of Willile Kirkland at Thomasville, Georgia." Howard Washington Raper Papers, Series 3, Box 15, Folder 749, SHC.

Indian Echo 28 (1966): 147–60. Accessed through Ancestry.com on June 10, 2022.

"The Jackson Movement Information Bulletin: Murder Inc." NAACP. Circa December 1963. Civil Rights Movement Archive. https://www.crmvet.org/docs/6312_jax_murder.pdf.

Jackson Municipal Separate School District v. Darrell Kenyatta Evers, Biloxi Municipal Separate School District v. Gilbert R. Mason, Jr., and *Leake County School Board v. Dian Hudson et al.*, Nos. 21851–52, No. 21878, United States Court of Appeals Fifth Circuit, January 26, 1966. https://openjurist.org/357/f2d/653/jackson-municipal-separate-school-district-v-evers-biloxi-municipal-separate-school-district.

"Jim Crow Laws." National Park Service. April 17, 2018. https://www.nps.gov/malu/learn/education/jim_crow_laws.htm.

Jones, Mark. "Eat Anywhere! Mary Church Terrell, the Lost Laws, and the End of Segregation in D. C. Restaurants." WETA, June 8, 2017.

Kincannon, A. A. "Manner of Apportioning Common School Fund." *Biennial Report of the State Superintendent of Public Education to the Legislature of Mississippi for Scholastic Years 1897–98 and 1898–99*. Jacksonville, FL: Vance Printing Co., insert 1.

King, Martin Luther, Jr. "The Look to the Future." Speech, Monteagle, Tennessee, September 2, 1957. Duke University. https://repository.duke.edu/dc/broadsides/bdsal40033.

Leach, Christopher. "Troubled Water: The Wade-Ins of Dr. Gilbert." WGNO. February 18, 2020.

"Lee's Obituary." Marshall Funeral Home. April 2001. https://www.marshallfh.com/obituary/lee-owens-jr.

Lund, Jim. "African Americans Stage a Wade-In on the Beach in Biloxi on April 24, 1960, to Protest the 'White-Only' Status of the Beaches." *Daily Herald*, April 24, 1960. https://www.wlox.com/2019/05/15/community-comes-together-remember-biloxi-beach-wade-ins/.

Lund, Jim. "A Group of Whites Chase Blacks." *Daily Herald*, April 24, 1960. https://www.sunherald.com/article145247704.html.

MacKenzie, Morgan. "American Lightships, 1820–1983: History, Construction, and Archaeology within the Maritime Cultural Landscape." Master's Thesis, East Carolina University, 2011. https://media.defense.gov/2020/Sep/28/2002507185/-1/1/0/LIGHTSHIP_AMERICAN_HISTORY%201820-1983.PDF.

"Malcolm Hoyd Jackson." Find A Grave. findagrave.com.

Mason, Aria M. "The Woman Behind the Man: The Life and Work of Natalie H. Mason." https://gilbertrmason.com/the-life-of-natalie-h-mason.

Maxson, Michael. "Medgar Evers." Ferris State University. 2015. https://www.ferris.edu/HTMLS/news/jimcrow/witnesses/medgarevers.htm.

Memorandum for the United States in Opposition to Defendants' Motion to Dismiss (May 1, 1963). *US v. Biloxi Municipal Separate School District et al.*, Civil Action No. 2643. and *US v. Gulfport.*

Meraji, Shereen Marisol, and Gene Demby. Interview with Peniel Joseph. "Unmasking the 'Outside Agitator.'" *Code Switch*, NPR. June 10, 2020. https://www.npr.org/2020/06/09/873592665/unmasking-the-outside-agitator.

Miller, Ronald W. National Register of Historic Places Inventory—Nomination Form. Magnolia Hotel. November 10, 1972. https://www.apps.mdah.ms.gov/nom/prop/9845.pdf.

Mimeographed Record, *United States v. Biloxi Municipal Separate School District et al.*, (US Court of Appeals for the Fifth Circuit), Docket Number: 63-02643. https://clearinghouse.net/doc/78366/.

"Mississippi." United States Census Bureau, 26. https://www2.census.gov/prod2/decennial/documents/06229686v20-25ch3.pdf.

Municipal Separate School District et al., Civil Action No. 2678. Civil Rights Litigation Clearing House.

"Myrtle's Obituary." Marshall Funeral Home. October 2015. https://www.marshallfh.com/obituary/5056736.

"Nolan McSwain." Marshall Funeral Home. https://www.marshallfh.com/obituary/5057694.

Novoa, Cristina, and Jamila Taylor. "Exploring African Americans' High Maternal and Infant Death Rates." Center for American Progress. February 1, 2018. https://americanprogress.org/issues/early-childhood/reports/2018/02/01/445576/exploring-african-americans-high-maternal-infant-death-rates/.

"Numbers of Negroes Registered by County." SNCC report, Civil Rights Movement Archive. https://www.crmvet.org/docs/610000_sncc_vr_stats.pdf.

Nuwer, Deanne Stephens. "The Seafood Industry in Biloxi: Its Early History, 1848–1930." *Mississippi History Now*, June 2006. https://mshistorynow.mdah.ms.gov/issue/the-seafood-industry-in-biloxi-its-early-history-1848-1930.

"The Old Shoreham Hotel at 15th and H Streets NW." Streets of Washington: Stories and Images of Historic Washington, DC, January 03, 2010. http://www.streetsofwashington.com/2010/01/old-shoreham-hotel-at-15th-and-h.html.

"Our History." Infinity Funeral Homes. Accessed August 9, 2012. https://www.infinityfuneralhomes.com/about-us/our-history.

"Our History." NAACP. Accessed May 6, 2022. https://naacp.org/about/our-history.

"Pauli Murray Organizes Howard Student Sit-Ins." Student Non-Violent Coordinating Committee Digital. https://snccdigital.org/events/pauli-murray-organizes-howard-student-sit-ins/.

PFC James William McKinley (9 Dec 1929–7 Aug 1990). Find a Grave, database citing Biloxi National Cemetery, Biloxi, Mississippi.

Pierre Le Blond de la Tour. Carte de partie de la coste du Nouveau Biloxy avec les isles des environs [map]. ca. 1722. "Research Laboratories of Archaeology. Early Maps of the American South—Local Haps: Harbors and Islands (Gulf Coast)." Last updated November 26, 2021. https://rla.unc.edu/emas/local-gulf-harb.html#Bilo.

Pilgram, David. "What Was Jim Crow." Ferris State University. September 2000. https://www.ferris.edu/jimcrow/what.htm.

Pitt, Matthew. "Civil Rights Watershed in Biloxi, Mississippi." *Smithsonian Magazine*, April 19, 2010. https://www.smithsonianmag.com/history/a-civil-rights-watershed-in-biloxi-mississippi-20888869.

"Plaintiff's Memorandum in Opposition (October 22, 1962): *US v. Harrison County, Mississippi et al.*," Civil Action No. 2262, Civil Rights Litigation. ClearingHouse.net.

Porter, Dawn, dir. *Spies of Mississippi: Spying on the Civil Rights Movement*. Trilogy Films, 2013.

P'Pool, Kenneth. "Historic Resources of Biloxi (Partial Inventory: Historic and Architectural Sites)." April 10, 1984. https://www.apps.mdah.ms.gov/t_nom/Historic%20Resources%20of%20Biloxi.pdf.

Rehofus "Rea" Staples Esters Sr. (18 May 1923–22 Sep 2014). Find a Grave, database citing Biloxi National Cemetery, Biloxi, Mississippi.

"Remembering the Struggle and Looking Back with Dr. Gilbert Mason Jr." *Go to Places Monthly*, February 5, 2013. https://gotoplaces.wordpress.com/2013/02/05/1345/.

Reynolds, Elizabeth P. National Register of Historic Places Inventory—Nomination Form. Pradat House, Toledano House, Philbrick House, Red Brick House, Tullis House. United States Department of the Interior, National Park Service. August 26, 1976. https://www.apps.mdah.ms.gov/nom/prop/9880.pdf.

Salvatore, Susan Cianci, et al., "Civil Rights in America: Racial Voting Rights." National Park Service, 2009.

Shafer, Ronald G. "The 'Mississippi Plan' to Keep Blacks from Voting in 1890: 'We Came Here to Exclude the Negro.'" *Washington Post*, May 1, 2021. https://www.washingtonpost.com/history/2021/05/01/mississippi-constitution-voting-rights-jim-crow/.

SNCC Digital Gateway. https://snccdigital.org/.

Solly, Meilan. "What the First Women Voters Experienced When Registering for the 1920 Election." *Smithsonian Magazine*, July 30, 2020. https://www.smithsonianmag.com/history/what-first-women-voters-experienced-when-registering-1920-election-180975435/.

Spruill, Marjorie Julian, and Jesse Spruill Wheeler. "Mississippi Women and the Woman Suffrage Amendment." *Mississippi History Now*, December 2001. http://www.mshistorynow.mdah.ms.gov/articles/245/mississippi-women-and-the-woman-suffrage-amendment.

"Table 11. Infant Mortality Rates by Race: United States, Select Years 1950–2015." Centers for Disease Control and Prevention. 2016. www.cdc.gov/nchs/data/hus/2016/011.pdf.

Trenholm, Sandra. "Robert Kennedy on Civil Rights, 1963." The Gilder Lehrman Institute of American History, 2012. Transcript January 24, 1963. https://www.gilderlehrman.org/sites/default/files/inline-pdfs/05630_FPS_0.pdf.

Truly, Jeff. *Artificially Stimulated Immigration*. Jackson, MS: Tucker Printing House, 1907. Mississippi Department of Archives and History. Broadside file/Politics/20th century/Folder 4/1907/2.

United States v. Harrison County et al., Civil Action No. 2262. "Amended Complaint." https://www.clearinghouse.net/chDocs/public/PA-MS-0003-0002.pdf.

Woodruff, Richard. Letter to Erle Johnston Jr. February 3, 1965. SSC 99-89-0-116.

Zhou, Li. "The Trope of 'Outside Agitators' at Protests, Explained." *Vox*, June 3, 2020. https://www.vox.com/2020/6/3/21275720/george-floyd-protests-outside-agitators-ferguson-civil-rights-movement.

INDEX

Adam, Cayton Bidwell, 62
Adams, O. L., 8
Adams, Sam, 117n32
Addison, Clarence, 64
A. E. Perkins Elementary School, 72–73, 86
Aid to Dependent Children, 155n20
Alcorn Agricultural and Mechanical College, 20, 73, 88
Allen, J. L., 74
Allen, Percy, 86
Allen, William, 82
Alpha Phi Alpha, 105
American Academy of Family Physicians, 102
American Board of Family Medicine, 102
American Civil Liberties Union (ACLU), 108
American Medical Association, 15
American Red Cross, 103
Andrews, Robert, 47, 50
Anglado, Anthony, 50
anti-protest legislation, 50–51. *See also* Mason Bill
Aregood, John M., 81–85, 101, 110, 152n85
Aregood, Joy (*née* Hartman), 83, 135n18, 152n85
Army Corps of Engineers, 8, 60, 64–65
Arnn, Gene C., 154
Askew, Henry, 7, 117n32
Asmar, Celeste, 114n16
Asmar, Charles/Chalot, 114n16
Asmar, Madeline, 114n16
Asmard, Julia (*née* de la Brosse), 114n16

Atlanta Constitution, 117n32
Austin, Joseph, 29–33, 125n9

Back Bay Mission, 40, 44, 51, 81, 85, 135n18, 141n22. *See also* St. Paul's United Church of Christ
"Back-of-Town" (historical African American section of Biloxi), 6–8, 14–15, 35, 39–40, 44, 46, 52, 69–72, 83, 98, 102–4, 109. *See also* Kendall brickworks; redlining
Bailey, Constance, 110
Bailey, Walter A., 23, 58, 68, 75, 91. *See also* Ku Klux Klan of Mississippi (KKK)
BAM, Black Angry Men (and Women), 33, 80
Bancroft Day School, 94
Baricev's Seafood Harbor Restaurant & Lounge, 42
Barnett, Ross, 34, 37, 49–50, 59, 68
Barrett, Richard, 106
Barrett, Walter C., 51
Batia, William "Billy," Jr., 96, 151n61
Battle, Clinton, 33, 56, 105
Beaches, Blood, and Ballots: A Black Doctor's Civil Rights Struggle, 12, 68
beach road. *See* Highway 90
Beauvoir Elementary, 97
Beauvoir historic plantation, 6, 69, 141n17
Beauvoir United Methodist of Biloxi, 85
Bell, Derrick, 76, 87, 92, 97
Bellamy, Alexander, 97
Belzoni, Mississippi, 22

Benoit, Bernard, 114
Benoit, Theodore, 114
Biloxi, Mississippi: indigenous people (*see* Tanêks); police station, 7, 27, 35, 45, 47–49, 82, 96, 125n19; schools, 6, 26, 52, 70–77, 80, 84, 86–88, 91–92, 94–100, 103–4, 109, 133n69, 142n24, 154n15 (*see also* Biloxi Colored School; dual school system; Nichols High School; school desegregation)
Biloxi Beach Property Owners Protective Association, 60, 65, 78
Biloxi Black Cats, 125n13
Biloxi Business Club, 8
Biloxi Chamber of Commerce, 15, 55
Biloxi City Hall, 27, 82, 125n21
Biloxi Civic League, 103
Biloxi Colored School, 6, 70–71
Biloxi Community House, 143n38
Biloxi High School, 71, 88, 98–99
Biloxi MacArthur Hotel, 40–41
Biloxi Planning Commission, 103
Biloxi Stadium, 101
Birmingham, Alabama (1964), 129n2
Black, Adele Mingo, 76
Black, Diane, 76
Black, Gary, 76
Black, James, 39, 42–43, 57, 81
Black, Jerry, 76, 91, 98
Black, Lewis, 76
Black Baptist Church (Biloxi). *See* First Missionary Baptist Church of Biloxi (Main Street)
Black compliance: as peer pressure, 17, 146n15; SSC informants, 23. *See also* Black press
Black Contributions to America, 106
Black cultural education events, 104, 107
Black femininity, 9, 13, 17, 42–44, 48, 62, 71–72, 80–82, 86, 103, 105–6, 120n18, 128n64, 135n18. *See also* Black maternal and infant mortality rate; women's suffrage
Black Interdenominational Ministerial Alliance of Gulfport, 53

Black maternal and infant mortality rate, 15–16
Black press, 23, 49, 55–56, 80–81, 119n3
Black separatism, 29
Black Spring Break, 110
Blessing of the Fleet, 78
Blum, Steve, 91
Boglin, Daryl, 76
Boglin, Harold, 76
Boglin, Myrtle Shirley, 76
Bolton, Eldon L., 81
Boston Globe, 97
bousillage (houses), 4
Bousqueto, Arthur, 80
boycotts, economic, 21, 32, 35, 57–58, 67, 146n15. *See also* tourism
Boy Scouts, 11; Eagle Scouts, 11, 107; Mason's Biloxi troop (416), 15, 26–27, 68, 104, 144n53; Pascagoula Troops (407 and 430), 144n53; Pine Burr Council, 56. *See also* Camp Attawah
Braxton, Floyd, 82
Bridges, Frank, 48
Broadus, Dennis, 137n68. *See also* Harrison County Board of Supervisors
Brown, Ellis, 42, 131n22
Brown, Henry, 19
Brown, Johnnie Mae Collins, 76
Brown, Mary, 91
Brown, Paul, 50
Brown, Reuben, 91
Brown, Richard Jess, 85
Brown, Robert D., 96
Brown Funeral Home, 45
Brown v. Board of Education of Topeka, 21–23, 31, 72, 75, 89, 91–92, 138n20, 143n38
Bruce, Blanche K., 17
Buckley, Luther, 98, 144n53
Buena Vista Hotel, 35, 42, 43
Bullock, Luzell, 41
Burkett, Willie, 64
Burns, James Albert, 7, 116n29
Butterfield, Ray, 51

INDEX

Calhoon, Solomon, 18
Camp Attawah, 26, 124n9
Campbell, H. A., 65
Cannon, Harry, 84
Carden, Vincent, 143n38
Carlos, John, 99
Carney, G. W., 42
Carney, Le'Roy, 41
Carroll, John, 130n17
Carter, Hodding, II, 87, 89, 92–93
Carter, Robert L., 57
Carthage, Mississippi, 74
Central Elementary, 142
Cesareo, Thomas C. Rinera, 132n63
Chamber of Commerce: Biloxi, 15, 55; Jackson, 92
Chaney, James, 90, 93, 95
Chapman, Johnny, 47–48, 50
Cherry, Gene A., 64
Cherry, Linda, 98
Chicago, Illinois, 12
Chickasaw tribe, 3
Choctaw tribe, 3, 124n9
Chrisman, J. J., 17
Christian Association, 30
Church of God, 82
Civil Rights Act (and Bill), 79–80, 86, 90, 97
Civil Rights Address, 79
Clarion-Ledger, 36, 48, 98–99
Clark, Emmett, 75
Clark, Kenneth B., 89
Clark, Mamie, 89
Clark, Robert, 109
Clarksdale, Mississippi, 76
Clarksdale School (Jackson), 94
Clippinger, D. L., 15
Coast Counties Medical Society, 14, 102
Cold War, 124n40
Coleman, James: as federal judge, 100–101; as governor of Mississippi, 22–23
Colfax Massacre, 121n3
Coliseum Commission, 103
College Hill Baptist Church, 11
Columbus, Mississippi, 74

Communism, 18, 24, 55, 93, 106, 124n40, 138n20, 146n15
Community Relations Committee, 83
Congress of Racial Equality (CORE), 55, 68
Constitution of the State of Mississippi, 18, 60, 101
Constitution of the United States of America, 5, 17, 21, 22, 31, 51, 60–61, 108, 143n38
Cook, Marsh, 18
Cook, Tom, 64
Cook, Walter, 47
Coquet Furniture Company, 47
Council of Conservative Citizens, 109
Council of Federated Organizations (COFO), 67, 91
courtesy titles, 16
Courts, Gus, 22
Cox, Murray, 62
Cox, William Harold, 100
Craft, C. W., 63–64
Cristianson, Roger L., 132n63
Cuevas, Milton, 63
Current, Gloster B., 144n52
Currie, Lucille, 64

Daily Herald (Biloxi, Gulfport), 7, 31–32, 40–41, 48–53, 61, 71–72, 81–83, 85–86, 88, 98, 101, 117n32, 154n15
Daniels, Sandy, 41
Davis, Cheryl, 91
Davis, Elaine, 91
Davis, Henry Lee, 76
Davis, James F., 43
Davis, Jefferson, 6, 69
Davis, Jessica, 76
Davis, Linda, 76, 91, 99
Davis, Myrtle (*née* Bridges), 47–48, 50, 81, 107, 128n64
Davis, Thomas, 76
Debro, Joseph, 11
DeCell, Hal, 24, 26
Declaration of Constitutional Principles, 22
Dedeaux, Curtis, 28, 34, 36–41, 46, 55, 57, 59, 63–64, 69, 129n96, 130n17, 137n68

DeDeaux, Roy, 137n68. *See also* Harrison County Board of Supervisors
Deer Island, 114n19
De la Beckwith, Byron, 79
Delta Sigma Theta, 106
Department of Education: Mississippi, 21; United States, 97
Department of Justice, 59, 75, 81
Derouen, L. J., 47, 50
desegregated events, 28, 42, 44, 56, 81, 85, 88, 91, 99, 135n18, 141n22, 144n53, 147n19
desegregation: hospitals, 13–14, 96, 105, 151n61; law enforcement, 70; medical associations, 102; politics, 11, 17–18, 22, 103, 109; public accommodations, 109; school board, 109; transportation, 12, 99. *See also* Civil Rights Act; school desegregation
Desoto National Park, 63–64
Desporte Agency, 82
D'Iberville, Mississippi, 114n19
Dickey, Marvin, 41, 45, 103
Dickey, Ruby, 45
Diggs, Charles L., Jr., 64, 76
direct action, protest of segregation, 13, 21–22 27–28, 30, 32, 34–36, 39–48, 80–81, 86, 90, 99, 129n96. *See also* Entertainment Committee; Food and Restaurant Committee; Public Accommodations Committees
disciplinary discrimination, 49, 109
"Dixie" (song), 99
Dolive, William L., 8, 64
Double V campaign, 13
Downing, Virgil, 67
Draughn, Daniel, 98
Dryden, Richard, 43
dual recreation system, 19, 104–5, 116, 125; exclusion from extracurricular activities, 98, 109. *See also* Biloxi Black Cats
dual school system, 6, 10–12, 19–21, 70–73, 88–89, 103–4, 142n24. *See also* Biloxi Colored School; Nichols High School; night school; remedial education; school desegregation; standardized testing; white flight
Duc du Maine (slave ship), 4
DuKate Elementary, 95
Dunn, Felix, 13, 28–36, 38–39, 45–46, 48, 57, 64, 75, 80, 83, 101, 107, 129n96, 133n69; family of, 36
Dunnam, Maxie D., 52–53, 84

Eagle's Nest, 7, 118n34
Easom, P. H., 72
East, Percy "P.D.," 23
Easterly, Clay, 33
Eastland, James, 59, 90, 150n35. *See also* Declaration of Constitutional Principles
Eatman, Gifford, 47, 50
economic boycotts, 57–58, 146n15
Edgewater Gulf Hotel, 62, 69, 90, 141n17
Edgewater Plaza, 91
Edwards, Glorhea Diane, 76
Edwards, Samuel, 76
Eisendrath, Cosman, 52, 61
Elder, Roy, 51
Elks Club (Black chapter, Biloxi), 25, 50, 57, 74
Ellerbrake, Johann Havenner, 135
Ellerbrake, Richard, 40, 44–45, 49, 51, 54, 61–62, 79–81, 111, 138n18, 141n22
Ellis, Charles, 41
Ellzey's Hardware, 106
Elzy, Janice, 76
Elzy, John, Jr., 76
Elzy, John, Sr., 48, 76
Elzy, Blanche Avery, 48, 76
Emancipation Proclamation, 5
emigration, Black Americans to Soviet Union, 124
Enforcement Acts, 121
Entertainment Committee, 90
Epworth United Methodist, 84
Equal Rights Amendment, 106
Esters, Barbara Carter, 76
Esters, John, 76, 98
Esters, LaValeria, 76
Esters, Michael, 76

Esters, Rehofus, Jr., 76
Esters, Rehofus, Sr., 76
Ethridge, Tom, 48
Evans, Wilson, II, 36, 129n85, 129n96
Evers, Charles, 90
Evers, Medgar, 49, 57, 73–75, 77, 79–81, 105, 144n52, 146n15
Evers, Myrlie, 79

Fair, Ernest, 50
FBI, 23, 31, 46, 60, 81, 83, 95, 141n22
Ferdinand, John, 47
Fernwood Junior High, 97
Ferrell, Gerald, 147
Fielder, Gilmore, 41, 50
Fifteenth Amendment, 17–18
Fifth Circuit Court of Appeals, New Orleans, 86–88, 92, 100
First Methodist Church of Gulfport, 85
First Missionary Baptist Church of Biloxi (Main Street), 6, 15, 71, 74, 100, 135n18
fishing culture of Harrison County, 5, 9, 39, 71, 91, 102, 135n18, 142n24
Fleeton, Gloria, 42
Fleeton, Myrtle Jeanette (née McSwain), 42, 131n28
Fleeton, Walter James, 42, 44–45, 131n28
Flemming, Rena, 147n19
Flemming, Rose, 74
Fletcher, Bernell Burney, 41, 44
Flowers, Alvin Arnold, 51
Floyd, Charles, 15
Floyd, Otha Lee, 27, 144n53
Food and Restaurant Committee, 90
Ford, Emma Lou, 14
4-H club, 155
Francis, James, 50
Free Blacks, 5, 6, 114n16
freedom of choice, 89, 94, 103, 152n72
Freedom School of Biloxi, 90–91, 94, 99
Freedom Summer, 90–95
Freedom Waders, 58
French, Nick, 137n68. *See also* Harrison County Board of Supervisors

Gaddis, William, Jr., 64
Gallagher, Roger G., 81–85
Galloway, Dorothy, 42, 45
gambling, 7, 104, 118n34, 133n69
Gayarreé, Charles, 4
Gayden, Demetrius, 107
Gerow, Richard, 94
gerrymandering, 68, 109
Giannoutses, John H., 82
Gilbert R. Mason Jr. et al. v. Biloxi Municipal School District (1971), 103
Gilreath, Mack L., 132n63
Girl Scouts, 12, 106. *See also* Boy Scouts
Gleason, Thomas Henry, 117n32
Gooden, James, 87
Goodman, Andrew, 90, 93–95
Gorenflo, Irma Dukate, 71
Gorenflo, William, 71
Gorenflo Elementary, 95
Green, Arnold W., 46
Green, Winifred, 60
Greene, Percy, 23, 55–56
Green Oaks Hotel, 4
Greyhound Bus station of Biloxi, 46, 86
Griffin, William, 91
Grimes, S. E., 16
Gruich, Frank, 15, 56
Guice, Daniel, 70, 78–79, 81, 85, 91, 100
Guice, Lee Dicks, 60–61, 65–66, 78, 137n68
Guice, William L., 60, 65–66, 78
Guidry, Francis, 50
Guidry, Nick, 68
Guinn Memorial of Gulfport, 84
Gulf Coast Medical, Dental and Pharmaceutical Association, 102
Gulf Coast Medical Association, 56, 101
Gulf Coast Unitarian Fellowship, 105
Gulfport, Mississippi, 8–9, 13, 15, 25–26, 28–30, 32, 34, 36, 46, 48, 52–53, 55–56, 62–64, 67–68, 73, 75, 79, 82–85, 90, 95, 101, 103, 105, 107, 117n32, 129n96, 133n69, 143n38; elementary schools, 73
Gulfport Pictorial Review, 28–29
Gulfport Recreation Department, 32
Gulfport Rotary Club, 55

Haberyan, Henry, 69
Haiti, 4
Hamill, C. C., 54
Hamilton, David, 45, 50
Hanshaw, Spencer, 50
Harlem Theatre, 52
Harris, Barbara, 76
Harris, Oscar, 76
Harris, Robert, 64
Harris, Robert (Cpt.), 51
Harrison County Board of Supervisors: (1959), 28, 30–31, 34, 137; (1960), 34, 37, 54, 56–59, 60, 65; (1962), 78; (1973), 155n22
Harrison County Civic Action Committee, 29–30, 33–34, 39, 103–4, 155n22
Harrison County Democratic Executive Committee, 103
Harrison County Health Department, 56
Harrison County Jail (Gulfport), 36, 82
Harrison County Mental Health Association, 105
Harrison County School Board, 73, 76–77, 87–88, 97–98, 109
Hartman, Joy, 83, 135n18, 152n85
Hattiesburg, Mississippi, 98
Hattiesburg American, 90
Hattiesburg Progress, 117n32
Hausen, Elzie, 7
Hayes, Eleanora, 43, 50
Head Start, 104, 106
Helmantoler, Willis L., 51
Helper, Paul D., 132n63
Henry, Aaron, 76
Heritage Crusade, 143n38
Highway 90 (Biloxi), 8, 40–41, 43, 45, 52, 65, 69, 107
Holleman, Boyce, 51, 57
Holmes County, 92, 109
homeowners vs. board of supervisors, 60–61, 64–66
Hope, Bobby C., 43, 69
Hotel Markham, 90
Hotel Riviera, 91

House of Representatives, 11, 18, 64, 76, 79, 99, 121n3
Houtz, George, 143n38
Howard, T. R. M., 33, 56
Howard Memorial Hospital, 81, 96, 102, 104, 151n61. *See also* New Biloxi Hospital
Howard University, 12–13, 21
Hoze, Jackie, 27
Hoze, James, 27
Hoze, Jimmie, 27
Hoze, Gloria, 27
Huggar, Janice, 91
Humes, H. H., 23
Humphreys County, 22
Hurley, Ruby, 146
Hurricane Camille, 102–3
Hurricane George, 8, 65
Hurricane Katrina, 107
Hurricane "New Orleans," 8
Hursey, Francis, 37

Inez Cafe, 107
integration vs. desegregation, defining terms, 5, 12, 24, 32, 53, 86–87, 93, 135n18
International Longshoremen Association, 129n96
International Women's Year (IWY) State Coordinating Committee, 106
intimidation/coercion, 7, 9–10, 17–19, 21–24, 28, 30–33, 35–37, 40–46, 50–51, 56–57, 62–64, 67, 73–75, 79–80, 82–83, 85, 90–91, 94, 96–100, 102, 109, 121n3, 129n96, 133n69; bribery, 129n96. *See also* lynching; Subversive Activities Act (1950)
itinerant workers, 6

Jackson, E. L., 81, 135n18
Jackson, Malcomb "Papa" Hoyd, 50, 68–69
Jackson, Mississippi, 10–11, 13, 57, 64, 74–75, 77, 79–80, 87–90, 92, 94–97, 103, 105, 146n15
Jackson, Tommy, 91
Jackson Advocate, 49, 55–56, 80
Jackson Daily News, 34, 56
Jackson State college, 100

James, Willie C., 43
Jeff Davis Elementary, 95
Jenkins brothers, 117n32
Jet, 52, 67, 74, 95–96, 131n22
Jewishness/Jews: involvement and conflation with Black civil rights, 24, 55, 124, 138n20; refugees, 12
Jim Crow, 12, 17–21, 79. *See also* segregation laws and practices
Jimerson, Clemon, Jr., 107
Jimerson, Clemon, Sr., 39, 42–46, 74, 84, 100–101, 107, 111, 130n13, 144n53, 149n20
Jim Hill Jr. High, 10
Johnson, George, 64
Johnson, John, 108
Johnson, Leroy Word, 64
Johnson, Paul, 89–90
Johnson, Phillip, 144n53
Johnston, Erle, 108
Jones, Albert, 61
Jones, Oscar, 47
Jones, Sam, 50
Jordan, Clarence, 44
Jordan's Grocery, 47
Joseph, Givonna, 107, 111
Joseph, Jack, 7
Juba, West Africa, 4

Kappa Alpha Psi, 26
Keesler Air Force Base, 7–8, 14, 26, 30, 42–43, 45–46, 54, 75, 80, 88, 104; staff and airmen, 44–46, 51, 54–55, 63–64, 76, 88, 104
Kemp, Cornelius, 84, 147n40
Kemp, John, 107
Kendall, W. G., 5
Kendall brickworks, 5, 114n19
Kennard, Clyde, 22, 73, 105, 148n48
Kennedy, Janice, 43. *See also* BAM, Black Angry Men (and Women)
Kennedy, John F., 73, 79–80, 86
Kennedy, Robert, 75, 88
Kennedy, Rose Fitzgerald, 73–74
Kincannon, A. A., 21
King, Clennon, 73

King, Martin Luther, Jr., 24, 74, 80, 100–101
King Edward Hotel, Jackson, 13
Kitty-Cat Cafe, 47
Knight, Haywood, Jr., 64
Koinonia Farm, 44
Kropp, Algot L., 132
Ku Klux Klan of Mississippi (KKK), 23, 33, 58, 68, 75, 91, 121n3, 150n35. *See also* Bailey, Walter; Heritage Crusade; White Citizens Council
Kyle, William P., 120n27

Ladiner, Milton, 129n94
Ladner, Gatha, 37, 137n68. *See also* Harrison County Board of Supervisors
l'Afriquian (slave ship), 4
L & N railroad, 103
Laurel Leader-Call, 96
Lawrence, Dewey, 30–31, 65, 137n68, 145n1. *See also* Harrison County Board of Supervisors
League of Women Voters, 92
Leake County, 77, 87–88, 94, 97
Le Blond de la Tour, Pierre, 4
le Courier de Bourbon (slave ship), 4
Lee, George, 22, 105
le Fortune (slave ship), 4
Leggett Memorial Methodist Church of Biloxi, 53, 84
Le Moyne d'Iberville, Pierre, 3
Le Moyne de Bienville, Jean-Baptiste, 3
le Neride (slave ship), 4
Leon, Sylvanie, 116n29
Leonard, George, 87
Lewis, Debora, 97
l'Expedition (slave ship), 4
Lidy, Henry, 7, 116
lighthouse (Biloxi), 35, 40–42, 53, 81, 107
lighthouse (Ship Island), 114n19
lightship (Ship Island), 114n19
Lips, Howard T., 53
Little Apple Bar/café, 47, 69
Little Rock, Arkansas, 54, 97
Lizana, Daniel Lee, 105
Lonberger, Joe, 41, 50, 131n22

Longfellow House, 42
Longino, Andrew, 117n32
Lopez, Eurilda Seal, 82
Lopez Elementary, 95, 151n50, 152n85
Lott, Adell, 27, 35
Love, J. P., 92
Lowe, Zeb, 50
lynching: "bees," 7, 40, 69, 117n32, 148n48; list of lynching victims in Harrison County, 117n32

Magnolia Hotel, 4
Main Street Revitalization Project, 103
manumission, 114n16
Maples, Luther, 84–86
Martin, Adrienne, 76, 98
Martin, Jack, 76
Martin, Rosa, 81
Martinolich, A. K., 15
Marshall College (Wiley, Texas), 144n53
Mary Holmes College (Community Education Extension), 104
Mary Mahoney (restaurant), 42
Mary Michel Junior High (Biloxi), 99, 142n24
Mason, Aria, 107, 111
Mason, Gilbert, Jr., 13, 14, 27, 36, 48, 56, 70, 73–74, 76, 80, 84, 86, 94–97, 98–103, 106–7, 120n35, 134n17, 144n48
Mason, Gilbert, Sr., 9–16, 21, 25–41, 44–46, 48–50, 53–54, 56–58, 64, 66, 68, 73, 75, 78–84, 90, 95–96, 99–101, 103–4; medical clinic of, 14, 25, 32–33, 39, 40, 43, 45–46, 83, 102
Mason, Natalie Lorraine (*née* Hamlar), 12–15, 26, 35–36, 45, 64, 73, 79–80, 96, 100–101, 105–6, 120n25, 126n24
Mason Bill, 50–51, 59, 64
McArthur, Arthur, 65
McClocky, Edward G., Jr., 46
McDaniels, Dorothy Holley, 43
McDaniels, Wilmer, 36, 42–43, 45
McDonnell, Edward E., 67, 90
McDonnell, Herbert, 25, 30, 34–35, 37–40, 52, 56, 59, 124n2, 137n68

McElhaney, Famous, 53
McGee, Alteese, 43
McGowan, Alethea (*née* Bridges), 47, 48, 50
McGowan, James, Sr., 44–45
McKinley, James, Jr., 76
McKinley, James, Sr., 76
McKinley, Maude Brown, 76
McKinley, Sylvia, 76
McNair, Donna, 91
McNair, Elnora Mary, 47
McSwain, Nolan, 42–43, 46
McSwain, Willie Jean, 42, 98
Meadows, Reginald "Billy," 36, 79, 83–84, 101
Medical Committee for Civil Rights, 102
Meredith, James, 73–74
Miley, Benjamin F., 7
Miley Hotel, 7, 71, 118n34
Miller, Claude, 41
Mississippi Advisory Committee, funding of, 104. *See also* US Civil Rights Commission
Mississippians for God, Country and Family, 106
Mississippians for Public Education, 92
Mississippi Cooperative Extension Service, 155n20
Mississippi Council on Human Relations, 98
Mississippi Gulf Coast Young Democrats Club, 106
Mississippi legislature, 17–20, 30, 32, 72, 87, 89–90, 92, 99, 108–9, 117n32, 141n22, 155n20. *See also* anti-protest legislation
Mississippi Medical and Surgical Association, 102
Mississippi Senate Education Committee, 92
Mississippi Sheiks, 13
Mississippi Southern College, 73
Mississippi state constitution. *See* Constitution of the State of Mississippi
Mississippi State Medical Association, 14, 102
Mississippi Valley Produce Company, 129n96

Mize, Sidney, 60–61, 66, 76–78, 80, 87–89, 91, 94, 100
Mobile, Alabama, 7, 54
Moffitt, Barbara, 135n18
Money, Mary, 91
Money, Pat, 91
Moore, Albert, 47, 50
Moore, Inman, Jr., 53, 84
Moran, Joseph, 4, 5. *See also* Kendall brickworks
Morse, Stanford, Jr., 30–32, 56
Mt. Olive Baptist Church, 83
Mullens, George E., 25, 28, 34, 36
Mumford, Patsy, 76
Mumford, Rosa "Rosie," 76, 98
Murray, Pauli, 120
music scene, jazz, 7, 42, 100. *See also* Mississippi Sheiks; Presley, Elvis; Price, Leontyne
Mutual Association of Colored People South, 30

NAACP: Biloxi chapter, 57, 67, 68, 70, 81, 90, 107, 109; Biloxi Youth Branch, 68, 81; Gulfport chapter, 15, 26, 29, 36, 67, 133n69; Harrison County, 25–26, 30, 34, 51, 95; Jackson chapter, 11; national, 13, 21, 29, 45, 55, 58, 73–74, 94, 97; state (Mississippi), 57, 73, 85, 105
Nabrit, James, 31
Nance, Robert, 82
National Association of Colored Women, 13
National Association of Social Workers, 106
National Council of Juvenile Court Judges, 84
National Council of Negro Women, 103
National Medical Association, 15
National Science Foundation, 107
Negro Business League of Biloxi, 7
Negro Health Week, 71
Negro Juke Box and Cigarette Machine Co., 38, 129n96
Negro Ministerial Association, 26
Negro Peace Conference, 30
Negro Youth Council, 26

Neshoba County, 90–91, 95
New Bethel Church, 45
New Biloxi Hospital, 14, 40–42, 56, 96. *See also* Howard Memorial Hospital
Newcomb, L. S., 64
New Orleans, Louisiana, 4
news coverage bias, 23, 31, 49, 55–56, 64, 88
New York Times, 97
New York World's Fair, 147n19
Nichols, Fannie L., 71
Nichols, Marshall F., 71–72
Nichols High School, 26, 31, 39, 50, 63, 69, 72–73, 75, 88, 104
night school (Back-of-Town), 71. *See also* remedial education
Nineteenth Amendment, 18–19
Nixon, Richard, 104
Nixon, Walter L., Jr., 103–4
Nunley, Clifton, Jr., 76
Nunley, Clifton, Sr., 76
Nunley, Doretha Pitts-Hall, 76
Nunley, Gretchen, 76

Ocean Springs, Mississippi, 7, 71, 117n32
O'Keefe, Jeremiah, 143n38
Old Biloxi Cemetery, 27, 130n13
Omega Psi Phi, 26
Operation Surf, 34–36
O'Shea, Michael Vincent, 20, 73
Owens, Lee, Jr., 43, 128n64
Owens, Vernon R., 50

Palmer, Merle, 143n38
Parker, A. J., 50
Parker, James Moore, 82
Parker, Mack Charles, 28, 31, 60
Pascagoula, Mississippi, 68. *See also* Boy Scouts
Pass Christian, Mississippi, 64, 26–27, 114n16, 117n32, 129n94; "Rice Fields," 9, 26, 62–63, 99. *See also* Free Blacks; Hursey, Francis
paternalism, 21, 54–55, 71–72, 94, 96. *See also* racism: psychology of
Patterson, Roma Mae, 47

182   INDEX

Patton, Luther, 79
pay gap, 116n29
Pease, William, 5
Pelman, Phillip, 129n96
Perkins, Archie E., 70, 72
Petal Paper, 54, 61
petition to desegregate Biloxi schools (June 4, 1963), 76–77, 87–89, 91, 94
Phillips, Rubel, 15
Philmont Ranch (Cimarron, New Mexico), 144n53
Pittman, Kay, 94
Plessy v. Ferguson, 19, 89
Poe, Dave, 117n32
Poinsett, Alex, 52, 67, 131n22
Point Cadet, 40, 64, 91, 142n24
Port of Gulfport, 129n96
Powers, George, 82
Presley, Elvis, 103
Price, Gerald V., 62
Price, Leontyne, 103
Primos, Alec, 87
Pringle, Victor, 88
Progressive Baptist State Convention, 30
Prohibition, 7, 118n34
Pruitt, Thomas, 155n20
Public Accommodations Committee, 90

Quave, Laz: as chief of police, 8; as mayor of Biloxi, 27–28, 36–38, 49, 51–52, 54–55, 59, 61, 66, 70, 126n24, 137n68, 143n38, 155n22
queer culture, intersection of, 120n18

racial murders, 22, 28, 33, 60, 64, 68–70, 79, 93–95, 105, 116n31
racism: class intersection, 5, 23, 36, 75–76, 96, 114n16, 144n47; distancing from KKK, 143n38; healing of, 53, 94, 99; psychology of, 3, 8, 16, 18–22, 26, 28, 34, 38, 54–55, 59, 87–89, 93, 117n32, 138n20. *See also* Free Blacks; intimidation/coercion; paternalism; segregation laws and practices; slave trade; white alliance; white femininity

Ragusin, Anthony, 55
railroad (Biloxi), 5–7, 69, 103, 117n32
Rainbow Beach, Chicago, Illinois, 58
Rainey, Ethel, 39–43, 46, 57–58, 129n2
Rainey, Gary, 43
Rainey, Jesse James, 41–42
Rainey, Ruby Hawkins, 41
Ramsey, Clara Bradley, 81
Rand, Clayton, 55, 62
Rankin, Levanie, 47
Ranston, Tom, 117n32
Reconstruction, 17
"Redemption," 17
redlining, 6, 8, 12
Regional Council of Negro Leadership, 25
Regional Economic Commission, 104
religious response, 6, 8, 12, 30, 40, 52–53, 61–62, 75, 141–42, 152n85; nuns, 28; ostracization of religious leaders, 61, 81, 83, 85, 138n20, 141n19. *See also* desegregated events
remedial education, 104. *See also* night school
Republic of New Afrika, 29
Revels, Hiram, 17
Rice, Robert L., 143n38
Richardson, Rachael, 142n24
Riley, George, 47
riots: prevention of, final wade in, 81–82; "race," 55; at third wade-in, 41–48, 58, 68, 103, 134n17; at University of Mississippi, 74. *See also* anti-protest legislation
Robinson, Candy, 91
Robinson, Herbert, 91
Robinson, Lodie, 91
Rock, Robert H., 46
Rogers, Earnest, 91
Rolkosky, Leo, 47, 50
Rosado, Bernard, 76
Rosado, Christopher, 45, 76, 126n24
Rosado, Ernest, 76
Rosado, Ruth Elmer, 76
Rosetti, George, 63
Rossotti, Louis, 79

Rozetta, Inez, 91
Rusch, C. W., 51
Russell, Ed, 7, 117n32
Russell, Leo, 100
Ryker, Harold, 85

Saenger Theatre, 90
Saucier, Murray, 27, 125n19
school desegregation: Biloxi, 95–98; of Catholic schools in Mississippi, 94; general, 6, 54, 67, 70, 74–77, 84–85, 87–92, 94–100, 103–4, 109, 154n15; Jackson, 97; Leake County, 97; around military bases, 75, 80. *See also* freedom of choice; King, Clennon; *United States v. Harrison County*; white flight
Schneckenburg, Alvin, 84
Schneckenburg, Clarence, 84
Schutt, Jane, 80
Schwan, Jules A., 37
Schwerner, Michael, 90, 93–95
Scruggs, A. E., 72
Seall, George, 50
Sears, Roebuck, 46
seawall, 8, 32, 40–41, 60, 65
segregation laws and practices, 6–12, 16, 17, 19, 23; Biloxi mall, 147n19; courthouses, 37, 84, 143n38; Harrison County jails, 82; hospital and medical conferences, 14–16; public accommodation, 12, 13, 31, 37, 86, 147n19. *See also* Back-of-Town; Black maternal and infant mortality rate; dual recreation system; dual school system; Mississippi legislature; *Plessy v. Ferguson*; redlining; "separate but equal"
segregation of Harrison County beach, 6, 8–9, 26–28, 34–36, 54, 58–59; eminent domain, 60; federal contract, 59–60; littoral privileges, 60, 101
Sekul, John: as attorney, 35; as judge, 83–84, 143n38
Selma, Alabama (march across Edmund Pettus Bridge), 134n17
Semski, Lawrence, 143n38

"separate but equal," 13–14, 29, 38, 55–56, 70, 93
Seymour, Bernard, 70
sharecropper, 33
Sheely, Delores Steward, 42, 44
Ship Island, 114n19
Shirley, Ann, 43, 50
sickle cell anemia, 102
Skrmetti, Paul M., 60, 65
slave trade, 3–4, 113n9, 114n16, 114n19
Smith, Carolyn, 91
Smith, Lester, 91
Smith, Robert L. T., 11
Smith, Tommie, 99
Southern Christian Ministers' Conference of Mississippi, 128n65
Southern Kitchen, 47
Southern Manifesto, 22. *See also* Declaration of Constitutional Principles
Soviet Union, critique of race relations, 55, 124n40
Stamps, Rozelia (*née* Mason), 105
standardized testing, 92, 109
Standard Station, 47
STAR vocational program, 104
State Advisory Committee on Education, 104
State Department of Youth Services, 106
State Manpower Council, 104
State Sovereignty Commission (SSC), xi, 22–26, 29, 31–34, 36–37, 40, 44–45, 54, 56–57, 61–62, 64, 67–68, 72, 78–79, 88, 90, 100, 102, 108, 123n31, 128n65, 133n69, 138n20
States' Rights Party, 55
Stennis, John, 59. *See also* Declaration of Constitutional Principles
Steps Coalition, 107
stereotype of native peoples, 4. *See also* Chickasaw tribe; Choctaw tribe; Tanêks
Stewart, Warren, 117n32
Still, Larry, 74
stipend, education of Black doctors, 12

Stockstill, J. E., 138n20
St. Paul's United Church of Christ, 44, 61, 81, 85, 141n22. *See also* Back Bay Mission
Strong, George, 69
Strong, Willie "Bud," 68–70, 131n33
Student Nonviolent Coordinating Committee (SNCC), 68
Subversive Activities Act, 72
Sugar Bowl, 95
Summer, Albion F., 108
Sun 'n' Sand, 90
Sutherland, John R., 51

Tanêks, 3
Tate, Joel Overton, 82, 124n9
Taylor, A., 75
Taylor, Andrew, 47
Taylor, Jerry, 14
tax: beach, 8–9, 26–29, 32, 53, 60, 62–63; government uses for segregation, 23, 61, 90, 108. *See also* tourism; votership; white flight
Tennessee Agricultural and Industrial State University (TSU), 12
Terrell, Mary Church, 13
Texas Christian University (El Paso), 144n53
Thames, Kenneth, 41
Thames, Marzine, 41
Thirteenth Amendment, 17
Thomas, Bob, 57, 68
Thomas, Janice, 91, 99
Thomas, John Ed, 84
Thompson, Allen, 87
Thompson, Clay, Jr., 93
Thompson, Doug, 63
Tichell, Florian, 70
Till, Emmett, 28, 31, 33, 64
Tilley, John C., 132n63
tokenism, 94, 98
Tonkel, Keith, 84
Tougaloo College, 11
tourism, 4–9, 22, 30, 54, 63, 66, 90, 95
Trahan's Hardware, 43, 57
Trinity Methodist Church of Gulfport, 52
Truly, Jeff, 20, 73

Turnkey Program (Gulfport), 103
Twilight Grill, 47

United Benevolence Association Hall, 136n60
United Church of Christ, 135n18
United Service Organizations (USO) of Biloxi, 104
United States v. Cruikshank, 121n3
United States v. Harrison County, 58–62, 74–75, 78, 100–101. *See also* homeowners vs. board of supervisors
University of Mississippi, 73–74, 88, 97
University of Southern Mississippi, 22, 88
US Civil Rights Commission, 62, 75, 80, 82, 104, 155n20
US marshals, 74, 97
US Supreme Court, 13, 19, 21, 57, 72, 74, 86–87, 89, 92, 101, 121n3

Vancleave, Mississippi, 7, 117n32
Van Horn, Lucille (*née* Kinney), 9
Van Landingham, Zack J., 31–32
Vann, Eddie, 69
Vardaman, James K., 19
Vermillion, David, 132n63
veterans, 22, 33, 42, 53, 76, 80, 143n38
Veterans Administration Hospital of Gulfport, 9, 45, 55, 60, 78, 105
Vietnam, 123n31
Vincent, Elvin P., 82
violence against women, 7, 47, 117n32. *See also* Black femininity; white femininity
votership, 17–19, 22, 25, 29, 67–68, 70–71, 73, 80, 90, 109; grandfather clause, character requirements, and literacy, 18, 19, 109; jury of peers, 17; poll tax, 18–19, 109. *See also* Enforcement Acts; Colfax Massacre; League of Women Voters; *United States v. Cruikshank*
Voting Rights Act (1965), 109

wade-ins: Biloxi, 27, 35, 41–45, 81–82; Gulfport, 36; national, 58; trespassing charges, 82–86

Waits, Jim, 84
Walker, Elliott L., 132n63
Walker, Kirby, 94
Walker, Knox, 31, 33, 35, 37, 129n96
Waller, Bill, 106
Ward, James M., 56
Warren, J. W., 63
Washington, DC, 12–13
Washington Post, 97
Watson, Clara, 9, 44
Watson, Tom, 18
weathering model, 15–16
Weathersby, Carolyn, 91, 94
welfare bias, 155
Wesley, Velma, 13–14
West End Elementary school, 151n50
Wheatley, Howard B., 64
White, Alice, 32
White, Eulice, 30–33
White, George, 18
White, James A., 11
White, Marshall, 84
White, Melinda, 91
White, Walter A., 117n32
white alliance, 15–16, 44–45, 56, 61, 82, 89, 93–94. *See also* League of Women Voters; Mississippians for Public Education; religious response
White Citizens Council, 23–24, 33, 38, 61–62, 70, 76, 79, 87, 93, 108–9, 150n30, 150n32
White Community Project. *See* Council of Federated Organizations
white compliance: coercion and encouragement of, 18–20, 24, 28, 33, 36–38, 40, 42, 44, 51–53, 58, 62–63, 68, 72, 81, 83, 85, 91, 93, 97, 103, 141n22; in favor of desegregation, 75–76, 91, 93, 95–96
white femininity, mobilization of, 28–29, 56, 65, 71, 74, 81, 92–93, 106, 135, 141n22. *See also* women's suffrage
white flight, 90, 92–94, 109, 154n16
white moderates, 93, 143, 154n16. *See also* religious response; white compliance
Whitfield, Henry, 20

Whitman, Gren, 91
Whitsun, Linda, 91
Wiggins, Mississippi, 26–27
Wilkins, Roy, 58, 146
Williams, Myrtle Corrinne (*née* Strong), 69, 70
Williams, Robert, 91
Williams, Sanford, 41
Williams, Walter, 34, 37, 40
Winterstein, Christinia, 117n32
Wittman, J. J., 26
Witzel, E. F., 67
women's exclusion: Coliseum Commission, 103; juries, 106; medical societies, 14
women's suffrage, 18–19
Woods, Stanley, 144n53
World War II, 10, 13, 21, 67
Wright, George, 81–83
Wright, Glen, 63
Wright, Robert, 7

Young, Edmond, 116n31
Youth Corps, 104

Zingland, Mississippi, 62

ABOUT THE AUTHOR

The author and her daughter at Biloxi Beach, ca. 2011

Amy Lemco grew up sharing time between Biloxi, Mississippi, and Bonney Lake, Washington. A mother of two, she was inspired to resume her education and earned her degree in History and Creative Writing at Emory & Henry. Traversing parallel dimensions by day, in the evening Amy tutors ESL students from around the world. Whenever travel on this plain is possible, she enjoys finding her city soulmates, like Santa Fe and Montreal. Biloxi remains one of her most beloved places. You can follow her for upcoming projects at AmyLemcoAuthor.com and Instagram.

www.ingramcontent.com/pod-product-compliance
Lightning Source LLC
Chambersburg PA
CBHW030110170426
43198CB00009B/559